DRIVEN

DRIVEN

The Men Who Made
Formula One

Kevin Eason

HODDER

First published in Great Britain in 2018 by Hodder & Stoughton
An Hachette UK company

This paperback edition published in 2019

3

B format ISBN 9781473684553
eBook ISBN 9781473684522

Typeset in Adobe Caslon by Hewer Text UK Ltd, Edinburgh

Printed and bound in Great Britain by Clays Ltd, Elcograf S.p.A.

Hodder & Stoughton policy is to use papers that are natural, renewable
and recyclable products and made from wood grown in sustainable
forests. The logging and manufacturing processes are expected to
conform to the environmental regulations of the country of origin.

Hodder & Stoughton Ltd
Carmelite House
50 Victoria Embankment
London EC4Y 0DZ

www.hodder.co.uk

To the talented and generous sports editors of *The Times* – David Chappell, Keith Blackmore and Tim Hallissey – who offered me the time and space to revel in sports reporting, and the Fleet Street gang who kept me sane over hundreds of thousands of miles of travelling with the Formula One circus, particularly Bob McKenzie and Jonathan McEvoy. And to Bernie Ecclestone and his incredible gang of entrepeneurs. It was a privilege to be a small part of their story.

CONTENTS

INTRODUCTION

THE verbal tirade came from somewhere above me. I couldn't see where, but I would recognise that Irish brogue any day. Eddie Jordan was on a balcony of the Yas Marina circuit and spotted me wandering in the paddock below.

After almost 300 grands prix, Abu Dhabi would be my last as motor racing correspondent for *The Times* and Jordan, the first team owner I met in Formula One, clearly wanted to mark the occasion. 'We're better rid of you,' he shouted, turning into a character that could come from *Mrs Brown's Boys* on television. 'You were never any good. You know fuck-all about Formula One anyway.'

You know what? He was right. Jordan's tongue was in his cheek but, compared to him, I didn't know much, even after 20 years at the heart of this most extraordinary of sports. Like Jordan's exit from Formula One as a team owner, though, my timing was perfect.

This was November 2016, and I was quitting my job at the end of an era when Jordan and a cohort of fellow entrepreneurs ruled the most glittering sporting extravaganza in the world. Bernie Ecclestone didn't know it then, but it would be his final grand prix in charge of a sport he ruled for almost forty years; Ron Dennis, the titan of McLaren, had gone just before this race and the rest – Flavio Briatore, Luca di Montezemolo and so many others – had disappeared in dribs and drabs.

To be a sports journalist is a great job; to be a sports journalist at *The Times* is a privilege; and to be a sports journalist in Formula One ... well, it was a blast.

Unlike so many in the Formula One media centre, who are essentially fans, I had a long career before Formula One (a proper job, I always said), coming through local newspapers where my first interview as a callow 17-year-old trainee was with Evelyn Harrison, a tiny woman with a purple bob haircut and wearing a 1920s flapper dress, who insisted on feeling the bumps on my head to ascertain whether I was trustworthy before telling me about her lonely hearts club. I passed the bump test. I interviewed Prime Minister Ted Heath about Britain joining something called the Common Market, and reported on the miners' strike and thousands of redundancies in Britain's car industry. I joined Fleet Street as an industrial correspondent, and followed Neil Kinnock on his 'red rose' general election tour of 1987, clutching my first mobile telephone (it never worked). But I also stood in a field close to the jet that crashed at Kegworth in 1989 killing forty-seven passengers, and later that year leaned on the wall overlooking the Thames at the hulk of the sunken *Marchioness* pleasure steamer, in which fifty-one party-goers lost their lives. In 1997, I was on the road for the general election again and was part of the team reporting on the death of Princess Diana that year.

I was also motoring editor, a diminutive version of Jeremy Clarkson if you like, driving every type of car you could imagine in every corner of the globe, crashing a famous Ford GT40 at Silverstone and spinning a Ferrari 360, appropriately through 360 degrees, to applause from Ferrari mechanics. It must have been an audition because in March 1998 I was on a plane to Australia to cover my first grand prix. After reporting on strikes, deaths, elections and cars, I was sent to watch the world's most expensive soap opera – and it was fascinating. There were glorious winners and plucky losers, whose stories could be just as compelling.

I thought I had seen it all in journalism, but I was mesmerised, not just by the cars, the paddock and parade of famous faces (I bumped into George Harrison coming out of the loo), but the people.

Sepp Blatter ran FIFA, football's world governing body, like a medieval prince with a subservient court, but he had 'no skin in the game', as they say. It wasn't his money or his neck on the line if things went wrong, unlike Eddie Jordan, who risked every penny he had on Formula One. Blatter hadn't had to watch footballers die horrifically on the pitch or lose a best friend in a fiery blaze in the middle of a game, like Sir Frank Williams or Bernie Ecclestone. Blatter hadn't risked his livelihood and still built an empire like McLaren's Ron Dennis.

This book is not a history, nor an investigation – there are authors like Tom Bower, Tim Collings, Susan Watkins and Richard Williams who have examined the inner workings of the sport forensically and with excellence. It is not really about motor racing. Instead, it is a series of memories, snapshots and anecdotes from a journalist who had a seat at the top table of Formula One, an attempt to put some colour into characters who seemed to me to appear in monochrome in television interviews, and to review the events that shaped them. I met up with them again for this book to help me remember the flipside of their personalities so rarely revealed. And to remind me that the men who made Formula One, who transformed the sport into a global phenomenon worth billions of pounds and engaged the interest of tens of millions of people, were extraordinary and unique. They were quite simply driven.

1

THE MAN WHO
MADE US RICH

7 MARCH 2017: Nineteen words in silver lettering on the invitation to dinner summed up a life: 'A tribute to Bernie Ecclestone, the man who made Formula One great.' And then the afterthought: 'And made a lot of people rich.'

The invitation could have gone further, for this was not just a tribute to a man, but to a unique era in all of sport, marking the end of an age of extraordinary entrepreneurs, led by Ecclestone, who transformed Formula One from a rabble of enthusiasts scraping a living from motor racing into a £1 billion entertainment behemoth.

They were giants of men, yet ruled, ironically, by the smallest. At 5 feet 3 inches, Ecclestone looks as though a gust of wind would blow him over, but you would be wrong. He was tough enough to trade second-hand cars in London and take care of himself among plenty of East End hard men, scaring people twice his size half to death in his prime before muscling into Formula One where he became the P.T. Barnum of sport, the Great Showman, the ringmaster with his incredible flying circus travelling to every corner of the world to thrill and entertain millions.

Not any more, though, for his extraordinary reign had come to an end. Ecclestone, who had ruled like a dictator for forty years, had been unceremoniously deposed from the sport he had created in his own image. For the first time in his eighty-six years, Ecclestone was out of work, and, for the first time since anyone could remember, there would be no Bernie when the new Formula One season opened just nineteen days after this celebratory dinner with fifty or so of his high-rolling associates and chums in a swish Chelsea restaurant.

As each guest arrived, they were given a souvenir programme and a mask emblazoned with Ecclestone's face, so that they could welcome the guest of honour with a spooky array of Bernie visages.

David Coulthard, the ex-driver with Williams, McLaren and Red Bull and winner of thirteen grands prix, was master of ceremonies and assigned the job of welcoming each guest, including me, the lone journalist and an interloper in a room crowded with multimillionaires. Formula One had, unfortunately, not made me rich, unlike Flavio Briatore, the former head of the world championship-winning Benetton and Renault teams, who had organised the dinner at Sumosan Twiga, a curious Japanese-Italian fusion restaurant at the end of Sloane Street, one of the most glamorous thoroughfares in London. This was part of Ecclestone's 'manor', the area of Chelsea and Knightsbridge where he had set up home and presided over Formula One from his tiny headquarters within walking distance of Harrods and Harvey Nichols, the department stores for the ultra-chic 'Made in Chelsea' set, and the line of expensive shops, from Bulgari to Tom Ford, Louis Vuitton and Versace that attracted wealthy tourists.

Sumosan Twiga nestles up against the Jumeirah Carlton Tower, a hotel where Middle Eastern royals park their gold Lamborghinis and inhabit suites that can cost as much as £2,600 a night. Once, Formula One was sandwiches and bottles of beer, but by the end of Ecclestone's reign, it was champagne and Chelsea.

Each time Sumosan Twiga's double doors opened, a familiar face from the world of Formula One – Bernie's world – would appear. Luca di Montezemolo, the aristocrat forced out of the Ferrari business he had rescued and rebuilt, had flown in from Rome, looking slender and immaculate, much as he did in his prime when he transformed Ferrari into the wealthiest and most successful team in Formula One. And then there was Piero Lardi Ferrari, the illegitimate son of Enzo and last family link to the great founder of Ferrari and pioneer of Formula One.

Across the room, clutching his glass, was Vijay Mallya, the Indian drinks billionaire once behind brands like Kingfisher. That was before the Indian authorities decided to pursue him on a series of corruption charges that Mallya condemned as the victimisation of a celebrity for political ends in his homeland. No one here cared much about that, and the owner of the Force India Formula One team was resplendent as always in huge diamond earrings and chunky gold jewellery.

Toto Wolff, the lanky Austrian head of the Mercedes F1 team, arrived with his wife Susie, closely followed by Christian Horner, the Red Bull team principal and Ecclestone's best man at his wedding. They are the new boys, the corporate youngsters who moved in to take over from the entrepreneurs who had risked their own money and livelihoods to go racing. Horner's wife Geri, the former Spice Girl, was on her usual bubbly form, and soon hooked up with David Coulthard's wife Karen and Susie Wolff to claim their 'women only' table, where they would be isolated from the testosterone-fuelled banter of the overwhelmingly male guests.

HRH Prince Salman bin Hamad Al Khalifa, Crown Prince of Bahrain, short and dapper and clutching his trademark cigar, was the first royal to turn up. Bahrain's crown prince was behind the radical plan to build a $150 million racetrack in the desert, a palace of speed of absolutely no interest to many of the ordinary people of his country and the subject of years of protest. No matter, he liked it and insisted his motor-racing palace built on a sand dune was of great benefit to his tiny island nation.

Prince Salman was followed by more minor royalty, this time Prince Albert of Monaco, in grey suit and open-necked white shirt. Formula One is in the Grimaldi family blood. They have been organising grands prix around the narrow, twisting streets of their toy-town principality since 1929. Monaco remains the jewel in the Formula One crown, which is probably why it is the only race that pays nothing for the privilege of staging a grand prix. The prince can look down from the battlements of his castle onto the most famous race-track in the world around streets described by Somerset Maugham as 'a sunny place for shady people'. Perhaps that was true once, but many in Formula One – like Lewis Hamilton, David Coulthard and Eddie Jordan – succumbed to the attraction of the tiny tax haven clinging to cliffs on the Côte d'Azur because of its fine weather and safe community away from the prying eyes of the public.

As the room filled and the noise level rose, I spotted the pale, lean figure of Max Mosley in a corner. Mosley was one half of the partnership that once ran Formula One – Ernie Wise to Ecclestone's Eric Morecambe, if you like. They were the most unlikely of friends: Mosley, a cerebral, aristocratic lawyer, who inherited the family fortune, and became president of the Fédération Internationale de l'Automobile, the governing body of motor racing, and Ecclestone, the used-car dealer from a tiny village in Suffolk, who ruled Formula One through a combination of fear of retribution and the lure of hard cash.

They had a vision for Formula One and shared something else that bound them closely – a delight in mischief-making. No wind-up was too great, no character in the sport too pompous to be embarrassed. They had connived and run Formula One like their own fiefdom since dislodging the ruling elite, but now the old pals were both out of the sport they had dominated for so long. Mosley isn't much of a party man either and preferred to stay in the background, sipping quietly at his champagne, modestly dressed in sports jacket and black roll-neck sweater. 'I wonder if Bernie will be able to retire?' I once asked Mosley. 'He thinks of nothing else from waking up to going to bed. It has been his life. Do you not miss it, Max?' 'No, not at all,' Mosley said. 'There are so many things to do now I don't have all that fuss with the teams and so on. There are so many books to read that I never got around to. Then again, I don't suppose Bernie reads much.' That was true, I reflected, of a man whose reading matter had likely only ever been contracts.

Then, the chatter died down. Briatore was at the front of the crowd, signalling silence. The doors swung open and there was Ecclestone, characteristically dressed in a handmade, dark grey suit with blindingly white shirt, blinking as the room erupted and he faced fifty paper Ecclestone faces staring back at him. As the comedy masks came off, his wife Fabiana took his arm and guided him into the melee. Ecclestone looked shell-shocked and desperate to slink away, but there was no escape from the adoration as everyone removed their masks to reveal their identities. After dinner came the grand finale – the cake. It was enormous and covered in pictures of Ecclestone's decades in the sport. He was handed a huge knife to carve, but looked positively tentative, as if not wanting to destroy the images of a lifetime. Fabiana, almost half a century younger than her husband, took charge, as she seemed to whenever Ecclestone suddenly looked his considerable years, and helped him to cut through the sugary layers. At the end, Ecclestone made his way around the room to speak to everyone there. He spotted me and touched my arm. 'Thanks for coming, sport,' he said, before moving on, as though looking for a convenient exit. The party was over . . . in more ways than one.

2

FRIENDS AND ENEMIES

THEY were chalk and cheese, apples and oranges, night and day – take your pick of simile. The entrepreneurs who created Formula One for the modern era ranged across the spectrum of shapes and sizes, intellect and upbringing, and the only thing this disparate band of brothers seemed to share was their obsession with perfection in a sport that ruled their lives to the exclusion of everything else.

They might not have been much alike, but they operated like a sporting Mafia family, outwardly close and united, but sometimes bitter enemies behind the closed doors of the negotiating room. They competed on the track and scrapped to outdo each other's bank balances, yet whenever the shit hit the fan, they closed ranks like the Corleones, the fictional clan of 'The Godfather' movie series, with every man watching the back of every other with a ferocity that could repel even the most powerful critics.

Some started with eye-watering overdrafts, but they all ended up with eye-watering wealth. The money seemed almost obscene, as each of these men became multimillion-aires and Bernie Ecclestone gained infamy as Britain's highest-paid executive in the 1990s, at a time when a billion-aire was a rare breed.

The rows were very public and the threats of a split constant and it sometimes seemed as if Formula One was in a perpetual state of war over who should get the biggest slice of the sport's ever-growing financial cake. David Richards, now in charge of the Motor Sports Association, is one of the most intelligent men in motor racing and steered Colin McRae and Richard Burns to World Rally championships before running both the Benetton and BAR Honda teams. He sees it differently: 'It's competition and bragging rights. It's not about money. The most competitive people in the world were around that Formula One table. They were extraordinary and would be extraordinary in any walk of life.'

Bernie Ecclestone, born in 1930, is the son of a Lowestoft trawlerman and the antithesis of Max Mosley, born ten years later to the fascist leader Oswald Mosley and his wife Diana, the couple notorious for their admiration for Adolf Hitler. Ecclestone and Mosley became as close as Siamese twins when they ruled Formula One together, although Mosley could perhaps have used his experience to advise Ecclestone not to tell *The Times* of his respect for Hitler's ability to 'get things done' in an interview in 2009. Mosley understood more than most just how contentious that would be.

The aristocratic Luca Cordero di Montezemolo was born, in August 1947, into one of Italy's most privileged families in

Bologna, while Ron Dennis, just two months older, came from a semi-detached home in Woking, a commuter town along the M3 corridor in the south of England. Montezemolo is multilingual, urbane, and was courted to become president of Italy; Dennis invented a strangulated version of English called 'Ronspeak' and confesses to suffering from Obsessive Compulsive Disorder, but nevertheless dragged McLaren into position as the most successful Formula One team in history after Ferrari. Both men, as different in temperament and style as it is possible to be, left a legacy of two companies – Ferrari and McLaren – whose brand names are famous the world over and bywords for technological and engineering excellence.

Sir Frank Williams was born five years before Montezemolo and Dennis, and a world away in South Shields, a fishing town in the northeast of England, where he lived until his parents split up and he was sent away to boarding school. By then, Sir Jackie Stewart, born in 1939, was being prepared for a life in his family motor business, dealing in Jaguar and Austin cars. Both men became motor-racing knights, yet their lives are marked by their differences.

There were significant others who came and went, like Eddie Jordan, born in 1948. The Irishman risked everything – his home, his future and his family – but walked away with a fortune because of his frenetic and indefatigable will. And there was the latecomer who knew nothing of motor racing: Flavio Briatore, flamboyant, opinionated and accused of cheating on an epic scale, was born in 1950 in the small town of Verzuolo in northern Italy. One of his early jobs was assistant to a businessman rumoured to have Mafia connections after he was killed by a car bomb, a glamorous embellishment of the story of the man whose brash confidence and business acumen helped turn the Benetton fashion brand into a household name before he moved into Formula One.

Put all of these characters into the same room and it would be impossible to fathom what they might have in common, save for one thing: Formula One. And maybe a second: they were all utterly driven to succeed. Perhaps one day a psychologist could prise open their skulls and tell us why such a small group of maybe half a dozen men, with some notable additions, could arrive in a single sport as contemporaries and turn it into their personal property, as well as propelling its image onto tens of millions of television screens around the world and generating billions of pounds of wealth.

There could be nothing but Formula One in their lives. Ron Dennis's neurosis turned out to be both affliction and strength. Was that what drove him as a youngster to work day and night with no time for an evening at the pictures with his arm around a girl, or a day at the seaside with his mates or a holiday at the beach? He simply never stopped.

'If you want to be the best in our world, everything else has to come second. To be focused and dedicated you need to be full of passion. My passion was extreme,' he told the American Academy of Achievement when it honoured his life in 2017.

'There was no room for girlfriends in my life, even in my early twenties, and I had no opportunity to spend my money because I didn't socialise because I was always working.'

Dennis didn't marry until he was thirty-eight. He was divorced from Lisa, his wife of twenty-two years, in 2008. They were a formidable combination, and there was a wistful note in his voice when he added to his analysis of the passion that has driven him. 'Sometimes you don't have time to decompress when you leave work. You are still at work when you get home and your family gets it.'

Claire Williams felt the restless quest that overshadowed these lives acutely, growing up with a father who invested everything he had in Formula One. Having succeeded once, Sir Frank Williams then had to overcome terrible disability, confined to a wheelchair for more than three decades. His private apartment is on the boardroom floor of the Williams factory, just around the corner from the buzz of office secretaries, designers and engineers. The longest-surviving tetraplegic in medical history, Sir Frank no longer plays an active role in the eponymous team he founded and nurtured into one of the most successful of all time, but he still could not let go of the sport that had been his life. According to Claire Williams, even her father's disability has had to take second place to his obsession with Formula One.

'The only thing my father did for me – from primary to boarding school and to university – was attend one single parents' evening. I don't begrudge that because Dad achieved so much. If you are going to be successful, you have to have that single-minded focus. But to give your whole life, to be so consumed, to be so obsessed and not have any other passions or pastimes, I find difficult to compute.'

To those outside Formula One, none of this makes sense in the real world, where people go shopping, take the kids to the playground and have something called hobbies. Then there is the sport, a curious combination of geeky obsession with mechanics and aerodynamics, tyres and computers, all contained in a glittering bubble that looks like something plucked from an edition of *Vogue*. Formula One has long been sporting Marmite: people love it or loathe it; there is rarely ambivalence. Newspaper, television and radio sports editors, usually steeped in football, cricket and rugby, cannot understand the jargon and the intricacies, never mind the constant references to huge amounts of money that seem to be the driving force. Reader comments below Formula One stories will often be populated by snarling, insulting remarks, usually summed up as: 'It's not a sport.'

There is little comprehension of why men like Frank Williams should be so hooked on the thrills of speed and danger, or why fans are so desperate to peek into the conspicuous opulence of the paddock with its supermodels and yachts.

Instead, Formula One is despised by many, who simply see it as a monotonous sport for anoraks. Worse still, the chattering classes often make a virtue of denigrating a sport that has appeared dedicated for so long to consuming so much. Take this withering description by Camilla Long in *The Sunday Times* in February 2018, a few days after Formula One's new owners Liberty Media announced that they were banning grid girls, one of the more infamous appendages of Formula One for generations, because they no longer fit the sport's 'brand values'. Long pulled no punches: 'I was fascinated to hear what F1's "brand values" actually were as I can't think of an industry more predicated on naked curves and the ogling of giant pneumatic breasts than the gas-guzzling, sock-on-the-head git circus that is automotive racing.'

That is a superficial assessment from a writer whose speciality appears to be grinding axes, but it might echo with millions, particularly women who see Formula One as a 'male only' preserve in these days of the #MeToo movement. Claire Williams felt it acutely at her first meeting with the sport's top executives as her father's new deputy team principal: 'We are all around the table and every so often Luca [Di Montezemolo] would look at me. It was all very awkward and embarrassing. Eventually, he got up and stopped behind me and said, "Now I know who you are. You are little Claire. I have known you since you were so small. You were that little person and now you are here." And he pats me on the head. I wanted the chair to swallow me up. Can you imagine someone doing that?'

It might have been a patronising moment, but there is a place for women. Apart from Claire Williams leading a famous team, check the garages during a broadcast and there will be women at laptops, others in overalls pitching in with the men at all levels of the teams. The missing link is a driver: women have had their chances – Maria Teresa de Filippis in the 1950s and Lella Lombardi twenty years later are the only two women to have started a grand prix – but no one knows why they fail to make the grade. Then again, plenty of men fail the ultimate test of Formula One. Perhaps salvation lies with Jamie Chadwick, a feisty young Briton, who won her first race in British Formula Three in 2018, the same series that groomed drivers like Martin Brundle, Mika Häkkinen and Ayrton Senna. She says that motor racing is desperate for a female champion – and she is right. Sponsors and teams would fall over themselves for a brilliant young woman to break up the ages-old male cartel.

But perceptions are everything, and Formula One's image has been forged over generations. Outsiders often only see the glitter of gold from the paddock and fail to understand the rich seam of passion that runs through the sport, as well as the technical brilliance admired around the world. There is little credit given for the creation of a magnificent, world-leading British industry, which has Formula One at its apex. From a clutch of garage enthusiasts, Formula One led British motorsport to become a £9 billion industry involving 4,500 companies, which export 87 per cent of everything they make and employ more than 41,000 people, according to figures calculated by the Motorsport Industry Association in 2013. That is, by any measure, huge.

Yet Formula One is rarely lauded and decades of bickering over cash has led to the assumption that this is a cold, calculating industry built on a thirst for riches at the expense of all else. Little wonder, then, that politicians and virtue-signallers will not allow any leeway for a sport that has garnered a reputation for excess and flirted with allegations of corruption and cheating on a scale that takes the breath away.

The drivers are the combatants on the track and grab the headlines with their exploits and their seven-figure salaries and many have forged their names onto the public consciousness to become unforgettable monuments of sport. Juan Manuel Fangio, Stirling Moss, Jackie Stewart, James Hunt, Michael Schumacher and Lewis Hamilton are among the poster boys who have thrilled millions with their exploits and shared grief when one of their own failed to return from a race.

But motor racing is not all cosseted drivers, conniving bosses and wall-to-wall champagne, it is men and women from ordinary families who have chosen to work in a business that demands loyalty, precision, dedication and just as much passion as from any of the superstars who hog the television interviews and parade around the paddock in front of millions. They are unseen and largely unsung, but their emotions run just as deep.

Flavio Briatore knew nothing of Formula One when he arrived from the United States, having helped transform Benetton into one of the world's biggest fashion brands. Briatore thought it was just another job, but soon realised how wrong he was when he turned up at the Benetton factory in rural Oxfordshire in 1990.

'I couldn't understand what was going on. It wasn't a business, like Benetton, because people were very emotional about the racing, right down to the guy sweeping the floor,' he told me. 'There was a big accident at a test and the car was very badly damaged. Everyone, including the secretaries, came into the courtyard to look at the car. I thought they were all mad. What is my secretary doing looking at the car? She can't fix it. Everyone was so emotional, so taken up with the cars and how they looked, how fast they were and who was driving them. This wasn't business for them. Formula One is noise and speed, but more than that, it is a lifestyle.'

Finbarr O'Connell is as far from being a motor-racing nut as you can get. In the City headquarters of Smith & Williamson, O'Connell is a star administrator, handling some of the firm's biggest accounts, trying to sort out failed businesses. He has run gold mines in Ghana, worried about wheat in the Ukraine and was involved in sorting out the mess of Boris Becker's bankruptcy. But Formula One, that was different. When he walked through the gates of the collapsed Caterham team in Leafield, Oxfordshire, in October 2014, he found himself staring at some of the most glamorous pieces of engineering in British industry and meeting a workforce that refused to give up, take their redundancy and slink into the countryside. 'One thing I will always remember is the team spirit – the guys, mechanics, all of the staff,' O'Connell says in his soft Irish burr.

The easy way out would have been to close the doors of the factory and sell off all the shiny chassis parts and carbon fibre, but O'Connell was inspired to try a last throw of the dice to keep Caterham alive. He started a crowd-funding page to get the team to the final grand prix of the 2014 season in Abu Dhabi. They had missed two races after the finances dried up, but O'Connell was hoping someone would spot the dedication and passion of the team members and step in with an offer to buy, if he could get the squad to perform one last time. The crowd-funding raised more than £230,000 and another £500,000 worth of sponsorship was enough to get the team on its way. Any bitterness among the workers was put to one side as the Caterham men and women scurried into action. That alone was impressive, but O'Connell had to bear in mind that this team was no world-beater: Caterham had not scored so much as a single point in five seasons in Formula One. There had been no celebratory champagne in the dark green Caterham motorhome, and not a single hurrah from five seasons of slog with no reward from one side of the world to the other.

In a sport deliberately skewed to favour the rich and powerful over the underdogs, you wondered why small teams like Caterham bothered. They could never win or even catch a close-up glimpse of a trophy, unless one of the big teams dropped one in an airport lounge. Every grand prix was a hopeless quest against the odds – but it was *their* hopeless quest. Perhaps the doggedness was built in, for this was their team, and their sport, and they weren't giving up that easily. O'Connell appeared an unlikely leader – a bespectacled accountant with greying hair and a twinkly smile – but where he led, the Caterham people were willing to follow.

If O'Connell was surprised at the readiness of mechanics

and engineers to work unpaid for almost a week under the intense sun of the Middle East and knowing their futures were on the line, he was amazed when he entered the Abu Dhabi paddock a little over a month after taking over. Suddenly, Formula One made sense to a man who had never seen a race or heard the blast of a Formula One engine. Money dripped from the sand-coloured walls of the hospitality offices, where Arab sheikhs mixed with European business-men, and champagne flowed into the night illuminated by thousands of high-powered floodlights.

'At that point, I got it,' O'Connell says. 'Here I could see all the attractions and why people get so passionate about it. They were just excited at being there. If you were a skilled mechanic servicing very wealthy people's cars, you would make twice as much money as you would make as a Formula One mechanic, but that isn't what they wanted. You could see they were all loving it.'

Entertainment in the paddock had once been rickety deck-chairs and trestle tables groaning under the weight of sand-wiches, with bottles of beer and the promise of cake, and shel-ter was a motorhome with an awning stretched out from the roof of a van that carried the tools as well as the food. If it rained, you got wet; if the sun shone, you got hot. Now Formula One entertains in huge, air-conditioned 'hospitality centres', where supermodels and business tycoons rub shoul-ders with stars like Michael Douglas, Al Pacino, Rihanna, David and Victoria Beckham, or chef Gordon Ramsay.

The people were beautiful, the food was beautiful and the wines fine, and the paddock was a paradise only accessed by an electronic pass issued with the personal approval of Ecclestone. That pass unlocked the gates to a parallel universe of wealth and glitter and everyone's aspiration was to get into that paddock. Those locked out were left with their envy. Every glitzy moment was a product of the Ecclestone gang's obsession with neatness, shiny metal and precision, and the Yas Marina circuit, the hub of more than $40 billion worth of investment by Abu Dhabi, is the zenith of their achievements.

This gang of entrepreneurs succeeded because they couldn't curb the compulsion to compete and those who didn't commit themselves body and soul discovered that there was no place for them in this strange asylum of people chained to their obsession. David Coulthard has lived his entire adult life in Formula One, first as a driver at Williams and McLaren, then Red Bull, where he transformed himself into a television pundit and successful businessman with his own television production and events companies. This is what he says of Ecclestone and his unique circus of speed: 'They are all on the spectrum, wrapped up in total belief. Where other people would give up because they are tired or cold or hungry or fed up, these guys can't. The majority of people go to a desk and work nine to five and then leave the job. These guys live their work. You either get swept up in this industry of Formula One – or you get chewed up and spat out.'

3

THE PIONEERS

THE inbox in Kimi Räikkönen's email account pings to signal a new message arriving just hours before he pulls on his red overalls to drive for the most famous Formula One team of them all. Räikkönen, poker-faced and almost mute in public, is a friendly and garrulous man in private, capable of extreme warmth and fun, according to his biggest fan, Brenda Vernor.

Brenda worries that he gets tangled up too often in crashes and incidents with that young kid Max Verstappen. 'I told Kimi something should be done. It is absolutely wrong and no driver in the past has been like that.'

Brenda should know because she has been friends with so many drivers down the years. Kimi was always a favourite of Brenda's, and she was protective of the young Finn she first met when he replaced Michael Schumacher at Ferrari in 2007. She wasn't that keen on Schumi, the way he assumed that he could take up residence in Enzo Ferrari's cottage in the middle of the Ferrari test track at Fiorano when he came to put his latest Formula One car through its paces. He would demand clean sheets every day and let his dog eat off the kitchen floor, she says, and then order takeaway food from the nearby Montana restaurant, a favourite with the Ferrari team, to eat alone. No, she was sorry for Michael, but she never warmed to him.

He wasn't close like Kimi or Jody Scheckter or Gilles Villeneuve, or the many who passed through her life since she'd pitched up in the little industrial town of Maranello, a young woman from Croydon who taught herself Italian with the distinctive Modenese accent of the region and with an attitude. She got a job teaching English to a teenager called Piero Lardi and encountered a grey-haired man in formal suit often lingering outside the room. She discovered that he was more than a visitor and that Piero was his illegitimate son, although she had no idea who Enzo Ferrari was. Then he phoned one day and offered her a job as his secretary. If she knew nothing of Ferrari then, she is encyclopaedic now. Drivers had to pass muster with Brenda before they got to Enzo Ferrari's inner sanctum, and she was the contact point for Bernie Ecclestone and his British *garagistes*, the upstarts who stole the thunder from the world's most famous racing marque. She was the gateway to Enzo Ferrari, the 'Old Man'.

Brenda is eighty-four when we meet and takes me to one of her favourite haunts, a trattoria down the road from the Ferrari factory gates where the scene is much the same as when she worked there, the only English voice in Maranello and the only woman among 200 men on the race team. She would rally round the mechanics she regarded as her family, taking trays laden with Lambrusco and prosciutto to keep them going through long nights when the red race cars were being prepared for their next grand prix. She washed overalls for the drivers and sewed on their sponsor patches She laughed and dined with them and then sat in rueful silence if they didn't return from a race, another cross on the casualty list. They were the days when she avoided the Old Man, as she calls him. He never showed his emotions and he never cried in public. A driver died but Ferrari lived on.

The Ferrari name in yellow is still over the rectangular tunnel entrance to the factory, and the walls remain a murky terracotta. Every now and again, a car emerges, its nose covered in sheets to disguise its sleek features, to set off down the narrow road, its engine barking like an angry dog.

Schumacher didn't make Brenda's favourites list, and nor did Alain Prost or Mario Andretti, but plenty of others did: Ayrton Senna was a gentleman, she says, and she remembers Jochen Rindt's eyes as the most beautiful, while Carlos Reutemann left her speechless because he was so handsome. She is still in touch with Jody Scheckter, Jean Alesi and Gerhard Berger, who used to change into his race overalls in her office before heading off to test drive his Formula One car.

She adored Gilles Villeneuve, his playfulness, like a child who couldn't grow up. He scared her so much driving to dinner one night that she insisted he stop so that she could get out. He once sent her a note and, instead of addressing it to Brenda Vernor, care of Ferrari, he addressed it to Ferrari, care of Brenda Vernor, almost acknowledging her role as the mother hen. She kept the note. His death at the 1982 Belgian Grand Prix was devastating, yet she knew deep inside that his risk-taking would end in tears. Enzo wouldn't have a word said against his favourite, even when the engineers complained that Villeneuve was wrecking their machinery with his hard-driving style. There is a picture of the two men together, Villeneuve with a bottle of fizzy Lambrusco in hand and Ferrari wreathed in smiles. After Villeneuve died, nothing was said. 'Gilles was like a son. Monday morning was like any other Monday morning. I didn't knock on the door. I just left the Old Man alone. It was business as usual.'

Lorenzo Bandini, dark-haired and with a lust for life, lived in her apartment building. 'He was a naughty boy. He used to be out until the early hours and I would have to cover for him. He was great fun.' Brenda was in Monte Carlo on that day in May 1967, when Bandini lost control of his Ferrari and flipped into the primitive hay bales that passed for a safety barricade. Suffering chest injuries and 70 per cent burns, Bandini died three days later. 'I said I wouldn't ever return to Monaco and it was ten years before I could go back,' Brenda says, visibly saddened as she cradled her small glass of Sangiovese, wine from grapes that grow in fields around Maranello. There were no special words for Bandini, dead at just thirty-one and no commemoration. But then, it would need a huge monument to pay tribute to all of the drivers who had died racing in a Ferrari. So much talk of sadness and lost friends makes the short return journey into Maranello more subdued.

We pass the main roundabout that signifies that Maranello is not so much a one-horse town as a Prancing Horse town, because its existence is dependent on Ferrari. On the roundabout, there is a statue of the horse rearing on its hind legs – the famous *Cavallino Rampante*, the symbol of Ferrari. It is the first thing to greet you if you drive the ten or so miles from Modena along the same winding roads, through olive groves and rows of vines, that Enzo Ferrari would have taken on his daily commute to his factory in the centre of Maranello.

The roads were full of traffic, including many red or yellow Ferraris, their exhausts rasping as enthusiastic drivers planted their feet on the throttles in an exhibition of Italian horsepower. The locals don't even bother to look up – they know all about Ferraris. The Ferraris head for the museum dedicated to the man who founded the legend they worship. It is difficult to imagine such pilgrimages to Woking or Milton Keynes, as successful as Ferrari's British rivals have been, because they don't have the mystique, the history, or the towering figure who created the myth. Crowds of people of all ages throng the concourse in front of the museum, taking the inevitable selfies, while inside families pose in front of one car after another. One floor is all Formula One cars and the other is devoted to cars for the road, including the Enzo, a 220 mph monster named in honour of the founder. Only 399 were built, with an on-the-road price of $659,000 in 2002; you would be lucky to get one at auction now for less than $3 million.

All this for an old man with claustrophobia and a complex love life, with his tempers and his authoritarianism, who loved the opera of Puccini and Verdi but hated travelling, and who shunned riding around in a Ferrari and drove a little Renault 5 instead. He was aloof and austere yet kind and generous, and he built one of the greatest symbols of all Italy, not a Formula One team but a national monument to an intoxicating, thrilling way of life. And he was never satisfied. When asked once which was the best Ferrari, he said simply: 'The next one.'

Only one name has been a constant in the modern era of Formula One, only one team has contested every season of the Formula One world championship since it was inaugurated in 1950, and only one team can be recognised from one side of the world to the other, from housewives in Los Angeles to schoolchildren in Shanghai: Ferrari. More than that, Enzo Ferrari was the bridge from the old world of motor racing to the new age of entrepreneurs who made Formula One their own. Enzo Ferrari was revered in his homeland as 'Il Commendatore', the Commander, but he preferred the simplicity and the meaning of 'L'Ingegnere', the Engineer. He might more accurately have been called the Pioneer.

It seems impossible to imagine now, but Enzo Ferrari was

born in 1898, just a dozen years after the date that experts regard as the birth of the motorcar. He was only ten when, in 1908, his father Alfredo took him to watch the Circuito di Bologna, a 50-kilometre course that followed public roads surrounding the city before hurtling back down the Via Emilia, the main drag towards Bologna Station. The red Fiats dominated, with Felice Nazzaro winning at an average of 74 mph, on the straight, dusty roads. It must have been a thrilling spectacle for a small boy, and you can almost imagine him going home to Modena, his head brimming with the sights and sounds that decades later would still hold their extraordinary grip on his life.

Enzo achieved his dream of becoming a driver with the Alfa Romeo company, a dominant force in the early days of motor racing, and won at the Circuito del Savio near Ravenna, where he met Count Enrico Baracca, the father of Francesco, the wartime fighter ace who was in the same air squadron during the First World War as Enzo's late brother Alfredo. Aware of the link between the families, Countess Paolina asked Ferrari to use the Prancing Horse emblem that had adorned her son's primitive aircraft before he was shot down and killed. According to legend, a humbled Ferrari did so, adding the yellow background, the colour of his home city of Modena.

The Prancing Horse is emblematic of an era when racing drivers were adventurers, risking as much as the tragic Francesco Baracca did in his rickety aircraft in the skies over war-torn

Europe. The cars were heavy, awkward and primitive, and death was ever-present. Ferrari held Ugo Sivocci, an early mentor and teammate, in his arms as his life ebbed away after a crash at the Circuito del Savio and was shattered in 1925 by the death of another friend and teammate, Antonio Ascari, who was killed at the French Grand Prix. It has been said that grand-prix racing was war without the shooting, and here was proof.

Driving gave way to running his own operation, but during the Second World War, Ferrari moved his factory from near the railway lines of Modena, which were vulnerable to Allied bombing, to a patch of agricultural land a dozen miles south in Maranello where his business made valuable components for the war effort. But his head was full of his beloved red cars and racing. The war was barely over before he switched back to car production and, by 1949, his cars had won the Le Mans 24 Hours Endurance Race and added the Targa Florio and the Mille Miglia to the trophy cabinet. Now he was ready to race the mighty Alfa Romeo and Maserati squads with his own cars in the new Formula One world championship inaugurated in 1950.

Two years later, in 1952, Alberto Ascari, the son of Enzo Ferrari's late colleague and friend, became the first Ferrari world champion, after a dominant season in which he won six of the eight grands prix. The legend of Ferrari was born.

As Ferraris were roaring around the tracks of Europe, Britain was still recovering from the pain of the war years. But a spirit of enterprise was also dawning, fuelled by a lust for life in the aftermath of so much destruction. The fledgling National Health Service was taking shape, a medical student called Roger Bannister had run the first four-minute mile and the world's first jet airliner flew from the De Havilland airstrip in Hatfield in Hertfordshire. Sedate dances were giving way to skiffle and raucous pop music, performed by young men with swaying hips and slick hair. Youngsters flocked to the cinema for their Friday night entertainment, not for cheery musicals and Westerns but to watch hard-hitting social dramas, in which they were given a voice of defiance against the establishment. The world was changing fast and so was the world of Formula One.

There was passion enough for motor racing in Britain, but not the infrastructure that the Italians had built up around Modena, Italy's engineering epicentre, where Enzo Ferrari could take his pick from the artisan workers who specialised in skills like welding and machining. But a generation of engineers in Britain had been trained in the Royal Air Force, often in only a few weeks, learning to work fast and smart, youngsters like Ken Tyrrell, who served in bombers as a navigator, and Colin Chapman, who completed his National Service with the RAF.

Money was scarce and the grandeur of grand-prix racing was largely beyond the stretched finances of those left after the hostilities with Germany had ended. Tyrrell was in the family timber business, although he looked as though he was made of granite. He was a useful centre-half with the village football team and joined in when they decided to throw some crates of beer onto a bus and drive up to Silverstone to watch the BRM cars in action at the 1951 British Grand Prix. The Alfa Romeos of Giuseppe 'Nino' Farina and Juan Manuel Fangio dominated the BRMs, but Tyrrell was still captivated. For his biography, he told Christopher Hilton, a friend and journalist: 'I had never even read anything about motor racing before that, but it really got to me. As soon as I saw it, I fell in love.'

But grand-prix racing was not for the masses yet. Instead, motorcycling – cheap and easily available – was big business and fertile ground for a young man whose fledgling business career had started in the playground, selling buns and pens to classmates to turn a few quid like an apprentice market trader. Bernie Ecclestone was a natural salesman, as a teenager able to turn on the charm and make a sale before his customer had time to blink. He left school at sixteen to work for the Gas Board, but spent all of his time on the company phone finding motorbikes to buy and sell and cleaning his treasured stock. Ecclestone knew his way around a motorcycle after starting to race as a sixteen-year-old from 1946 as the debris of war was cleared, competing in hill climbs and scrambles before taking his motorcycle to Brands Hatch, where there would be thousands of spectators yearning for cheap and cheerful excitement after the privations of war. It was entertainment for the crowds, but dangerous for the participants, and Ecclestone was carted off to hospital concussed and bruised more than once.

For Ecclestone, it was all about the next move, the next deal, the next victory. The £5-a-week wage at the Gas Board was soon ditched as he discovered he could make more money from selling motorbikes. He set up his nascent business in a garage in Bexleyheath in southeast London called Harcourt's, but, just eighteen months later, moved across the road to share a bigger and better forecourt at Compton & Fuller. There he could see more trade and more profit, buying in motorbikes, cleaning and repairing them before selling at twice the mark-up – and then dashing off to a race for his adrenalin rush.

A legacy of the war was redundant airfields: Spitfires and Hurricanes had flown out of West Hampnett next to Goodwood House, and paratroopers in gliders left Thruxton to take part in the D-Day landings. In Northamptonshire, Wellington bombers trundled into the skies from a flat, treeless expanse with long runways near the village of Silverstone – an ideal location for a racer with a thirst for speed and with what should have been little risk. In September 1947, a group of pals led by Maurice Geoghegan, who lived in the village, raced over a two-mile circuit along the runways that had once carried their deadly cargo to war. There was a single casualty this time: Geoghegan hit a wandering sheep and the car was written off. The event was commemorated as the Mutton Grand Prix.

The Royal Automobile Club saw the potential for a permanent home for British motor racing – minus the sheep – but it was a time of austerity, with little money available for a project that would be seen as frivolous and for the benefit of a few privileged and wealthy drivers and a host of foreign manufacturers. Silverstone, however, provided a cheap and reasonable proposition, positioned almost in the centre of England, and with land to spare as well as asphalted runways and perimeter roads. It was ready-made for action. A year after the Mutton Grand Prix came the official British Grand Prix, attended by more than 100,000 spectators, who were helping to establish the circuit as a permanent feature of British sporting life.

The 1949 grand prix was to entertain yet more huge crowds, but also provide a platform for a man who would become as much part of Sunday life in Britain as roast beef and Yorkshire pudding. Murray Walker was brought up in the world of motorcycles, his father Graham competing at the Isle of Man TT races, but he remembers being taken from his Warwickshire home to the Donington circuit in 1938 as a fifteen-year-old, where he met Tazio Nuvolari, dressed in his blindingly white overalls before he drove the fearsome Auto Union to victory. After fifty years at the microphone, commentating on grands prix and meeting almost every key figure in Formula One, Nuvolari remained his hero.

Walker was sent to the 1949 British Grand Prix, to make his commentating debut, installed in a makeshift wooden box at Silverstone's Stowe Corner to report on the action, although he barely knew what was happening. There was none of the coverage of today, with computers and high-definition cameras and clever electronic timing boards. He was alone with a microphone, a set of notes and a great deal of hope. The huge cars snarled past, their tyres squealing, leaving behind an odour trail of oil and petrol. Suddenly, an English Racing Automobiles car belonging to John Bolster cartwheeled past him end over end. Bolster was thrown clear and landed bleeding badly, almost at Walker's feet. All that the fledgling commentator, later to be affectionately known as 'Motormouth', could think to tell his listeners was: 'And Bolster's gone off.'

The adoption of Silverstone was a physical landmark in the revolution starting to take place in a sport now known and accepted as Formula One, and the old airfield was to provide the stage on which to launch history. The grid for the first Formula One world championship race for drivers – the British Grand Prix at Silverstone on 13 May 1950 – was dominated by the powerful Alfa Romeo and Maserati works squads. Only five British-made cars were entered, all from English Racing Automobiles, better known as ERA, the marque started before the war by Raymond Mays from a garage behind the family home in Bourne in Lincolnshire.

Enzo Ferrari refused to send his Scuderia to this gala attended by 150,000 spectators and the King and Queen, Princess Margaret and Earl and Countess Mountbatten. In a huff over the prize money on offer, Ferrari took his team to a minor Formula Two race at Mons in Belgium, while his countryman, Giuseppe Farina, dominated at Silverstone, with pole position and victory for Alfa Romeo. The man from Turin,

Fiat's city, would go on to become Formula One's first official world champion.

Apart from the odd foray, British marques were largely absent from the early post-war years of Formula One and the first world champions drove cars from Italy or Germany – Alfa Romeo, Maserati, Mercedes and, of course, Ferrari. Imperceptibly, though, a cluster was forming: long before the concept of Silicon Valley, the south of England was becoming the world's motor-racing valley, its boundaries at first set from north London, running south to affluent Surrey.

In north London a young man, fresh out of the forces, wanted to put the engineering knowledge he had gleaned – first at University College London and then in the RAF – to good use. There wasn't much in the way of family money behind Colin Chapman. His father ran the Railway Hotel in Hornsey and when he married Hazel, his new father-in-law let him use his lock-up garage for the princely rent of ten bob a week – 50 pence in today's money. Chapman was never that good with money and the ten shillings probably never changed hands. Hazel was a driving force, though, and it was her £25 that paid for the start-up of Lotus Engineering in 1952. It was hand-to-mouth stuff, with Chapman initially rebuilding Austins and Fords, but slowly Lotus cars began to take to the tracks and his major success came with the Lotus 7, a light-weight two-seater that doubled up as a road and track car. He sold more than 100 in 1956, and his career as an engineer and team owner took off.

Stirling Moss was Britain's flag bearer, becoming the nation's first driver to win a world championship race in 1955 at the British Grand Prix on the old Aintree circuit on Merseyside, although he had to do it in a Mercedes from Germany, and then Tony Brooks signalled Britain's emergence from the domination of foreign constructors when he drove a Connaught car, which came out of a garage in the small village of Send in Surrey, to victory at the non-championship Syracuse Grand Prix that same year. Two years on, Stirling Moss and Tony Brooks jointly won the British Grand Prix at Aintree in a Vanwall built in Acton, west London. It was a first for a British constructor in the modern era of the world championship, and a glorious triumph on home ground.

British drivers were in the ascendance, followed by British racing teams, accelerated by the ingenuity of a father and son who ran a garage business from Surbiton in Surrey. Surbiton is a quiet town south of London, probably most famous as the epitome of suburban life (the popular TV comedy *The Good Life* was set on one of its middle-class housing estates), rather than for being home to Charles and John Cooper. To call their operation a factory might be overstating it – John Surtees, the only man to win world championships on two and four wheels, thought it was little more than 'a blacksmith's shop', so rudimentary was their engineering, as they took suspensions from Fiat road cars, fitted telescopic dampers and then stuck a 500-cc JAP motorcycle speedway engine at the back. It might seem now like a sophisticated idea to put the engine behind the driver, but it had to go into the rear simply because the motorcycle engine drove the rear axle with a chain.

These tiny, buzzy cars provided a few giggles for the royalty of motor racing, who laughed at their elementary engineering, and Enzo Ferrari mocked his new rivals as *garagistes*, jumped-up garage owners, because they were not like him, making both engine and chassis as a dedicated manufacturer in Formula One. It was a curious cottage industry and drivers would gather at the Coopers' garage to hang around, making sure that their car was completed with all of the components they had ordered.

One of those lurking in the background was a young man making a name as a used-car dealer. Bernie Ecclestone had moved up in the world from motorcycles and was selling – and racing – cars. The Cooper cars were quick and they were fun, and provided the training ground for some of Britain's greatest racing drivers, from Surtees, Moss and Brooks to Peter Collins, Mike Hawthorn and Ken Tyrrell. And a novice called Ecclestone.

The world of motor racing sat up to take notice at the first Formula One grand prix of the 1958 season in Argentina, when Stirling Moss drove Rob Walker's privately entered Cooper T43 to victory, chased by the twin Ferraris of Luigi Musso and Mike Hawthorn. That was the first win for a rear-engine car in the new world drivers' championship, and a first for a privateer, but it was more than that: the Coopers had demonstrated that a new breed of lightweight, aerodynamic cars, handled by adventurous young drivers like Moss, were the way ahead for Formula One, once the preserve of the privileged and wealthy or the huge European manufacturers. Formula One was now open to entrepreneurs with ideas and enthusiasm.

Mike Hawthorn was Britain's first world champion driver in 1958, at the wheel of a Ferrari. It was momentous for the nation, but there was greater significance on the results sheet at the end of that season, for eight of the ten official championship races were won by Vanwall and Cooper, and Vanwall were Britain's first world champion constructor. Apparently, John Cooper had a habit of doing forward somersaults in the pit lane after each victory, and there would be plenty of those to come as Jack Brabham, an Australian who emigrated to the new home of motor racing in Britain, took successive drivers' championships in 1959 and 1960, with Cooper as the champion constructor.

Enzo Ferrari's world had turned, and the wretched little teams based in England that he had mocked were making Formula One their own. Enzo hated the concept of a rear-engine car – the horse pulled the cart, he said – but these new teams were small and nimble, clever and innovative and passionate about the sport.

Ecclestone loved this world. He was lauded for some of his exploits in Formula Three, proving to be an aggressive and ambitious driver, and was good enough to be competing against men like Stirling Moss and at major circuits, including Germany's infamous Nürburgring. But there were too many crashes: at Brands Hatch in 1951, he was hit by a stray wheel and careered through a fence into spectators, knocking over an eight-year-old boy who fractured his thigh. Another time, he flipped over a fence and landed in a car park. He was getting £100 from Shell to race, but the appearances became more sporadic. There was no big money in driving, not like in his business, where the cash registers were ringing like a frantic peal of church bells. He told his friends he couldn't race seriously any longer because he couldn't afford it. He was selling cars thick and fast, with his trademark handshake as his currency. If he made a deal, he made a deal. Max Mosley, later to become his confidant and greatest ally in Formula One, told me: 'Bernie used to say: never put anything in writing because then you can't argue that you didn't say this or that if there is a dispute. I think he learned all this off the Tottenham Court Road as a car dealer. If you wanted to learn about wheeling and dealing, that was the environment for it.

'He heard about a scheme run by dealers in Manchester, who would go to an auction to bid against each other and then go to the Queen's Hotel and swap whatever they bought between them. He was introduced as this green guy from London, but he was sharper than all of them. He would introduce a couple of fictitious cars into the dealing and then the cars would go around this bargaining table and at the end of the evening he would end up with his two fictitious cars back plus two or three more. Inevitably, he started to get bored with all this, so the next time he went up, he introduced an articulated lorry into the swap. At the end of the evening some old dealer said, "You'll be wanting your artic back then, son." No one figured it out. But he was always looking for the next deal.'

Even now, Ecclestone haunts the auction rooms. One of his big deals before Formula One came from selling his Weekend Car Auctions business to British Car Auctions, and there must be something in the air that makes sniffing a bargain irresistible. 'You will find him at the auction at Lots Road in Chelsea on a Sunday morning,' says Christian Horner, principal of the Red Bull team and best man at Ecclestone's third wedding. 'It's all about the deal. It doesn't matter if it's a crappy £200 sofa or a £200 million television deal with a broadcaster, it is about the deal – and if he can make it as confusing as possible so you don't understand what is going on, then all the better.'

Confusion, Ecclestone's strategy. He was so clever at making sure that the detail of any deal was correct to the letter. His letter. One story, recounted in Tom Bower's biography of Ecclestone, called *No Angel: The Secret Life of Bernie Ecclestone*, tells how he took revenge on a dealer who had tricked him. Ecclestone tracked him down and offered him a Mercedes 230SL hard top at a knockdown price. The dealer was surprised but shook hands and asked where the upmarket convertible car might be. Ecclestone pointed to the street – and there on the pavement was a hard top for a convertible car. Just no car. The deal was the deal and to the letter of the offer.

Bernie Ecclestone wanted to be part of that 1958 season,

entering himself in the Monaco Grand Prix in a Connaught. Jack Brabham was in a Cooper with Moss and Brooks driving Vanwalls, while Mike Hawthorn, Peter Collins and Luigi Musso led an exciting Ferrari challenge. Stuart Lewis-Evans, a young driver from Luton rapidly forging a friendship with Ecclestone, was also in a Vanwall. There was to be no glory for the two pals: Ecclestone was among fifteen drivers who failed to qualify, while Lewis-Evans was the first to retire his car, which overheated after just eleven laps.

There was no thought of death or injury in Ecclestone's mind as he tried to wrestle the unwilling Connaught around Monte Carlo's winding streets. The Formula One cars that thrilled this generation were fast, but also horribly fragile. They were basic machines knocked together with hammers and prone to fractures and breaks and tyres that would explode on tracks that could be bumpy and potholed. It was racing at the extreme, often with violent and catastrophic consequences.

The 1958 season has been called a 'Golden Year' for British motor racing, and the legend was burnished by the golden boys from Britain, Collins and Hawthorn, who were driving Ferrari towards the world championship. But it was a season punctuated by too many funerals and would almost destroy Ecclestone's passion for speed.

Musso was killed at the French Grand Prix in July; a month later, in Germany, Collins – gifted, handsome and still just twenty-six – was also dead. In Morocco, the final grand prix of the year, Lewis-Evans crashed when the engine of his Vanwall seized and he smashed into the barriers. The dark green Vanwall's fuel system ruptured and the car burst into flames. Lewis-Evans ran clear, but he was on fire and horribly burned. Ecclestone flew with his injured friend back to England in a plane chartered by the Vanwall owner Tony Vandervell, and to the Queen Victoria Hospital in East Grinstead, which had treated wounded pilots during the Second World War. Stuart Lewis-Evans died after five days in hospital, aged twenty-eight, leaving a wife and two children. Just five days later, Ecclestone, too, turned twenty-eight. He walked away from Formula One, leaving behind the smell of death in Morocco and a loss he had never before experienced.

Enzo Ferrari could not walk away. Motor racing was his life, and he demanded that his drivers gave everything – and more. He had little time for the careful or thoughtful. He wanted drivers with a forceful right foot and a gut full of courage, even when it risked pushing them over the limits of mortality. But that meant that death would not leave Enzo Ferrari or Formula One. In later life, Enzo Ferrari was able to voice the terrible burden of sending out drivers who never came back. 'If you visit the cemetery as often as I do, you will find yourself staring into the mystic face of death,' he said in a television interview in Italy. 'What can you think in that moment? All those worries, all those issues, all those fights to come to this. I question myself profoundly. I feel many things, too many things – for instance, the frightening frailty of human existence.'

4

THE BRITS
ARE COMING

THE Warren Street traders, who bought and sold cars in the street bounded by London's Marylebone Road and Tottenham Court Road, were a tough crowd. Mingling with the dealers on the crowded pavements would be gangsters and ruffians, cheats and swindlers, but Bernie Ecclestone had their measure, even though he was the smallest of the lot, nicknamed 'the Whippet' because of his speed of thought and action, nipping between his rivals and giving prices on the spot – always to his advantage, of course.

He was never cowed by bigger men or scared of the gang warfare that haunted the backstreets of London. The deals were paid for in 'readies', rolls of banknotes that even fifty years on was Ecclestone's preferred way of settling up. He was clever and he was sharp, dressing in the most fashionable suits bought from Edward Sexton on Savile Row, where Mick Jagger or Paul McCartney might show up for the latest in trendy menswear. His slicked-back hairstyle of the 1950s gave way to the more familiar 'moptop' of today, and Ecclestone revelled in London, the epicentre of cool.

Ecclestone was also buying property, investing the money that was rolling in, as well as enjoying the nightlife of the hottest city in the world. Dinner might be in Park Lane followed by a session at Crockfords, the upmarket casino in Mayfair where he was prepared to lose not just hundreds, but thousands. He was mixing with show-business stars, like Val Doonican, the popular singer who was watched by millions on television, or the Eurovision songstresses Lulu and Sandie Shaw. The cars had gone upmarket, too, and Rolls-Royces and Ferraris joined the showroom.

The Sixties were Swinging and the Union Jack was the emblem of a nation rebuilding its confidence to lead the world in fashion, music – and motor racing.

The Coopers were still the British flagship in Formula One, but Colin Chapman's Lotus cars were becoming the new stars of the show. Like Ecclestone, Chapman wore sharp suits and ties but, unlike Ecclestone, he liked to sport his thinning hair swept back, accompanied by a natty moustache that was more Leslie Phillips, the popular rakish lothario of British cinema, than John Lennon.

Chapman emerged from the RAF to start applying aircraft principles of lightweight and aerodynamic streamlining to his cars. The cars were quick until he found a driver who could make them even quicker. A quiet young man from a Scottish farm near Fife called Jim Clark could drive anything – give him a lawnmower or a milk float and he could pilot it at breakneck speeds, yet still smoothly and comfortably within his limits. It was God-given talent. Chapman decided to give him a test, measuring the youngster against some of the best drivers of the day, including Graham Hill, who was to be a two-times world champion. After an early trip across the grass, Clark went faster and faster, eclipsing even Hill. 'God, this bloke's quick. Bring him in, for God's sake, before he kills himself,' Chapman muttered in awe. Clark would be in Chapman's Lotus 18 for the 1960 season, and he would never drive any other type of Formula One car.

Clark was one of the Lotus drivers lined up for the 1961 International Trophy meeting at Silverstone, alongside Stirling Moss, by now a household name as the public thrilled to his exploits on the track and his delight in what he described happily as 'chasing crumpet'.

It was a filthy wet day as the crowds gathered at Silverstone to see the Lotus drivers. On a grassy bank stood a newly married couple. Max Mosley was tall, handsome and extremely clever, but harnessed to a family name that would haunt him. He was the son of Oswald Mosley, the fascist party leader who had triggered riots across Britain and become a pariah in British society. His mother Diana was a great society beauty in her time, but notorious for her admiration for Adolf Hitler. The couple had even married in Germany, with the Führer as a witness and in front of the highest officers of the Third Reich. Mosley was training as a barrister and had no thoughts of motor racing until his wife, Jean, was given two tickets to Silverstone. His feet wet and his clothes soggy, he watched enthralled as Moss won and crowds cheered their British hero. He was hooked, so he taught evening classes in law to raise the money to buy his first racing car, based on a Lotus 7.

Enzo Ferrari didn't care much for fashion, even though his road cars had rapidly become the must-have machines for the glitterati of Hollywood and high-rollers of Europe. A trip along the mountainous roads of the Côte d'Azur or along the Californian coast was made for a red Ferrari, the top down, hair blowing in the breeze, with passers-by stopping to gawp and admire. If only that easy glamour could follow on the track where Lotus and Cooper had parked their cars on Ferrari's private territory.

In 1961, there was revenge of sorts, but overshadowed by tragedy: at the Italian Grand Prix, Wolfgang von Trips needed to finish third to become world champion, while Phil Hill, his Ferrari teammate, would have to finish second to snatch the title away. Monza was in the grip of a hot Italian summer, and spectators crowded into the royal park, hoping for shade among the tall trees that lined the circuit, but desperate to see the Ferraris with their flared 'sharknoses'. Coming into the Parabolica, a long right-hand bend, Von Trips touched the back of Clark's Lotus. The Ferrari was catapulted into a chain-link fence designed to protect spectators; it didn't, and fifteen people died, along with the German. Clark remembered nothing, except seeing the body of Von Trips and feeling 'sick through and through'. He was spirited away from the Carabinieri, who were seeking a culprit for the accident, by

Chapman. Phil Hill won and was world champion by a single point from his dead teammate. There was no celebration in Monza or in Hill's home nation, the USA. Ferrari pulled out of the final race of the season, the US Grand Prix, which meant that the champion from Miami was denied the adulation of his countrymen.

Ferrari didn't like Phil Hill much, considering him too nervous and careful to be a true Ferrari hero. Hill was a quiet, gentle and introspective man, who freely admitted he didn't have the same ruthless streak that drove so many of his rivals. The American was all too aware of the atmosphere at Maranello, where conflict appeared to be part of the diet and as predictable as the heat and sun of an Italian summer. Tim Collings, in *The Piranha Club*, his definitive examination of Formula One's modern era, quotes Hill as saying: 'They think I should go out there in an inferior car and sacrifice myself to the honour and glory of Ferrari. There have been too many sacrifices. I won't be another.'

There had been no thanks for Hill from the Old Man, not a word after everything that had happened during that gruelling season of 1961. When Hill returned to Maranello, he found deep unrest and a mass walkout of senior staff, fed up with the autocratic regime where drivers were considered to be of no more importance than the components in the machinery being turned out of the low cluster of factory buildings.

The Old Man had coveted a driver whose bravura style and

raw courage allied to sublime skill marked him out from the rest. He wanted Stirling Moss, the driver who had beaten Juan Manuel Fangio, the five-times world champion, and who could drive sports cars, saloon cars – any car – and conquered the feared Mille Miglia at an average of almost 99 mph. Enzo was so desperate, he even offered to paint Moss's Ferrari in the blue of the Cooper Climax in which he had won the 1955 Argentine Grand Prix for Rob Walker's privateer team. It was an offer Moss didn't have the chance to refuse.

Born in 1929, Stirling Craufurd Moss might have spent a lifetime cursing his oddball name, but he relished it. His mother Aileen was Scottish and could trace her roots back to William Wallace, the thirteenth-century freedom fighter depicted on film by Mel Gibson in *Braveheart*. She named her only son Stirling, after the town where she was born, and he was rather proud of it, regularly pointing out: 'It's better than Tom or Dick, isn't it?' His father Alfred was one of Britain's most successful dentists and had dabbled in motor racing as a student at the University of Indiana, taking a drive in the Indianapolis 500. Racing was in the blood.

Moss drove an old Austin Seven around the orchard of the family home in Bray on the banks of the River Thames and was desperate to try his hand at racing. His father had drilled into him a respect for money, and when it came to acquiring a tiny 500-cc Cooper, his father loaned him the money but insisted it was to be repaid. Alfred needn't have worried, for his son was a driving prodigy, storming through the ranks and driving any car he could get his hands on, until his final tally was an astonishing 212 career victories in 529 races, including 16 grand-prix wins. It is a total that perhaps no driver will ever rival.

That he was never Formula One world champion never rankled or disturbed Moss. He was second or third in his final seven seasons in the world championship and only an act of the greatest chivalry robbed him of the greatest prize. During the 1958 Portuguese Grand Prix, he had spotted Mike Hawthorn trying to push his stalled Ferrari uphill to jump-start it. Moss slowed and signalled to let the car run downhill, which Hawthorn did and got going again. Hawthorn was disqualified for running against the direction of the race traffic, but Moss intervened with the stewards to speak up for his fellow Brit. Moss had won the grand prix and he knew full well what the outcome would be if Hawthorn's second place was reinstated. Still, he persisted on behalf of his countryman until the stewards relented. Moss won four grands prix that season to Hawthorn's one, but Portugal was enough to make the difference, and Hawthorn was world champion by a single point from the man who had so courageously stood up for him.

Such a chivalrous act seems unimaginable in the cutthroat world of modern sport, but it was perfectly natural to Moss. As we sat one day in 2015 in his house – a tall, thin building packed with gadgets, a bit like the Thunderbirds headquarters – just off Park Lane in Mayfair, he simply shrugged when I reminded him of that day. He has answered the question a thousand times over the years: why did he do it? 'I had to,' he said, 'otherwise it would simply not have been right.' Dressed in a colourful beach shirt and slacks held up with braces, he turned to the fun of motor racing and what had captured him. There was the speed, of course, the thrills, the travel and the friends he met in Hollywood and the camaraderie of his fellow drivers – and one other thing. 'Meeting crumpet all over the world. When Lewis Hamilton wins a grand prix, he goes off to talk to sponsors and to sign hundreds of autographs, but I used to chase crumpet.' To prove it, he has scrapbooks: a green one for his motor-racing exploits and a black one commemorating the girls he chased, a politically incorrect reminder of a bygone age when he often raced to avoid the paparazzi on the streets of London, once having to squeeze a girl down into the foot-well of his car so that she wouldn't be spotted with him.

The 1955 Mille Miglia will rank as his greatest feat. He was guided by Denis 'Jenks' Jenkinson, a journalist who had mapped the 1,000-mile route through Italy onto a twenty-foot-long paper roll, a bit like a giant toilet roll, so that he could give hand signals – left, right, straight on, fast or brake – to Moss as they swept through tiny villages between the cheering crowds. Moss won in 10 hours 7 minutes 48 seconds at an astonishing average speed of 98.53 mph, a record that will never be broken because the race was banned after the 1957 event, when the Ferrari of the Marquis Alfonso de

Portago killed nine spectators, including five children. The scale of Moss's achievement could be measured in coffins: almost sixty people died over thirty years of the Mille Miglia. The silver Mercedes 300SLR sports car – no. 722 – that Moss drove is commemorated on a plaque on the outside wall of his home.

Moss spoke lucidly of the accident that robbed him of his chance at Ferrari and ended his career – and almost his life. A month before the start of the 1962 season, he crashed at Goodwood during the Easter Monday Glover Trophy race. His injuries were devastating: a shattered left eye socket and cheekbone, a double fracture of the left leg and broken left arm. The driver who had once worried that wearing a crash helmet might mark him out as a 'cissy' suffered terrible head injuries. It took forty-five minutes to cut him free from the remains of his Lotus to get him to hospital, where he lay in a coma for thirty-eight days. The newspapers were full of this British hero, whose fame had gone beyond the sports pages and into the society columns. He was as well known to housewives as he was to Formula One fans, and policemen would ask speeding motorists: 'Who do you think you are, then, sonny? Stirling Moss?' Every day the British public waited for news and the switchboard at his hospital was jammed with calls, including one from an American friend called Frank Sinatra. At Maranello, a reluctant Phil Hill was given a contract for another year at Ferrari but vowed to drive within himself so as not to become another name on the Ferrari roll call.

Moss finally left hospital after three months and did so in customary style, his arms around some of the eleven nurses who had cared for him. Then, swaying unsteadily on his crutches, he insisted on taking them all to dinner and to the theatre in London to thank them. A year later, Moss tested a Formula One car again, but his reflexes had gone and so had his desire and so he hung up his helmet. But he had done as much as anyone to enhance the legend of Formula One, to underline its place as a sport only for the daring, the courageous and, in his case, the chivalrous. There is an old saying, often attributed to the great novelist and adventurer Ernest Hemingway: 'There are only three sports – bullfighting, motor racing and mountaineering; all the rest are merely games.' There was no world title for Moss, but he was rewarded with a knighthood in 2000 and still enjoys the deep affection of a British public who regard him as a sporting legend.

Without Moss, Clark and Graham Hill would become the superstars, as Chapman and the Brits tightened their grip on Formula One. In 1962, the order in the constructors' championship was BRM (British Racing Motors), Lotus and Cooper, with Graham Hill as world champion. A year on, Clark was close to unbeatable, with seven wins from ten races, plus two podium finishes.

Ferrari returned to win the world championship with John Surtees in 1964, but as usual there was rancour and division in the Scuderia. The man from Tatsfield in Surrey had earned his fame as a four-times 500-cc motorcycle world champion and was almost as irascible and determined as the Old Man. Their relationship was tense from the off, with the new British driver complaining that too much time and effort was being devoted to Ferrari's sports car programme to the detriment of Formula One because he could see the growing strength of the threat from the *garagistes*.

Ferrari were briefly revived, but the components that would bring together the gang who would rule over Formula One for almost forty years were slowly falling into place – and a new driver from Scotland followed in the wake of Jim Clark and with the potential to influence the sport he would briefly and brilliantly dominate. John Young Stewart – Jackie to everyone – had been spotted by Ken Tyrrell, who was running a Formula Three team for the Coopers and invited this precocious youngster down to Goodwood, where Bruce McLaren, an established driver, would be testing. Stewart was faster than the highly regarded New Zealander. After winning the Formula Three championship, Stewart was launched into Formula One with BRM in 1965, as teammate to Graham Hill. His salary was £4,000.

As Stewart took his place on the grid, Ecclestone was being drawn back into Formula One that same season. He had disappeared from the tracks, taking a sabbatical forced by his reaction to the death of Stuart Lewis-Evans, and immersed himself in business to dispel thoughts of Formula One with its carnage. John Cooper and Roy Salvadori, a former driver and a friend in the motor trade, took him to the Mexican

Grand Prix where they introduced him to a promising twenty-three-year-old Austrian. Jochen Rindt was born in Germany, but moved to Graz in Austria to live with his maternal grandparents after his parents were killed in a bombing raid on Hamburg during the Second World War. He was adventurous, even wild on the track, and in his first race he was black-flagged – meaning he had to pull into the pits and stop – for being reckless.

For some reason, these men from different nations and backgrounds hit it off, and Ecclestone became mentor as much as manager, just as he had been with Stuart Lewis-Evans. Rindt was a huge talent, and, by 1966, was making his mark with the Cooper team, so much so that he merited his own personal mechanic, an ambitious nineteen-year-old called Ron Dennis. Fascinated by mechanical things throughout his childhood, building Meccano and fiddling with metal, Dennis hung around Jack Brabham's factory in Chessington as a youngster, making tea and 'a nuisance' of himself as he watched the Formula One mechanics at work. As soon as he had completed a course in mechanical engineering at Guildford Technical College, he went to work for the Coopers, and was immediately marked out for his diligence and commitment. When Rindt moved to Brabham, he took his young mechanic with him to what Dennis called his 'old tea-making stamping ground', a suitably mixed metaphor for a man whose use of the English language would become legendary in itself.

As Dennis got to work on the cars, Rindt's star rose, and the Austrian became closer to Ecclestone, regularly calling at his home, then in Chislehurst in southeast London, usually not even bothering to knock, just walking in and dumping his bags. Soon, the pair were business partners, dealing in airplane components, with plans on the horizon for new ventures, such as sportswear. Leisure time was spent playing cards long into the night, and Rindt even took Ecclestone with his then partner, Tuana Tan, on honeymoon after marrying his wife Nina. Their relationship was that close.

Britain was the centre of the universe as the decade drew to a close. England had won football's World Cup in 1966 and created an icon in the shape of the team's blond-haired and elegant captain Bobby Moore, while the world was queuing to see a British spy in action on the screen. Sean Connery as James Bond was the biggest box office hit with his dark good looks and a British-built Aston Martin DB5 that became as desirable as any Ferrari. The Coopers also made it to the big screen with their souped-up Mini Cooper alongside Michael Caine in *The Italian Job*, the 1969 comedy caper. By the end of the movie, it was questionable whether it was Caine or the three Minis in their red, white and blue paint jobs that were the real stars of the film, as they ran rings around the hapless Carabinieri in Fiat's home city of Turin, and even sprinted around the company's rooftop test track. Colin Chapman was in on the act, too: the willowy Diana Rigg was a sensation around the world as the beautiful Mrs Peel in *The Avengers* television series; Steed, her urbane accomplice, drove a Bentley, but she had a cute, white convertible Lotus Elan. The car was so iconic that the Japanese manufacturer Mazda paid tribute by designing their MX-5 sports car to look like a chip off the Elan's block a quarter of a century later.

There was glamour on track and off it and a winning spree for Lotus, Brabham and Ken Tyrrell, running a Matra chassis coupled to a Ford engine. Only Ferrari was missing from the winner's roster. The Old Man needed a top-notch driver to replace those who had tragically died and those who had walked out. He had lost Moss, and Surtees had been the latest to hand in his notice after a series of rows, culminating in Ferrari's doubts over his driver's fitness for 1966. Surtees had crashed a Lola sports car and reports claimed that one side of his body had ended up four inches shorter than the other and was only corrected with surgery. They took their argument to Le Mans where Surtees assumed he would be the number one driver. He wasn't and he quit.

Enzo needed a driver who could bring glory and the world championship back to Maranello and he turned to another 'Brit' – Jackie Stewart, the diminutive Scot, who was at the height of his powers, but driving a BRM H16 that he reckoned 'carried more fuel, oil and water than the *Queen Mary*'. Stewart had been offered a drive by Chapman, but was wary of the reputation of his cars, which were superbly clever and light but not strong when it mattered. Then Enzo came calling. Stewart wanted desperately to join an outfit that promised to make any driver a legend, but he was on his guard, aware of the turmoil that seemed to surround the Ferrari name. Enzo, too, was wary when the Scotsman consulted his lawyers and then carefully set out his own demands as he sat across the desk from Il Commendatore.

'Enzo was really keen to get me,' Stewart says, 'but I realised I would need eyes in the back of my head. We shook hands for the 1968 season and that was that. It would have been worth $30,000, although I would have earned more with other things added – and this was when Enzo wasn't keen on paying drivers.'

Then Stewart bumped into Jacky Ickx, a former teammate. Ickx was clearly being played off against Stewart in an attempt to drive down his money. 'I phoned to tell Ferrari the deal was off because Jacky Ickx had been offered the same drive. They apologised and said it was all a mistake, but it turned out that the Old Man had been involved. I'm sorry. I couldn't drive for a team like that.' Perhaps Ferrari decided the Scotsman had broken his immutable rule that the driver could never be bigger than the team. 'I never regretted it,' Stewart told me. 'I never looked back at Ferrari and I went to someone I trusted.' That someone was Ken Tyrrell. It was the big man who pushed Stewart into Formula One and he knew his friend was out on a limb. 'Why don't you come and drive for me, Jackie?' Tyrrell asked. 'Er, because you don't have a Formula One team, Ken,' was the succinct and logical reply. But Tyrrell had a plan: he was going to start a Formula One team in his woodshed in Surrey, a far cry from the grandeur and history of Maranello.

Mosley would discover 1968 to be a turning point, too. He felt ready for the major step-up to International Formula Two. In those days, drivers switched readily between series, driving saloon cars one week and Formula One cars the next, and the best were in big demand – Jackie Stewart calculated that he drove fifty-three races in twenty-six different cars in one season. Mosley bought a Brabham BT23C from a young chap called Frank Williams, who was then dealing in racing cars, and, with one eye on safety, fitted seatbelts. Most drivers shunned belts, believing it was better to be thrown clear of a car that was little more than a high-speed bomb. The design then was a frame made of lightweight steel tubing, clothed in fibreglass, with the driver lying between two long petrol tanks either side of him. On impact, cars shattered like a bone china cup on a tiled floor. And then there was fire. 'It was crazy when you think about,' Mosley says. 'You are sitting in this tub of glass fibre and aluminium surrounded by fuel. It was a lethal combination, and it is hardly a surprise there were so many drivers maimed and killed during that period. Drivers were dying left, right and centre.'

Mosley's first Formula Two race at Hockenheim in Germany had attracted two of the great British drivers: Graham Hill and Jim Clark, both world champions and heroes of motor racing, instantly recognisable around the world. This was like promotion to the Premier League, where the best raced against the best. Before setting off to enter this daunting higher level of competition, Mosley had guaranteed his wife Jean that he would be 'very careful', because she was fully aware of the carnage on racetracks with deaths coming almost weekly. But there can be no such thing in motor racing as 'careful': relax or ease off and concentration wanes with speed. No driver worth a second's mention can do anything else but drive to their limit, something Stirling Moss liked to call 'ten-tenths'. Go to eleven-tenths and the price would most likely be death.

It was a wet day, and Mosley had almost no experience of driving on a damp track that was more like an ice rink and his heart was pumping with anxiety at the start. The spray was like a thick fog, forcing the drivers to peer into the gloom as they hurtled into the forest. Mosley says he used the tree tops as a guide to the circuit layout but plucked up the courage to put his foot down to overtake until he noticed an ambulance on a bend on a fast part of the track. His first reaction was that anyone going off there at 170 mph into the dense trees would not return.

He finished eleventh, relieved it was over, until someone approached to ask if Jim Clark was dead. The ambulance was for the Scot. Clark's Lotus 48 was wrapped around a tree, the engine and gearbox ripped off the chassis and fifty metres away in the forest. Clark's skull was fractured where his crash helmet ended at the neck. He was pronounced dead at the scene. The reaction in motor racing to the death of Jim Clark was like the impact of John F. Kennedy's murder – everyone can remember where they were on that day: 7 April, 1968. Jim Clark was in a line of descent from the true greats:

Nuvolari, Fangio and then Clark. Jackie Stewart has never doubted who was the greatest because it was his countryman and friend, the man he had shared digs with and the man he attempted to emulate.

Jim Clark was a shy farmer's boy who didn't make a noise or brag or play mind-games with his rivals. He had won the 1963 Belgian Grand Prix in the most atrocious conditions anyone could remember by almost five minutes from Bruce McLaren's Cooper Climax. In 1965 he became the first British driver to win the Indianapolis 500, and the first to win in a rear-engine car in a Chapman Lotus, as well as the only driver to win Indy and the F1 World Championship in the same year. He had won 25 grands prix in just 72 starts and taken 33 pole positions, and aged thirty-two would be approaching his peak.

No one could believe that Jim Clark made a mistake – he was too good. Jochen Rindt, a fervent admirer and friend, told an Austrian journalist: 'If Jim Clark isn't safe, what can happen to us?' Investigators thought perhaps he had a puncture and that was what everyone wanted to believe. Chapman was distraught. He had been closer to Clark than any other driver and vowed never to allow his emotions to become so entangled again. Chapman invited Mike Spence, a thirty-one-year-old from Croydon, to take over as replacement for Clark at the Indianapolis 500 a month later. Spence hit a wall and the right front wheel reared up and smashed into his helmet. He died later that day.

There was little Max Mosley could say to his wife Jean on his return from Germany. It was like a redemptive scene from a movie, the driver who had left full of bravado returning full of contrition, his wife anxious and fearful of their future. 'I suppose Jim Clark was driving carefully, wasn't he?' she asked, already knowing the answer. If motor racing had become Mosley's drug, safety was to become a mission.

Safety was first in Ecclestone's mind, too, when Chapman's sights settled on his friend, Rindt. Ecclestone took note when Stewart refused Chapman because he worried that his cars were too fragile. Ecclestone told his friend that his muscular style was too much for the Lotus cars, even though they offered the best chance of a world championship. 'The Brabham was safer,' Ecclestone said. His words were to prove prophetic.

Like his designs, everything about Chapman was innovative. With the future of sponsorship from key oil and tyre suppliers looking shaky, particularly after the sudden withdrawal of Esso, Chapman cast the net for alternative industries looking for the exposure Formula One could provide. When he found Gold Leaf cigarettes, even he wasn't bold enough to show his Lotus cars repainted from the tradi-tional British Racing Green to the red, white and gold of Player's tobacco brand on home soil, knowing there could be ructions, so he took his cars to New Zealand for the Tasman Series for a more discreet unveiling over the winter of 1967–68. The livery caused the expected shockwaves, but Chapman had struck tobacco gold and in May his cars lined up for the 1968 Spanish Grand Prix in their new livery. Graham Hill won, but the Gold Leaf name was discreetly blotted out so as not to cause offence. Nevertheless, title sponsorship had arrived in Formula One and tobacco money would help revolutionise the sport, financing startling technologies and transforming drivers from enthusiastic amateurs to wealthy professionals.

Ferrari had not seen Chapman's innovative idea coming, and he went down the traditional route of trying to find an investor who could pump money into his Scuderia, but who could also be held at arm's length while he ran his team. Fiat held a minority stake and the owners, the Agnelli family, were anxious to increase their hold over Italy's most famous brand. The negotiations were long and hard, but Giovanni 'Gianni' Agnelli was a convert. Agnelli, the head of Fiat, was one of Italy's most powerful businessmen and loved to drive Ferraris – even breaking his legs in one, which left him with a permanent deformity that forced him to wear an orthopaedic shoe – and was desperate to be part of this dynamic racing business. The bargaining was hard and, ultimately, pleased everyone: Fiat got 40 per cent of the business, with Ferrari keeping half, although that would be handed over to Fiat on his death. Piero Lardi Ferrari, who had been kept from public knowledge until the death of Enzo's beloved son, Dino, got 10 per cent, a shareholding that would prove lucrative in years to come and make him a dollar billionaire.

Ferrari had the protection of Fiat's money, but he was still Il Commendatore. John Hogan, the man who took Marlboro's lucrative sponsorship into Ferrari, remembers that Gianni Agnelli boasted about owning Ferrari, but when he wanted to land his helicopter on a field belonging to Enzo, he was put in his place. 'That is Ferrari's field and no helicopters land there,' Enzo told Agnelli.

Ferrari had his money, his security and he was still the boss. Now all he needed was a world champion and a car that could compete with the damned British.

5

NEW FACES

A T the end of a rural track between the trees in dense Surrey woodland was a wooden shed with blue double doors. You would expect the makeshift wooden building to house lawnmowers and garden forks and smell of cut grass. But the smell was of oil and the tools were for producing world champions.

Ken Tyrrell was an archetypal Englishman, a man of solid oak whose large feet were planted on the ground. He was no nonsense, no guff, no frills. He just loved motor racing and, when he decided to construct his own car, he simply did it in his shed near the village of Ockham. Tyrrell's 'factory' would seem laughably quaint today in an era when it takes up to 1,500 people and as much as £300 million a year to construct two cars in gleaming bays that look like operating theatres. It was more cottage industry than high-tech laboratory, with just eight engineers involved when the first Tyrrell 001 car was put together over the winter of 1970. The finished car cost an estimated £22,000, about £320,000 at the time of writing – a pittance now, but no doubt a hefty investment for a Surrey wood merchant.

Tyrrell met Derek Gardner in a pub and shook hands on a deal to build a Formula One car – no contract or paperwork, just a gentleman's agreement. It was a leap of faith because Gardner had never designed a complete Formula One car before, working mainly on transmissions and four-wheel drive systems for the French Matra company that had supplied Tyrrell. Gardner worked at home in Leamington Spa in Warwickshire, 100 miles from Ockham, until he was ready to show a wooden mock-up.

Jackie Stewart was the reigning world champion in a car with a Matra chassis powered by a Ford engine, put together by Tyrrell, but he knew nothing of his boss's ambitions to become a fully fledged constructor. The Scot was the hottest ticket in Formula One, the natural successor to his country-man Jim Clark. He could name his price and his team as the biggest new star in the world of motor racing and had turned down Ferrari to stay with the *garagistes*. And here he was, staring at what would be his new Formula One car – in a domestic garage.

'It was just a terraced house,' Stewart mused. 'All we had was this balsa-wood mock-up and I sat in the car and got the measurements done for the seat.'

From the garage to the shed. Intensely practical, Tyrrell had spotted that the Ministry of Defence was selling off barracks used by the Women's Royal Army Corps at a base near Guildford. He bought a couple for £50 each and linked them to make one long wooden shed. Walter Hayes, the executive who took Ford into Formula One to produce the Cosworth DFV engine, which powered nine drivers to twelve world titles, put it simply. 'A dump,' he said.

Frank Williams would have been grateful for a dump when he started out in Formula One. Francis Owen Garbett Williams, to give him his full name, was an unlikely arrival in the sport. Born in South Shields to an RAF officer and a headmistress, he had almost no contact with motor racing in any form and was born in a part of the country 250 miles from the main action around London and the southeast. After his parents' marriage broke down, he was sent to boarding school in Scotland, and it was a ride in a Jaguar XK150 sports car as a sixteen-year-old that changed his life, for he was suddenly enthralled by cars and speed. He got a job as a travelling salesman but, as soon as the weekend arrived, he would hang up the suit he wore for his sales job and be off racing wherever he could, becoming enmeshed in the fabric of the racing community and meeting a young man called Piers Courage, who would become his flatmate and closest friend. Born into the wealthy brewing dynasty, Courage was a glamorous and charismatic figure, just as determined as Frank to get to the top of Formula One.

Frank always seemed at full throttle, and even his relationships demanded utter commitment, as Virginia Berry was to discover. She was preparing to marry when she first met this young man on a mission, and they would have a torrid affair, right under the nose of her husband Charles. In her moving autobiography, Virginia told how she would invite Williams to her marital home, then wait until her husband was asleep before sneaking into her lover's bed. The first sentence of her book says: 'The first time I saw Frank I fell in love with him.' She would need the strength of that love for all that came afterwards.

In 1966, aged just twenty-four, Williams had founded his own racing team, even if it was a beg-steal-and-borrow operation, running cars mainly for Courage. The motor racing was serious, but the methods were haphazard, with Williams borrowing money wherever he could to keep the show on the road. On one occasion, he managed to raise £900, which was enough to get the team of seven – Williams, three mechanics, a truck driver, Courage and his wife Sally, who was their time-keeper – to a race. The money was so stretched that Williams had to ask Courage to pay the hotel bills.

Williams acquired an Italian De Tomaso, an overweight, bulky machine, for Courage to drive in the 1970 season. It wasn't up to much, but it was all they had. The fifth grand prix, at Zandvoort in the Netherlands, came not quite three weeks after Bruce McLaren had died testing a Can-Am car at Goodwood in West Sussex. The New Zealander left the legacy of a team that would emerge later in a new and formidable guise in the hands of a Williams contemporary.

McLaren's death was another on the list, another to mourn, but not enough to stop the show. The Dutch Grand Prix would go on. Courage was running consistently in the middle of the pack when his car careered off the circuit. The front wheel broke away and hit Courage in the head before magnesium in the chassis ignited and the car was consumed by fire. Sally Courage only realised something was wrong when she noticed a plume of smoke at the far side of the track. She waited with her stopwatch, but her husband – and father to their two boys – didn't come back. He was just twenty-eight.

While Frank Williams struggled and Ken Tyrrell plotted in secret, there was trouble at Lotus that was very public. Chapman was still experimenting with designs that risked lives, specifically those of Rindt and Graham Hill, his teammate. The fashion was for rear wings mounted on tall struts that looked like radio masts over the back of the car. The idea was that the aerofoils would provide much more grip at the rear of the car, but the extra downforce was so great it snapped the long struts holding up the wing. Unfortunately for Rindt and Hill, during the 1969 Spanish Grand Prix they snapped at exactly the same place around the tight Montjuïc course in Barcelona. Rindt suffered no more damage than a broken nose, bruised pride, and a dose of fury that his team owner would be so cavalier with the lives of his drivers. Rindt had six retirements in eleven grands prix in that 1969 season, while Jackie Stewart, who had turned down Lotus, romped to his first world championship title with Ken Tyrrell.

Rindt was concerned enough to write to Chapman, telling him that 'the point of no confidence is near'. Hill, who suffered more than his fair share of accidents, was at least able to adapt his own brand of laconic, stiff-upper-lip humour to the situation: 'Every time I am being overtaken by my own wheel, I know I am in a Lotus,' he said.

Ecclestone revelled in the banter and the characters of Formula One. Jackie Stewart's wife Helen was a glamorous fixture in the pits, acting as timekeeper for her husband, while Nina Rindt was a constant at the races. Graham Hill's wife Bette had small children – including Damon, born in 1960, who would emulate his father as Formula One world champion – but when she arrived at a circuit, she would call a meeting of the Doghouse Club, the nickname for the group of wives who watched and waited for their husbands and boyfriends to return safely from their racing. They would chat, share a glass or two of wine, and gossip about the men in their lives and their crazy world of travel and danger. The club still exists today, although under the grander title of the Women's Motor Racing Associates Club, raising thousands of pounds for charity, and the conversation is less likely to revolve around the fear of death and injury that once haunted the founders of the club.

Ecclestone's natural gift for dry humour made him a popular member of the in-crowd that travelled from race to race. He was a great admirer of Chapman, whose single-mindedness meant that nothing got in the way of his tightly controlled operation focused entirely on winning – and finding the money to do it. That reflected Ecclestone's own approach to life, although he lacked the engineering gifts of Chapman, who will forever be regarded as one of the greatest figures to emerge from Formula One. So much of Chapman's pioneering work laid the foundations for what followed, and Formula One cars today owe much to his original concepts.

The Player's Gold Leaf sponsorship deal had been financial manna from heaven for Lotus, because the cigarette maker was picking up the bills, including Chapman's, Hill's and Rindt's salaries, and helping to finance the racing in a deal worth about £100,000. But Ecclestone suffered the nagging doubt that the Lotus cars, fast as they were, wouldn't hold together to take his friend to the world title. Returning to Brabham for 1970 had been an option, but Rindt believed that Lotus still offered his best chance of success, and his feelings were underlined when he won five of the first eight grands prix of the year to put himself in a commanding position in the championship.

Monza was the final European destination of the season. Chapman had done away with the rear wing that had so upset Rindt, who set off in the qualifying session for the Italian Grand Prix in his red, white and gold Lotus 72. As Rindt entered the Parabolica corner, his car started to flick from side to side under braking, then veered into the Armco barrier, hitting a supporting post nose first. Rindt did not wear the crotch strap that formed part of his safety belts because he was terrified that he, like so many others, would be trapped in burning wreckage in the event of a crash, but that meant he slid downwards into the disintegrating cockpit. As the dust cloud cleared, spectators could see the front of the car had gone and Rindt was sprawled in what remained of his cockpit, his legs exposed and one of his feet amputated. His jugular vein was slashed on the buckle of his harness. A front brake shaft was thought to have broken.

Ecclestone ran to the scene, anxiety mounting as he closed in on the wreckage of the Lotus. There was nothing he or anyone else could do. Jackie Stewart was about to lose yet another friend, one of too many during his racing lifetime. 'I went over to see what was happening,' Stewart told me, 'but I could see immediately that there was no hope. There was a lot of blood, but Jochen wasn't bleeding so I knew his heart had stopped. The last time I saw Bernie, he was walking back to the pits carrying Jochen's helmet under his arm. He didn't speak, he just looked shocked.'

Stewart was still waiting to post a qualifying time. As he sat in the cockpit, he pulled down his visor and burst into tears.

Ecclestone went to the hospital in Milan where he waited with Chapman and Rindt's wife, unsure whether he was angry or stricken with grief. Jochen Rindt became Formula One's only posthumous world champion. He was just twenty-eight, the same age as Piers Courage and Stuart Lewis-Evans.

Chapman left the country quickly, only too aware that the authorities might be looking for someone to prosecute for the crash, and the formalities were left to Ecclestone. He asked Herbie Blash, who had engineered Rindt's cars at Brabham, to collect his friend's personal belongings and deliver them to the Rindts' home in Switzerland where Nina would be waiting. Jackie Stewart presented the world championship trophy to Nina Rindt at a ceremony in Paris, but he was still seething at this appalling parade of young men, crushed, incinerated and maimed, and he determined to change a sport that seemed to treat life so casually.

Four years earlier, he, too, had almost been a victim in Belgium when, in appalling wet conditions, he aquaplaned at 170 mph, hit a telegraph pole and then the side of a farmhouse before sliding into a ditch. Graham Hill had been following him and he slithered through the same river of water, coming to rest against a straw bale. He then spotted his BRM teammate trapped in his car.

There were no marshals or safety crews, and Hill had to borrow a socket set from the boot of a spectator's car to release the steering wheel trapping Stewart's legs. With the help of an American driver, Bob Bondurant, Hill pulled Stewart clear and into a barn, where they stripped off the petrol-soaked overalls that threatened to burn his skin. Hill sprinted away to find a phone box when, bizarrely, a group of nuns appeared; apparently unnerved by Stewart's lack of clothing, they proceeded to cover him again with the overalls stinking of petrol. A bus converted to an ambulance finally arrived and took Stewart to a medical centre, where he lay on a canvas stretcher. 'I will never forget it. I was alone and the floor was covered in cigarette ends. I thought that this cannot be right.' Another ambulance then took him to a hospital in Verviers, a city about seven miles away – and promptly got lost.

Decades later, Stewart shook his head as he remembered the carnage, the needless loss of young lives for what called itself a sport. He owns an apartment on a hillside just outside Geneva, minutes from the home belonging to Nina Rindt, still a friend and companion after all these years. 'We were very close to Jochen and Nina. It was very difficult to accept what had happened. Helen and I counted up one day that we lost fifty-seven friends in just over a decade. Imagine that. It is like a war. It couldn't go on. I had to do something.'

As head of the Grand Prix Drivers' Association (a trades union for drivers, which was formed in 1961 with Stirling Moss as chairman), Stewart pushed for fireproof overalls, full-face helmets and seatbelts to be compulsory, along with improvements to safety at circuits, but it was amid resistance from organisers and, astonishingly, drivers. He was accused of trying to turn Formula One into a 'milk and water' series for cissies by journalists who wanted their drivers to be muscular gladiators facing death with a smile. Max Mosley was once told by an official: 'No one makes you do it. If you don't like it, then don't do it.'

Mosley got out while he could. His driving career was short-lived, but relatively successful, with twelve victories registered from about forty races. He had given his wife an assurance that he would remain safe and he was ready to move on. As with Ken Tyrrell, there was a shed involved. Mosley teamed up with Robin Herd, a contemporary at Oxford, Alan Rees and Graham Coaker to form the March company (the name comes from their initials: M for Mosley, with an additional A to link Rees, Coaker and Herd), building racing cars for several different series. Each partner put in £2,500, although Mosley, who gave up the Bar, had to borrow his investment from his mother. The first March was built in 1969, a Formula Three car that emerged from the shed in Graham Coaker's garden. Soon, Mosley had found a factory next to a dairy in Bicester, near Oxford, where March built a car for Jackie Stewart to drive to victory at the 1970 Spanish Grand Prix, the first major win for Mosley's fledgling outfit.

Virginia Williams believed that grief would drive Frank out of Formula One and motor racing after Courage's accident, but four weeks later he was fielding Brian Redman at the British Grand Prix, and in a De Tomaso. Frank Williams was running again, chasing his dream from track to track, utterly relentless in his quest for success. Within two years, with backing from Politoys, the toy maker, he was in his own factory in Reading and ready to roll out the first Williams car. He had sold his watch, his stereo and his car, while Virginia sold her maisonette in London to loan him £4,000 to get started. It was a hand-to-mouth existence, constantly chasing the money, as Max Mosley remembers.

March were supplying cars to a variety of teams in junior series with a workforce of just 100 people, including a Formula One race team of eight. 'Our first year's budget at March, including paying the drivers, was just £113,000. In the early days Frank ran March cars. We had an absolute rule that you didn't let any parts out of the door unless they were paid for because dealing with people who run racing cars is like dealing with drug addicts – if you give them credit, you will never get the money back. Frank would call up and say a van was on the way for a new wishbone and the driver had a cheque with him. But then he would say, "Can you just hang on for a few days before you cash it." We had a paying-in book and I used to pin Frank's cheques to the top of the page and wait a while.'

Bernie Ecclestone admired risk-takers, gamblers prepared to take a chance. 'In the old days, people like Frank Williams would spend more than he had because he had balls. Frank was always coming to me for money. He would be looking for a few quid, say £12,000, and then he would come round with a cheque and leave it with me. We would have a chat and then, just as he was going through the door to leave, he would say, "Oh, any chance of a loan of £12 million, or something." It was hilarious. Still, he doesn't owe me one dollar. He always paid me back.'

Ecclestone's hyperbole over that £12 million masks the reality that Williams was an all-too-frequent caller on his financial resources and wasn't always quick to pay his debts.

Ron Dennis's methods were structured, cautious and meticulous. From the start of his career as a mechanic in Formula One, he was forever looking for ways to improve – anything that would separate him from the crowd. He had refused to follow Rindt from Brabham to Lotus, and instead became chief mechanic to Jack Brabham, the only man to have driven his own car to the world championship. Dennis was close to Brabham, whose factory he hung around as a youngster, and didn't want to work for another driver after the Australian decided he would retire in 1970. Dennis had graduated from mechanic to team manager, carrying out all of the key functions, from organising the travel to collecting the start money in cash to pay wages and expenses.

'I thought, "I run the team, the drivers came and went, I collect the money, so why don't I run my own team?"' It seemed that simple. One day, Graham Hill, who was contracted to Brabham for 1971, turned up and asked what Dennis was up to. He said he was building Brabham Formula Two cars to start his own team. Hill then offered to drive one of the cars to help out the youngster, provided that when the team started to make money, he and Dennis would go 50-50. Their first win was at their second race and the ball was rolling. At one time, Dennis had four teams in different categories, with mechanics being sent off in different directions to compete, with Hill as his leading light.

It was all going so well until the 1973 oil crisis. OAPEC – the Organisation of Arab Petroleum Exporting Countries – started an embargo against countries perceived to have supported Israel during the Yom Kippur war. The UK was one of the first nations to suffer, with the price of a barrel of oil quadrupling overnight. It was a potential disaster for motor racing and for Dennis in particular, as his key sponsor was Motul, a French company making the first synthetic motor oils. The company pulled out and Dennis became technically insolvent almost overnight. He needed a saviour, and it came again in the urbane shape of Graham Hill, who was starting his own Formula One team. He needed a factory quickly, and had heard that Dennis might be ready to sell. They did the deal and Dennis was able to walk away with his head held high, paying off his creditors and keeping enough money back for a rainy day.

Dennis was trying to find his place in a sport moving away from its formative stage and into a much higher gear, but it was all-consuming – too much for Jackie Stewart, who decided to retire from driving at the end of 1973. He had won two world championships and there would be symmetry at his final grand prix of the season, at Watkins Glen in the USA, which would be his hundredth, as well as the venue to celebrate his third world title.

Stewart was the most famous driver in the world, the first to earn more than $1 million a year, mainly thanks to personal sponsorship deals with blue-chip companies like Rolex and Ford. But the constant travel, the constant expectation, and the constant fear that he might be next was taking its toll, physically and mentally. He had been troubled by stomach ulcers and he knew that the pressure was telling on Helen. He couldn't even tell her he was retiring because he knew that she might be counting off each race to the end – a little like Nina

Rindt might have done, or Sally Courage, or so many of the wives and girlfriends left behind.

Stewart had also found his successor in a handsome young Frenchman. François Cevert was like a movie version of a racing driver, with his dark, wavy hair and striking good looks. Cevert was more than a teammate and friend, he was the protégé that Stewart believed might take his crown when he retired. On the Saturday morning of the US Grand Prix, Cevert steered flat out into the Esses, clipped a kerb and careered into the barriers on the right before slewing across to the barriers on the opposite side. He was dead on impact. It was described as one of the 'most savage accidents' seen in Formula One. Stewart approached the scene, realising something was wrong. He saw Chris Amon walking towards him, signalling that all was not well, so Stewart stopped, leapt from his car and ran to the wreckage. He described the scene to *Motorsport* magazine: 'Jody [Scheckter] was walking back towards me, and he said, "Don't go there, you don't want to see." But, of course, I had to, he was my teammate. It was a terrible sight. His body was horribly mutilated. I stood there two feet from him in total shock. Ken withdrew the team from the next day's race and my career as a racing driver was over.'

It seemed each triumph must be matched by tragedy. Stewart went into retirement, having made ninety-nine grands prix starts, and would never think of driving in a grand prix again, even when Bernie Ecclestone offered him £6 million to drive for his Brabham team. 'I don't know whether he was pulling my chain, but I didn't give it a second thought. I never regretted it, just as I never regretted not driving for Ferrari.'

Enzo Ferrari was isolated from this storm of activity in Britain where these young and ambitious team owners found their feet in the complex world of making Formula One cars. He came from a different generation, when the pace of change had not been so frenetic. There had been no Ferrari world champion since John Surtees in 1964, while Chapman had Clark and Hill, and Jack Brabham and Jackie Stewart were stars. After selling to Fiat, Ferrari had been engulfed in the motor giant's corporate structure, and Maranello was now packed with men from the Turin headquarters who knew little about the intricacies of Formula One. Ferrari seemed to have lost control of the glamorous empire he had spent decades creating. He needed help, he needed young ideas and energy.

Ferrari had a routine: each afternoon he would work in the office of his little farmhouse, which stands today in the centre of Ferrari's test track at Fiorano, neighbouring Maranello, listening to his favourite phone-in show on a big Bakelite radio on his desk. Someone rang in to complain about Formula One, how it was all about wealth and privilege, it was dangerous and bad for the environment. A listening student felt enraged by this and decided to call to defend the sport. His name was Luca Cordero di Montezemolo and the phone call was to prove momentous. 'I was angry, so I rang the programme live on air and I was tough with this critic and told him you don't know anything because there were hundreds of drivers and mechanics who were good people doing good work and, at the time, racing was a place where you could prototype components and ideas for road cars. Ferrari called in live and asked, "Who is this young Italian boy? He has balls. I want to talk to him."'

Ferrari was so impressed that a few days later he sent the outspoken youngster a copy of his memoirs, with a message: 'To Luca di Montezemolo, who has the courage of his words and his actions.' It came with an invitation to visit Ferrari at Maranello.

Luca Cordero di Montezemolo is an Italian blue blood. His father, Massimo Cordero dei Marchesi di Montezemolo, was a Piedmontese aristocrat who had settled in the hills south of Bologna, near what was to become one of Italy's most important industrial cities. The family had a long history of connections to the high establishment, and still runs the Cordero di Montezemolo winery, from a vineyard that dates back to the fourteenth century, making rich Barolo red wines.

Power and position surrounded his childhood. There is even a scurrilous rumour that Montezemolo is the illegitimate son of Gianní Agnelli, the most powerful man in postwar Italian industry. The Agnellis were a dynasty, the richest family in Italy, sometimes compared to the Kennedys in the USA, who founded Fabbrica Italiana Automobili Torino, Fiat, which became not only Italy's biggest business, but a symbol of the nation's industrial might. It was into this clan that Montezemolo was welcomed with open arms.

For Italians, motor racing is as much a national passion as football, and the country was steeped in the legend of Enzo Ferrari and his great Scuderia. Montezemolo had been taken as a child to watch the cars roaring by on the Mille Miglia, the fabled 1,000-mile race, which passed through Bologna. It was no surprise, then, that Montezemolo would want to try his hand at the wheel, although he chose rallying and started as close to the bottom as it was possible to get when still a law student, driving a tiny Fiat Nuova 500. 'I was a bit of a prodigy,' he says proudly. His co-driver was Cristiano Rattazzi, the son of Susanna Agnelli, Gianni's formidable sister. The link to the Agnelli empire was strengthened by association.

Montezemolo was one of the few who could call Agnelli by his first name, and many wondered how the head of Italy's biggest business could be so in thrall to this boy fresh from college. Sometimes they socialised, and it was often Montezemolo's role to act as gofer for Italy's most famous industrialist. Italian newspapers were always on the lookout for salacious gossip about the Agnellis, who were as close to a royal family as Italy could get. Photographers would be stationed at all of the hottest nightspots and restaurants around Rome, desperate to get snaps for the morning editions, and Montezemolo would often be sent ahead to restaurants to book a table, and then to make sure that Agnelli could enter by the back entrance to avoid the inevitable lenses.

When Montezemolo started work at Ferrari, it was in the commercial departments, learning how the Old Man operated and it was an eye-opener. 'We had forty or fifty cars unsold in the factory when two American collectors came to Maranello to buy from us. We had lunch and I sat in to translate. Enzo listened to what the Americans had to say about buying some Ferraris and nodded and said, "Yes, yes, yes. I will see what I can do, but you must understand it takes time because we haven't any cars available so you will have to be patient." I looked at him and then at the cars outside and I wanted to say that we had all of these cars and we could sell right now – but this was marketing by Enzo. He knew they wanted something and they had to want it enough. That was a lesson.'

Montezemolo was only twenty-five, skinny as a rake with a mop of long brown hair, when he was sent to the 1973 British Grand Prix. It was a chastening experience watching a once-proud team mired in chaos and humiliation. Montezemolo described what he found as a farce that deteriorated into a debacle: the 312B3 car was hopeless – some say the worst car built in the history of Ferrari – and Enzo was so angry after qualifying, with Jacky Ickx only nineteenth on the grid and Arturo Merzario not taking part, that he ordered the team to withdraw and bring the cars home. Montezemolo intervened and persuaded the Old Man they should stay, but it required all of his silver-tongued powers to calm down the boss and convince him that Ferrari must take part in such an important race in the world championship. Ickx raced and finished a fortuitous eighth, thanks to a huge first-lap pile-up caused by Jody Scheckter in a McLaren. Ferrari remained furious, though, and the cars were put into their transporters and taken back to Italy in disgrace. Ferrari did not race at the next two grands prix, in Holland and Germany.

It was time for Montezemolo to make his mark on Formula One. In an extraordinary leap of faith, he was promoted to *direttore sportivo*, sporting director, of the oldest team in the world championship. Montezemolo was fresh from Columbia University in the USA, he had never raced a Formula One car or run a team in his young life, and now he was being entrusted with a squad that verged on sporting royalty. He would not only have to convince the Scuderia that this youngster with the tight shirts and bell-bottom jeans was up to the job, but he would have to make his mark in the paddock, where there would be no welcome into the ranks, just suspicion of this suave, sophisticated smooth-talker, who seemed more public relations man than one of the oily-rag brigade.

'I was the first man not to be an owner – like Enzo or Ken Tyrrell – so I had to introduce organisation, team spirit, even communications, because Ferrari was infamous for his arguments with his drivers.'

Montezemolo set about invigorating operations at Maranello, bringing back Mauro Forghieri, who had designed John Surtees' 1964 championship-winning car, with orders to dismantle the useless 312B3 and start again. The next move would be to find a driver who could pilot Forghieri's car. James Hunt was briefly in the frame, but a serious young Austrian, Niki Lauda, had put his future on the line for Formula One after borrowing £30,000 to get a drive with Mosley's March team. March were not up to much, and Lauda had been forced to borrow more to get into BRM. There he had been partner to Clay Regazzoni, who then moved back to Ferrari in 1974 after a disappointing season with BRM. By the time Ferrari called Lauda to offer him a job – on the recommendation of Regazzoni who was happy to have him as a new teammate – the Austrian was £120,000 in debt. Thin-faced and with slightly protruding front teeth that earned him the nickname 'The Rat', Lauda was fiercely driven and utterly fearless. He would think nothing of banging on Ferrari's door to give vent to his opinions, unlike the staff who lived in fear of Il Commendatore.

The transformation was as rapid as it was remarkable. Montezemolo found he could bounce off Lauda's perfectionism and dedication. Lauda worked hand-in-glove with Forghieri, spending hours on the Fiorano test track over the winter of 1973, within sight and earshot of the founder, who would sit in his cottage there, observing the activity. Although Il Commendatore was aware of the great changes going on around him, he had become remote from the team he had built. Montezemolo says that Ferrari's divisiveness and apparent love of conflict and drama, always needling and upsetting his drivers, was married to a tendency to listen to acolytes who would tell him what he wanted to hear rather than what he needed to know, as well as bowing to the clamour of a demanding Italian press corps.

There was also a hint of jealousy, as Montezemolo caught the eye as well as the attention in Formula One. Phone calls back to Maranello would sometimes include the boss commenting on how well turned out his sporting director was, instead of asking how well the cars had run. Montezemolo's close relationship with Agnelli turned out to be a potent weapon, though, giving him an authority beyond his years to pull the team apart, with Lauda as his feisty accomplice.

The 1974 season was close, Regazzoni losing the championship at the final race of the season to McLaren's Emerson Fittipaldi, but the Scuderia would triumph a year later when Lauda carried off the first drivers' championship for Ferrari since John Surtees eleven years earlier. Emotions ran high, but there was no Enzo Ferrari to see the triumph. He remained at home in Italy and television coverage was scant, so it was up to Montezemolo to relay the news. He wasn't sure what the reception would be from the austere old man. 'There were no mobile phones in those days, so I had to find a telephone to call Enzo Ferrari to tell him that he had a new champion. You know, he just said, "Thank you", that was all, but I am sure there was a tear in his eyes.'

6

MONEY'S THE SCORE

B ERNIE Ecclestone was forty years old and trying to overcome his grief after Rindt's death. He was anxious, but still longed for the thrill of the racetrack despite losing two close friends in horrific crashes.

He had studied Colin Chapman and realised that there was an unexplored world of opportunity to make money beyond the simple gathering of dollar bills after each race, when teams would get their share of the start money in a brown envelope. Chapman had proved with Gold Leaf that there were companies wanting exposure as the power of television glued families to their sofas in living rooms around the world.

The youngster who had traded in buns and pens – and then motorcycles and used cars – had tired of the rough and tumble of the forecourt, and Formula One opened his eyes to wider and more glamorous horizons. So, he resolved to become a team owner, just like Colin and Enzo and Ken. As co-founder of Brabham, Ron Tauranac had taken over the team after Jack Brabham retired, but by the end of 1971 he was happy to sell at the right price. According to the account by Susan Watkins in her biography of Ecclestone, Tauranac valued the business at £130,000, and wanted to set up a trust fund for his daughters, when he was approached by Ecclestone. Tauranac thought the price was agreed, but when he prepared to sign the contract, Ecclestone's offer was for only £100,000 – way below expectations. By this point Tauranac was over a barrel and had no choice but to agree. He was bitter but realised that he had been negotiating with a hard-nosed dealer.

Ecclestone liked to trot out his version of the quote by Ted Turner, the CNN cable news magnate: 'Life's a game and money's the score,' and this was another victory, as well as early proof of how Ecclestone would tot up the score in Formula One.

What Ecclestone saw when he walked into his new place of work was typical for a Formula One garage in the 1970s – oil, dirt, rags and a general air of chaos. It was everything he hated. Ecclestone ordered new walls and doors to segment the open-plan garage, and then started throwing out anything he decided was junk, from posters to discarded metal or wood. In came the paintbrush, turning walls and benches white – even the cars, traditionally British Racing Green, became white.

The workforce could sense this was a man with purpose and were prepared to tolerate Ecclestone's outbursts. In Tom Bower's account of Ecclestone's life, he tells the story of a mechanic who damaged one of his benches and had his car headlamps kicked in by Ecclestone as a result. Herbie Blash, who became Ecclestone's team manager, remembers how the boss would go into empty offices to turn off lights and rip phones from their sockets if they weren't answered. If the floor needed sweeping, Ecclestone would sometimes pick up a broom and do it himself, and he often threatened to close the factory down if it was untidy or anything was out of place. It was detail, detail, detail – but it worked, and it was detail that others so often missed to their cost.

Ecclestone was now a team owner, the equal of Colin Chapman and Enzo Ferrari, the two men he admired most. He was also a fully fledged member of F1CA, the Formula 1 Constructors' Association, set up by Chapman in 1963. It was a loose union that had done little to advance the cause of the *garagistes*, whose financial struggles remained a source of amusement to Ferrari and the Formula One authorities, and promoters who had seen spectator numbers grow yet not increased prize money. Ferrari were always first in line for the biggest share of the money paid to teams who started a race, and the rest got what they could – if they got anything at all. It was a shambles, mainly because the team owners were not interested in anything other than racing and, as a result, every team apart from Ferrari was at risk of sinking into the financial mire.

At his first F1CA meetings, Ecclestone studied the faces around the table – the long, toothy visage of Ken Tyrrell; Colin Chapman, neat and tidy and full of restless energy; John

Surtees, pugnacious and determined; and a young ex-lawyer called Max Mosley. Ecclestone was conciliatory, friendly, even offering to pour the tea. He listened and waited and marvelled at their inability to negotiate as a unit. The team owners traditionally did their deals with all the circuits separately, and they were losing out everywhere, their money draining away when they should be cleaning up. Ecclestone cut through the discussion to suggest negotiating a collective deal with the circuits, including transport, so that everything was in one package. It would be faster, cleaner and cheaper. There were nods of agreement as each team owner saw the sense of the proposals and an opportunity to improve their precarious finances. But who would carry out the negotiations? No one stepped forward until Ecclestone said he would – for a cut of the profits. Perhaps even Ecclestone didn't realise it then, but he had timed his entry into Formula One perfectly.

So had Luca di Montezemolo: Ferrari was on its knees when he took over, the Old Man disaffected and battered by years of trying to hold the Scuderia together, and watching young men die in his cars. Ferrari was unique, but not beyond the buffeting of years of failure. Montezemolo and Lauda had brought him another world championship, but there was festering jealousy of their high profile – no one could be higher than Il Commendatore, even when Lauda forged his place in motor-racing history in 1976 during a season so dramatic that it was commemorated in the movie *Rush*, by the acclaimed director Ron Howard.

The challenge would come from James Hunt, a driver whose reputation for mischief and fun was way beyond any fame he garnered for his driving. It was the perfect rivalry – the straitlaced perfectionist champion Lauda against the playboy Hunt. For all his carousing, Hunt was highly intelligent and sensitive. He had been unnerved by the death of Jochen Rindt, with whom he had forged a friendship, but was sought out by John Hogan, Formula One's 'Marlboro Man', in charge of the cigarette brand's Formula One sponsorship programme at McLaren. Emerson Fittipaldi, McLaren's 1974 world champion, had left and the team wanted Jacky Ickx, but Hogan, the marketing man, pushed for Hunt. He tracked him down relaxing at the South Kensington home of Alexander Hesketh, who had brought Hunt into Formula One as a member of his avowed 'party team'. It was a 'cheap deal', according to Hogan, because Hunt had nowhere else to go. He had an offer on the table from Lotus, but refused it because he believed Chapman's cars were death traps after what had happened to his friend Rindt.

The fulcrum of this 1976 season would be at the notorious Nürburgring, known as the Nordschleife. Jackie Stewart called it 'The Green Hell', because the narrow track wound almost fourteen miles through the Eifel mountains, bordered on each side by dense forest. There was no run-off, no gravel traps, no safe haven for a driver who forgot any of the seventy-three corners. It was a track bordering on insanity, as Lauda had vociferously pointed out when he called for a boycott. It was not a question of cowardice, for Lauda was the fastest man there. Ironically, though, he would be its victim. On the second lap, Lauda's Ferrari snapped away from him and careered into a rock face before bursting into flames. Lauda was trapped in the cockpit, breathing the intense smoke and flames because his helmet had flown off in the impact. His fellow drivers, Guy Edwards, Brett Lunger, Harald Ertl and Arturo Merzario, desperately tried to pull him clear as flames from the ruptured fuel tanks licked around the sides of the Ferrari. In hospital, his condition was so poor that a priest arrived to give him the Last Rites.

Montezemolo remembered that Ferrari wanted a full report on what was happening. After hearing details of the accident, Ferrari asked his sporting director: 'Who will we get to replace him?' It seemed a callous remark as Lauda, his world champion, was fighting for his life, but Ferrari must have secretly been in turmoil. This was yet another accident, another driver to add to the casualty list that once prompted the Vatican newspaper, *L'Osservatore Romano*, to turn on Il Commendatore, describing Ferrari as like the god Saturn, who consumed his own sons.

Lauda's recovery and determination to get back into the car to pursue a world championship that was within his grasp is one of the most extraordinary of all sporting stories. He was on the grid for the Italian Grand Prix forty-two days after his fiery crash, missing just two grands prix. It was a sensation, and Italy's newspapers devoted their front pages to a young man whose face was horribly scarred by his burns, and whose still-healing skin came away with his fireproof balaclava when he took off his helmet. His ears and eyelids were burnt and he was in agony. Astonishingly, he raced to fourth place in Monza, the home grand prix for Ferrari, Italy's team. The crowds were delirious, for this was a miracle, but the only man in Italy who was not impressed was Enzo Ferrari. He was seething that so many column inches were being devoted to Lauda's bravery when it was the car that made history, not the driver. Ferrari called Montezemolo into his office. 'Enzo was always trying to get the maximum from everyone, not just his drivers but also collaborators, putting one against another in conflict. Sometimes, he went too far. When Niki came back after his accident, one of the biggest Italian newspapers urged all the fans to go to Monza to support him, but Enzo said to me, "Luca, this guy can drive a Ferrari or he can get on his bike." He was just jealous of his driver because it was all about the driver and not Enzo.'

It was typically thin-skinned of Il Commendatore, who was used to claiming the worship and adulation. If his self-centred view of the Formula One world had missed the point, John Hogan hadn't. He called 1976 'Year Zero for Formula One'. The Hunt–Lauda rivalry – the accident; the traumatic climax at the storm-sodden final grand prix in the shadow of Mount Fuji where Lauda retired from the race, unwilling to take any more risks, to leave Hunt to become world champion – turned Formula One into major box office.

Broadcasters flocked to Formula One when they realised how the season was unfolding. Bizarrely, only one broadcaster held back: the BBC wanted to cover the season but had reservations over the Surtees team sponsor – Durex, maker of condoms. Old Auntie clearly didn't want the viewers to have fainting fits watching the Surtees car with the logo paid for by the London Rubber Company, but Britain's senior broadcaster had to relent as the championship went to a thrilling climax.

There was a footnote to that tumultuous season of 1976: despite Lauda's terrible accident, there was not a single death during a grand-prix weekend for the first time since 1972.

Ecclestone could see the media circus grow with each race after the Nürburgring and, by Japan, broadcasters were desperate to get the race on air. As the F1CA representative, Ecclestone was ready to say yes, as long as they committed to show every race of 1977. It was typically canny as Ecclestone roped in television companies to start spreading the Gospel of the new Formula One and to pay for it. His methods were taking shape. He had vision and understood that personalities make the drama, and he singled out Hunt as a star with good looks and a racy lifestyle. The following year, he offered Hunt $1 million in return for all of his earnings for the season. Hunt was advised to turn down the offer, but it was a demonstration of how far Ecclestone was prepared to go.

Even Chapman, who had supercharged sponsorship in the sport, respected Ecclestone's eye for organisation. According to Hogan, there was chaos at one race when the start marshal disappeared at a crucial moment. Chapman marched in and demanded Ecclestone sort things out. 'This fucking sport's a business. Tell them to get on with it,' he yelled.

Ecclestone was getting on with it: he was rapidly reorganising the entire structure of the sport, and the three-way relationship between the circuits, the teams and the Fédération Internationale du Sport Automobile, or FISA, the sporting division of the FIA, as the regulatory authority. Payments could be haphazard, but he was also the teams' guarantor and, if it went wrong, it was Ecclestone who would pick up the pieces. But, as the years passed and Ecclestone's wealth grew, team owners started to believe that he was reaching into their pockets, even though they had happily sanctioned his offer to run their financial affairs. As one team owner observed: 'It is one thing to say you are taking 10 per cent, but to know what the 10 per cent is worth, you need to know what the 100 per cent is, but we never knew what the 100 per cent was.'

Ecclestone's demands of the circuit promoters shot up from $10,000 a race to $100,000 and then more, until by the end of his reign the price tag could be as high as $40 million to stage a single grand prix. He was also tying circuits into long-term contracts to guarantee their commitment and, in return, he guaranteed at least eighteen cars would turn up, with teams facing a financial penalty if they didn't attend. Television came next, and Ecclestone wrested the broadcasting contracts from the circuits and assigned them to F1CA, renamed FOCA, for the Formula One Constructors' Association (at the suggestion of Enzo Ferrari who told them that *fica* in Italian carried a certain erotic connotation that wasn't appropriate).

Ecclestone was refining the bargaining techniques he had learned as a used-car dealer – humour, distraction and insult. Team owners say now that they would watch in awe as Ecclestone put forward some scheme that would inevitably favour him. When it was thrown out, he would move on to a joke or a story that would distract everyone and then home in on one individual, taking the mickey and trying to turn everyone's attention away from his agenda, before neatly doing a reverse turn to somehow push his idea through. 'He did it time after time and so many didn't realise what was going on,' one onlooker said.

There was more than money, though: Ecclestone was also reorganising the way a grand-prix weekend was run. For all their supposed glitz, grands prix could be slapdash affairs and, in the early days, no one was quite sure who would turn up and how many cars would race. That offended Ecclestone's sense of order. Soon, he had regularised start times for practice and qualifying and introduced passes that would operate at every circuit, not just one. He also cleared the paddock of hangers-on who got in the way of mechanics attempting to get on with their strenuous and tiring work.

If Ecclestone was establishing himself as the Boss, then Max Mosley was becoming his *consiglierie* – the advisor, the good cop, the sensible one. Ecclestone was streetwise and a fighter, but he needed someone like Mosley – highly educated, sophisticated and multilingual – to navigate the corridors where he would feel out of place. FISA was a gentlemen's club for continental aristocrats, a gathering of titled blazers whose antagonism was growing towards the *garagistes*, the rough-and-tumble lot from across the Channel led by the brazen little emperor, and the organisation's grandees were livid at all this plotting. It is said that, at one point, federation officials were open to offering cash sweeteners to teams willing to break away from F1CA and Ecclestone's rule.

In the Brabham factory, Ecclestone was relentless. He had sacked the design team and promoted Gordon Murray, a South African who had come to England to try to break into Formula One. Murray, a tall guitar-playing designer with long hair and a penchant for jukeboxes, was just twenty-five when Ecclestone entrusted the team to what he hoped would be a visionary and an innovator in 1972. Five years later, Ecclestone moved Brabham from Weybridge to Chessington, to a factory with more space and better facilities, including timer switches on the lights, which would save Ecclestone the job of switching them off.

As frugal as he so often was, Ecclestone was prepared to risk big money on a driver who would bring sponsorship and attention to the team. That driver was Niki Lauda. Ecclestone knew Lauda was disaffected at Ferrari after winning back his championship in 1977 and the departure of Montezemolo. The Old Man was convinced Lauda hadn't recovered fully from his Nürburgring accident and was unnerved by Lauda's decision to pull out of that final race at drenched Fuji: when Lauda had pulled into the pits, the rain teeming down, Mauro Forghieri leaned down into the cockpit to find out what was wrong. Lauda told him the race was madness and he was pulling out, so Forghieri gave him the chance of an excuse and he would tell everyone that the car had engine trouble. Lauda being Lauda, forthright and honest, refused. He would tell it as it was.

Enzo had brought in Carlos Reutemann and was lining up Gilles Villeneuve to drive a third car for 1977, which antagonised the Austrian, who no longer felt valued, as he had with Montezemolo. Ecclestone, with his ear to the ground, picked up on Lauda's discontent and they shook hands on a $1 million-a-year deal for the upcoming 1978 season, which included bringing Parmalat, the Italian food company, in as sponsor. Lauda won the world championship for Ferrari at the US Grand Prix and then walked out of Maranello with two races of the season remaining.

Now Ecclestone needed a car for a world champion, and he let Murray have his head, although the designer was struggling to accommodate a big Alfa Romeo flat 12-cylinder engine, which made the Brabhams wide as well as horribly heavy. Murray was ingenious, and came up with one of the most notorious designs in the history of Formula One – the BT46B fan car. Colin Chapman's Lotus 79 seemed unbeatable because he had conquered the Holy Grail of aerodynamic ground effect, essentially tunnels beneath the floor of the car that helped suck it to the track for huge grip and stability. In the now iconic black and gold livery of John Player cigarettes, the JPS Specials of Mario Andretti and Ronnie Peterson were going to be uncatchable, and it would take something out of the blue to stop their winning streak in the 1978 season.

It came at the Swedish Grand Prix, when Brabham wheeled out the fan car. Ecclestone told everyone that the huge fan at the rear was to cool the engine. Even road cars used fans to cool the radiators, he said, and this was merely an advanced version of that, but when the engine was turned on, the car visibly dipped, sucked onto the track as the fan created a vacuum under the floor – a mere by-product of the cooling effect, according to Ecclestone, who had the cheek to carry through his version of events with a straight face. There was a rush to protest from the rest of the teams, not least because the powerful fan was sucking up every piece of debris from the track and flinging it into the visors of following drivers.

The stewards deemed the car legal. However, a little chicanery had to be employed to get the cars of Lauda and John Watson through qualifying without anyone guessing just how much downforce the fan was generating. Ecclestone ordered the fuel tanks full to the brim so that the extra weight would slow his cars down and, even then, Lauda was hard-pressed not to qualify on pole position, leaving the prime slot to Andretti's Lotus. In the race, the fan cars were extraordinary, accelerating where others had to lift the throttle. The beauty of the system was that, unlike the Lotus, which needed speed to generate downforce, the fan was instantly sucking the car to the asphalt. Watson spun off, but Lauda won by 34 seconds from Riccardo Patrese's Arrows.

The car was a triumph of innovation, but also a roadblock for Ecclestone's ambitions to rule the sport. Enraged rivals would not take kindly to being hoodwinked, even though a further investigation ruled that the car remained legal. Ecclestone withdrew the BT46B from the rest of the season.

Ecclestone seemed to have an answer for everything and he was usually smart when employing drivers and finding sponsors to pay their wages. 'He never spent his own money if he didn't have to,' says one rival team owner. Lauda knew his worth to Ecclestone, both as a driver and as a draw for sponsors stumping up the hard cash, and he was prepared to put himself on the market unless his $1 million salary was doubled. Ecclestone was on the verge of renewing his lucrative sponsor deal with Parmalat, but he needed Lauda to accompany him to the signing. The Austrian obeyed and bided his time until Ecclestone announced he was ready to sign and Lauda would be driving for the team in 1979. 'No, I'm not,' Lauda said, throwing the entire meeting into confusion. Ecclestone and Lauda went into a side room, where it became clear it was $2 million or no drive. Ecclestone agreed to pay up. Ecclestone was seething at first, but couldn't contain his admiration for a friend who had got one over on him.

The following season, though, the dynamic changed, for

1979 was a miserable year for Lauda with retirement after retirement – eleven in all from thirteen grands prix. By the Canadian Grand Prix, Lauda had had enough. The weather was miserable and so was he. He took part in practice, but he was, as he put it, 'tired of driving round in circles'. Lauda told Ecclestone he was retiring immediately and, at first, Ecclestone would have none of it. When he realised it was happening and Lauda was walking out with two races of the season to go, he said: 'If you're going, you had better leave your overalls behind.' Ricardo Zunino, a young Argentinian driver, was in the crowd on a weekend off. He had tested for Brabham and, before he knew it, he was driving in the Canadian Grand Prix – in Lauda's overalls.

7

THE ODD COUPLE

T HE hubbub died down immediately the wheelchair of Sir Frank Williams, Formula One's racing knight, appeared in the crowded room. We were at the top of the BT Tower, the lights of London twinkling below this landmark building. BT – British Telecom, as we used to know it – was to be a new sponsor of the Williams Formula One team, and Sir Frank was there to help toast the deal with a rare public outing. After decades confined to a wheelchair as a tetraplegic, his strength was not as it was in his audacious youth, when he was notorious for a surfeit of sometimes mischievous energy as he buzzed from bank to bank to try to get loans, cadged bits and pieces for his cars and then held out a hopeful hand for a few quid to get by.

The executives and staff were ready to hang on every word from one of the most successful and revered men in Formula One. In his customary blue V-necked sweater and white shirt, which had become almost a uniform in his years in the wheelchair, Sir Frank started to speak in that quiet, slightly breathy voice that was a legacy of his accident three decades before.

The body was weakened, but the mind remained sharp and the humour intact. He looked up slowly and smiled. 'I must say this is marvellous having BT giving me money for a change. There was a time when they were always cutting me off.'

The story of Britain's motor-racing knight pouring pennies into a coinbox to run his team is a cornerstone of the legend of Sir Frank Williams, but there was a daily reality to the struggle to succeed that once proved cruel in the extreme. In her autobiography, *A Different Kind of Life*, Williams's wife Virginia remembered being in agony when four-and-a-half months pregnant in 1974. Her husband was away racing and she staggered to the phone to call an ambulance, only to discover the line was dead. Virginia – known as Ginny to all in Formula One – lost the baby.

When fans see the pomp and glitter of modern Formula One, those days of struggle and pain seem so far away, but they were all too real for Frank Williams as he tried to stand shoulder to shoulder with team owners who were better funded and better organised than he was.

Five years younger, Ron Dennis lagged behind the man who would become a good friend and ally, for theirs was a rare rivalry, in which friendship was often locked and bolted out of sight as they stole each other's star men and sponsorship millions. They were friends and contemporaries, but ruthless within the confines of Formula One. Loyalty was rewarded, but defectors could be cast out with the utmost brutality. They sacrificed so much for their obsession and made enemies with the same vehemence as they clung to friends.

In any other walk of life, Frank Williams and Ron Dennis would have been marked out as an odd couple for a friendship pact pockmarked by their feverish, relentless desire to succeed.

Frank Williams seemed to make it up as he went along in the interminable search for cash to feed the open maw that is a Formula One team. He borrowed from Bernie Ecclestone and any bank who would tolerate his obsession with motor racing. The standing joke was that he was always walking out of banks telling them over his shoulder he would take his overdraft elsewhere. He had bounced cheques for a decade and lived on the edge, as he tried to gain respectability in the Formula One paddock with bailiffs following him around like old friends. He wasn't wealthy like Ecclestone or establishment like Enzo Ferrari and, as the 1970s passed, his contemporaries believed he would probably sink under a flood of debt.

An effort to launch a car in 1972, using the Politoys sponsorship, failed at the first race when Henri Pescarolo crashed and Williams was forced to turn again to Mosley's March outfit to supply him with a car. It was a losing battle and, in 1975, he bit the bullet and abandoned his independence by selling 60 per cent of his operation to Walter Wolf, a Canadian businessman, mainly to escape mounting debts that would be his responsibility if the business went under. Williams was supposed to remain as manager, but the relationship soured and he was shuffled aside to become an upmarket odd-job man, running errands for Wolf instead of leading the team. Williams wanted his independence back and to be his own man again, even if it meant giving up the financial security of a job with Wolf. He walked away, taking with him Patrick Head, a talented new engineer who had come through the Royal Navy before getting his mechanical engineering degree at University College London.

They found an old carpet warehouse in Didcot in Oxfordshire, cheap enough to set up their new venture in 1977 but also within striking distance of the fast-growing 'Silicon Valley' of motor racing so that the new company, Williams Grand Prix Engineering, would have access to experienced engineers and technicians. It also had an over-draft facility of £30,000, enough to send a shiver through those who understood Williams's inability to manage money, for any crisis was unlikely to deter him from his favourite handmade suits, expensive shirts and cashmere sweaters. No matter how hard times were, Williams acted like a top executive, dressing immaculately to conduct his interviews at plush London hotels, as though to the manor born. There was something of the Derek Trotter about him, the relentlessly optimistic hero of the classic *Only Fools and Horses* comedy series, who was always going to be a millionaire by 'this time next year'. Except for Williams, next year would bring a winning car.

Fortune turned when he found an unlikely source of

sponsorship from a name that would ring down the years –
Bin Laden. Williams had secured sponsorship from the Saudi
state airline and discovered that there was a rich seam of
money waiting to be mined in the Middle East. He set off
with Patrick Head for Saudi Arabia and soon the sponsor
roster included the Albilad hotel chain, owned by Mohammed
bin Laden, the father of Osama, who would become famous
for all the wrong reasons decades later. Williams wasn't stopping there, though, and Ginny Williams relates a story of
how her husband found out there was an Arab prince staying
at London's Dorchester Hotel. Williams had the logo of the
prince's company painted on the nosecone of one of his cars
and then sprinted from Didcot to London to show off the car.
The prince was so delighted that he insisted the car be reversed
off its trailer into the hooting horns of angry taxi drivers in
the dense Park Lane traffic.

Wheels were turning quickly now and Frank was running
from sponsor to sponsor, always in a hurry. His family tell
how even a drive to work would become a race against the
clock, and he would set his watch to see whether he could
better his time on each commute. It seems obvious now, but
Frank Williams was an accident waiting to happen.

If Frank Williams was running at high speed, the quest for
victory was slow in coming. When it did, it was in the perfect
setting of Silverstone, the home of British motor racing, but
with an Arab tinge. Alan Jones, a stocky Australian, had taken
the team's first pole position in the Ford-powered FW07 at

the 1979 British Grand Prix, but he was overtaken by his Swiss teammate Clay Regazzoni. The race was a hectic affair until Regazzoni emerged in the lead to take the chequered flag. Williams was thinking clearly enough to have a Saudi flag hoisted alongside the Union Jack, knowing that his Albilad sponsors were overjoyed with the victory they had paid for. He then had to send a discreet message to the podium to make sure that Regazzoni didn't drink any champagne out of respect for his sponsor's Muslim religion. Regazzoni got orange juice instead.

Frank Williams, that chap always cadging parts and tyres and asking for a loan here and there, was suddenly a legitimate player in Formula One. Alan Jones was his first world champion the following season, and Frank Williams was no longer the joke figure with his struggles to make ends meet and his cars that could barely make the grid. In a book called *Racers*, by Doug Nye, the racing historian, Williams said: 'It was a completely new world to me. I had difficulty coping with the enormity of it. For years, I had become accustomed to just hanging in there hoping to qualify and now we were showing signs of becoming really competitive.'

There should have been a celebration of the first order and a new house, a new car or, at the very least, a new dress for Ginny, his long-suffering wife. But Williams was now ruling out indulgence and free spending when there was a world championship team to run. Ginny Williams found herself eating in an all-you-can-eat burger bar from the $1.50 menu after Jones finished 1980 with victory and the title at the US Grand Prix at Watkins Glen.

Williams was showing all the signs of the obsessive drive that would characterise his contemporaries in Formula One. He hated holidays or any form of time off from his factory and would fret if he wasn't near his beloved race cars and team. Claire Williams remembers a childhood in which there were no extravagant luxuries or round-the-world trips or fancy cars or houses. Her father was largely absent, consumed with his team and Formula One, while her mother ran the household and the kids – her and her two brothers, Jaime and Jonathan.

'It was a bugbear for my Mum all through the years because Dad only took a salary. He just took enough to make sure the mortgage was paid off, Mum had enough for housekeeping and the school fees were paid. There were never any boats and yachts. It used to really annoy us because there would be other families from Formula One on their yachts and kids on private planes and there was me, Mum and the boys in economy flying to Marbella for our one week's holiday of the year.'

Family outings to the races were rare, too. Williams made it clear that he didn't like his wife and children around the team during a grand-prix weekend, saying that most people wouldn't take their family to the office when they were working. He would set off in a private plane to meet up with the team, leaving Ginny behind to round up the children and get them into the family car for the long drive.

'Dad was always averse to taking us to races, but Mum somehow convinced him to let us go,' Claire Williams says. 'We didn't go in the plane, so poor old Mum had to drive us down to the ferry. When I was very small, in the early eighties, Nigel Mansell was tasked with taking us to the funfair. We had funny little motorhomes and I stayed there making sandwiches or tea.'

It was obsession to the exclusion of all else. Williams couldn't do small talk, but he would come to life if the chat switched to engine components or the ability of drivers. According to Claire, her father never had much time for sponsors, only their money. 'If Dad had to go to a sponsor meeting, he would hate it because all he would want to do was be at the track with his cars and drivers.'

Ginny Williams recounts a story in her autobiography that is telling: as part of the Saudi connection, Mansour Ojjeh had brought his TAG group into Williams as a lucrative sponsor and asked for a meeting at his office in Paris before he handed over his cheque. Williams was accompanied by Charles Crichton-Stuart, a close friend, and grandson of the fifth Marquess of Bute. Crichton-Stuart was acting as commercial director, partly for his connections and his ability to smooth his way through any open door. His marriage to actress Shirley-Anne Field, who starred in some seminal British films of the early 1960s, meant he was regular fodder for the gossip columns. Crichton-Stuart led the way into Ojjeh's office and the chat was all about their holidays on sunny beaches, friends and entertainment. All the while, Williams stared out of the window. His wife's version of events went this way: 'There was a lull in the conversation and Charlie suddenly heard Frank say to Mansour with no preliminary niceties, "The budget is going up next year. It's got to be 1.3 million." It was his sole contribution to the conversation.'

The contest on the track had switched from Ferrari and Lotus to Ecclestone's Brabham and Williams. After Andretti's title for Lotus in 1978 came Jody Scheckter for Ferrari, but then Jones's breakthrough for Williams in 1980 was followed by Nelson Piquet in a Brabham. Keke Rosberg interrupted with victory for Williams in 1982 before Piquet took the honours again.

This new cartel would soon be smashed by a young visionary, who transformed a grand old name of the past into the team of the future. Ron Dennis came from an ordinary lower middle class home in Woking. His parents were originally from Hull in northeast England, but moved south to Woking, a commuter town in Surrey. Woking is of no great distinction or beauty, but it was located between two significant landmarks in motor racing – the Brooklands circuit, the first purpose-built racetrack in the world, and the Brabham Formula One team in Byfleet, about five miles across country.

Dennis's father was a salesman and drove a Ford Prefect, which was the apple of his eye and would be meticulously cared for at weekends with some spit and polish. His mother was the epitome of old-fashioned virtues, keeping her house spick and span and always pushing the vacuum cleaner round last thing at night so that her family could wake up to an immaculate home. Dennis was fascinated by anything mechanical, and the die was cast when his elder brother took him to Brands Hatch to watch some junior racing. Dennis was captivated and, as a schoolboy, hung around the Brabham works, making the tea and sweeping the floor until he was allowed to get near the precious Formula One cars and learn the tricks of the trade. Two mechanics, Tim Wall and Roger Billington, could see the burning interest in this youngster and started to give him some instructions. The first was: be meticulous. As Dennis once put it: 'Don't think about starting a job until you've prepared for it, like a surgeon laying out his tools before an operation.'

Joining Cooper as a mechanic was his entry point and his chance to prove himself, working eighteen hours a day if needed to make sure everything was perfect. By twenty-one, he owned a Jaguar E-Type, the sexiest sports car on the road, but was too tired to enjoy it after working day and night. He fell asleep at some traffic lights, woke abruptly and shot across the road and crashed. His hospital stay was lengthy and there was plenty of time for thinking while the physical scars healed.

After almost losing his shirt in the 1973 oil crisis, Dennis was back on his feet after accepting a deal to run two Ecuadorian drivers backed with big sponsorship. That evolved into the Project Four operation, winning in all sorts of series and picking up some limited backing from Marlboro. Meanwhile, the McLaren Formula One team, also sponsored by Marlboro, was on the wane. What both needed was a go-between, like John Hogan.

John Hogan was born in Australia, but sent to school in England, where he met a fellow pupil called Malcolm Taylor, who became the actor Malcolm McDowell. Together they went to the old Aintree motor-racing course to watch Jack Brabham win. And so his love affair with Formula One started. Without Hogan, there would perhaps have been no James Hunt: Hogan organised sponsorship worth £500 a race to get Hunt started before placing him at McLaren in 1976. Then he helped Rondel, the nascent motor organisation shared between Dennis and Neil Trundle, to find the Motul sponsorship that was their lifeline until 1973.

Hogan realised faster than most the potential of Dennis. Over lunch near Hogan's offices in London's Victoria, where he works for the CSM Sport and Entertainment group, still on the fringes of Formula One, he told me that Dennis exuded a quality that few others had. 'I knew he was different. Ron understood sponsorship, he understood how teams worked. He was brilliant with his technical people but also had an instinct for what was coming in the future.'

Hogan pushed McLaren, a mighty Formula One team, into a merger with Dennis's Project Four racing in 1981. It was an unlikely marriage – like a local pharmacy taking over Boots the chemist, Dennis says. Dennis then went to work creating his Formula One team, persuading Niki Lauda to come out of retirement for the 1982 season, hiring John Barnard, who had come through the ranks as a designer at Lola and Williams and worked in the United States, and then luring Ojjeh away from Williams, eventually to become his partner.

Most will concede that Bernie Ecclestone created the Formula One we know today, with its show-business and careful attention to detail, but it might be fair to say that Ron Dennis invented the modern Formula One team. Even Ecclestone's mania for cleanliness could not match Dennis's energy and rate of invention. He admits that his mother's obsession with a pin-neat home rubbed off on him, but he went further in his desire for perfection. Look around any modern Formula One garage and there will be something that derives directly from his pioneering days at McLaren.

He started by making sure he knew how every aspect of his cars worked. 'I built teams on the basis that I would do everything that I asked everyone else to do. I always felt I could contribute and push people to have ideas. I told them that the impossible just takes a bit longer to achieve.'

While Dennis went about revolution, the grandees of Formula One were falling into disarray once again. More than one mechanic noticed that when Ferrari arrived at a grand-prix track, they would open the rear doors of their truck and equipment would fall out because it was so badly packed and their Keystone Cops approach was in stark contrast to what was happening in the McLaren garage.

Dennis was all about the constant search for improvement and says that when the history of Formula One is written, people may see his fingerprints all over the sport. 'People laughed at us when we went in and painted the garages and laid tiles and then created the concept of using the interior of the garage as a promotional tool. We were the first to create hydraulic lifting equipment, for instance, at a time when mechanics would stand at each corner and lift the car onto stands, leaving them with back problems. Within two races, everyone had them. Go down the list of innovations and you will see them coming from McLaren. Extend that template to the way we ran the cars and you have our story.'

The turning point came from Barnard's discovery that he could use a new material – carbon fibre, a high-strength but lightweight composite far beyond anything used in Formula One at the time, and immeasurably safer than steel tubes and fibreglass or light aluminium bodywork. Gordon Murray had tinkered with this new material, but discarded the idea because a major problem was finding someone who could make a monocoque chassis in carbon fibre when the technology didn't exist in Britain or Europe. Dennis was convinced this was the breakthrough, though, and scoured the planet until he found an aerospace company in the United States working mainly on secret government projects.

'We wanted something unbelievably stiff so that the chassis wouldn't twist and bend like an aluminium structure when the aerodynamic forces were applied. I told John that if he designed it, I would find someone to make it. We found out about this company in America called Hercules Aerospace. We packed up our wind tunnel model and trekked to Salt Lake City. When we arrived at the gates of this aerospace company, we were looking at desert. After a mile of driving, we found one building. Everything was underground because they were making solid fuel missiles, so if one blew, the whole lot didn't go up. We finally got in and they were saying they would like to help, but they were bound up in government secrecy clauses.'

Dennis wouldn't take no for an answer and convinced the Hercules executives that although they couldn't talk about their secret government work, they could make a showpiece of manufacturing a Formula One car in this new wonder material. His persuasion worked and by the end of that 1981 season, McLaren had rendered traditional construction methods obsolete and had every team rushing to understand carbon fibre.

'We were self-sufficient in three years and leading the field. We would go into each season with everyone a year behind, which kept us ahead of the game for a long time,' he said.

Carbon fibre was a game-changer and so were Dennis's management techniques. Niki Lauda was Dennis's first world champion, in 1984, and champion for the third time. Alongside him was a young Frenchman called Alain Prost, who was quiet, but thorough and thoughtful. Meticulous even, just like Dennis. During that 1984 season, Lauda was following his teammate and suddenly realised just how fast and precise he was. Lauda was thirty-five and had driven for Ferrari, Brabham and now McLaren, and now he was following an ambitious driver, six years his junior. In 1985, he suffered eleven retirements in fourteen races and broke his wrist. Niki Lauda retired for the second time. He had no ears, no eyebrows, and awful scarring from that appalling accident at the Nürburgring. But he was alive.

8

WINDS OF CHANGE

THE pace of change in Formula One was as fast as the frightening speed of the rapidly developing cars throughout the 1980s. Frank Williams and Ron Dennis epitomised the new wave of team owners, with their innovation and unquenchable thirst for winning, and Colin Chapman and Enzo Ferrari – the pioneers – would soon be consigned to the past as they left the sport that they once bestrode.

Chapman was a colossus and, with Enzo Ferrari, will be considered one of the true geniuses of Formula One. His invention was without equal, his strength of character formidable and his vision enduring. He had been accused of producing cars that were death traps, yet Lotus was the first team to notch up 50 constructor victories in Formula One and Rindt, Mario Andretti, Jim Clark, Emerson Fittipaldi and Graham Hill were all world champions in cars that were fast and fragile, but there was genius in their design.

Friends sensed a waning of the spirit and a tiring of the intense politics of Formula One, and Chapman's home at Ketteringham Hall in Norfolk, in the far east of England, seemed part ideas factory and part bunker after Mario Andretti's championship year of 1978. The competition was becoming ever more ferocious and there were no victories to cheer for three years, and even Andretti's title was overshadowed by the death of his teammate Ronnie Peterson at the Italian Grand Prix.

After the glory, the innovation and the domination of Formula One, the finale was sad and unedifying. John DeLorean, a former General Motors executive, was rich, dated supermodels, and must have appeared as an industrial saint for a beleaguered Labour government led by Prime Minister James Callaghan when he turned up with plans to build a revolutionary stainless steel sports car in 1976. By the time production was ready, the so-called Winter of Discontent had crippled the country, with tens of thousands of workers on strike, inflation was in double digits and traditional industries were collapsing. The government tried to shore up the ailing motor industry, but it was a losing battle. Some of the greatest names disappeared – like Triumph, Hillman, Standard, Austin, Morris, Singer and Sunbeam – while the rest clung on for survival. DeLorean raised millions from investors – some high-profile, like America's most famous talk-show host Johnny Carson, and Hollywood singing star Sammy Davis Jr – and the Northern Ireland authorities, excited by the prospect of two thousand new jobs in an area where unemployment was as much as 20 per cent, ploughed in £100 million. Chapman's Group Lotus, the Formula One team and carmaking businesses now ensconced in premises in Hethel in Norfolk, were to be the main consultants for the project.

The publicity around DeLorean and his car, the DMC-12, was huge, from the factory in Belfast to the west coast of the United States, where the two-seater with its gullwing doors was launched with great fanfare. But the car was a dud and the promises soon turned to scandal, as a police investigation was launched into the disappearance of funds, as much as £10 million according to reports at the time. By the time the investigation reached its climax, Chapman was dead of a massive heart attack, on 16 December 1982. He was only fifty-four. Some say his huge workload and the travel and pressure of Formula One killed him, but there would always be the suspicion that the stress of the DeLorean affair played its part.

Perhaps it was a good thing that Chapman avoided what could have been a humiliating court case, for him, Lotus and Formula One, after a High Court judge reportedly surmised that the Lotus founder would have spent as many as ten years at Her Majesty's Pleasure. The Chapman legend was allowed to live on in Formula One, and the DeLorean car is not forgotten either. With its matt silver bodywork and sharp droop nose, the DeLorean never caught on in its day and hundreds went unsold, but the car became something of a cult when Marty McFly went *Back to the Future* in one in the Hollywood blockbuster of 1985.

There would be only a single victory for a Lotus car in the year of Chapman's death – for Elio de Angelis in Austria – as the next generation took over, led by Frank Williams, now owner of a world championship team, who was still keeping up his breathless assault on life, still timing his wild commute on the roads, still pushing harder and harder to stay in the big time. It was to cost him dearly.

In March, 1986, Williams had been working on his car for the new season with his test team at the Paul Ricard circuit at Le Castellet, about thirty miles south of Marseille, but wanted to get back to England to take part in a fun run the next day. Williams picked up team manager Peter Windsor and set off at his usual hair-raising speed, but he lost control and the car somersaulted into a ditch, landing heavily. Williams had broken his neck, and those years of struggle, building a team that could rank alongside the greatest in history, hung in the balance with his fate. Williams without Williams was unthinkable.

The offers of help flowed in: Bernie Ecclestone was on the phone immediately to say his private plane could be on the runway within minutes; Mansour Ojjeh, too, was ready to convert an aircraft to medical standards to airlift Williams out of Marseille, where he was being treated. Word of the accident even reached Downing Street, where Prime Minister Margaret Thatcher sent a message to the hospital that she wanted the best treatment for one of Britain's heroes.

The waiting was agonising for Ginny Williams, who was

left to wonder if she was about to join the ranks of Formula One widows. It seemed hopeless: patients with Williams' condition could usually measure their lives in days, not months or years, and treatment was scant and cursory. Doctors had given up and wanted to turn off his life support, but Ginny Williams refused and called Professor Sid Watkins, Formula One's senior medic and one of the most respected neurosurgeons in the world. He dispatched Dr Paul Yate, an anaesthetist from the London Hospital, who realised that Williams had to be returned to London. An air ambulance was readied and Ecclestone sent his plane to pick up Ginny Williams, while the British Embassy arranged a police escort from the hospital to the airport. Frank Williams was on his way home.

The first grand prix of the 1986 season was just seventeen days after the accident, in Brazil, where the Williams team had to regroup under Patrick Head, the technical director and Williams' partner, and somehow concentrate while their founder and leading light clung to life. They were not to know that he might be paralysed, but he was in the best hands in the business with Professor Watkins, the man everyone knew as 'Prof'.

I first met the Prof one sunlit evening, on the steps of a motorhome in the Formula One paddock. I was just leaving after a cooling glass or two of wine, and he was outside puffing on his cigar and clutching a glass of whisky. He cut a Pickwickian figure, if Mr Pickwick could be stuffed into tight-fitting, fireproof overalls. They were blue, with the word

'Doctor' emblazoned across the front, as if anyone needed telling that this most familiar figure was the man who stood between life and death on the track. On his head was a battered baseball cap carrying the FIA logo that had seen better days. I introduced myself and we exchanged pleasantries before he asked: 'Ever smoked, young man?' I had never smoked. 'Good chap. Stick to whisky,' he said.

As long ago as 1961, Watkins was the medic at the Watkins Glen circuit in the United States, while he was working as a young neurosurgeon at a hospital in Syracuse. He realised that he might be exposed if anything went seriously wrong, and in those days it did – often – so he took with him an anaesthetist and an orthopaedic surgeon to work as a team. The conditions were primitive and there were flies everywhere which had to be swept out of the trackside hut, which doubled as the medical centre. He then spread a liberal dose of disinfectant around his makeshift hospital. Watkins remembered that in 1969, when Graham Hill broke both his legs at Watkins Glen, he had been sent to hospital three miles away in Montour Falls, only for ambulance men to discover it was closed. They then had to drive on for almost an hour to the next one.

Bernie Ecclestone had done his research and knew all about the Prof when he called the London Hospital and asked for a meeting. He knew that Prof Watkins had trained at the Radcliffe Infirmary in Oxford, thirty miles south of the Silverstone circuit, where he had acquired huge experience in treating serious accident victims, particularly those with head trauma. Watkins was also a motor-racing fan, having 'messed with cars' in his father's garage as a child – and he had to be because Bernie wanted the Prof to become Formula One's first medical director, and the money wouldn't be much – just $35,000 and he would be paying most of his own expenses. Watkins' first race as chief medic was the 1978 Swedish Grand Prix, where he would see the debut of the infamous fan car. At the track, the Prof discovered a caravan with a hut extension in case there was an overflow of casualties and was told there would be no emergency helicopter for Friday practice sessions because practice wasn't dangerous. The Prof watched the grand prix from the base of the control tower and remembered in his autobiography that James Hunt waved to him each time he entered the pits as a mark of respect.

Formula One had medical facilities of sorts, but only because of the experience of Jackie Stewart and the generosity of Louis Stanley, who ran the BRM team. Stewart was in a BRM when he crashed at Spa and vowed to make Formula One safer and he found a willing partner in Stanley, a formidable figure in the Formula One paddock. They devised a mobile medical centre, which travelled to each of the European grand-prix circuits. Remarkably, some of the circuits refused to allow it entry.

Ecclestone wasn't having any of that nonsense and decided that whatever the Prof wanted, he would get. Soon, track medical facilities were among the best equipped anywhere; it is often said that if you decide to have a heart attack, do it on race day at a grand prix, because the treatment at the circuit medical centre will be second to none. It was all the doing of Prof Watkins and Bernie Ecclestone.

Recovery should have been a long haul for Frank Williams, but he was still running, mentally if not physically, and the drive to overcome his injuries and get back to work was overwhelming. Frank had been as close to death as any man can be, yet barely three months after his crash, defying doctors and medical science, Ginny Williams and three helpers manhandled him into a National Health wheelchair, with an oxygen tank on standby, to take him to the factory he loved and to the people who built his astonishing cars. In July, he was at the British Grand Prix at Brands Hatch for qualifying, carried by a helicopter ordered by Bernie Ecclestone. He was greeted by a three-foot-high banner, saying, 'Welcome Back, Frank', held by his fellow team owners, and a standing ovation. On the Sunday of the race, Williams was too tired to attend, but the helicopter was back to pick up Ginny, who watched Nigel Mansell win. At Patrick Head's insistence, she went to the podium, fighting back tears, to collect the trophy for the winning constructor. At the end of that season, Williams was the world champion constructor for the third time. The story of Frank Williams has passed into living legend, and he was rewarded with a knighthood in 1999.

Williams and McLaren were the future, while the years were passing Enzo Ferrari by. His last world champion was Jody Scheckter in 1979 and he had invested his hopes in

Gilles Villeneuve, a Canadian with flair and a sense of fun, who was Scheckter's teammate that season. Villeneuve had a special place in the Old Man's heart. He loved his absolute commitment on the track and adored his lust for life. Most drivers have a self-preservation switch in their heads that tell them when they have reached the limits, but not Villeneuve. He was wild, flamboyant, and almost frightening in his refusal to be afraid on the track, and he was a perfect combination with the exacting and studious Scheckter; it was racing yin and yang. 'Gilles used to listen to Jody and they would discuss everything,' Brenda Vernor told me. 'Jody used to tell Gilles, "You will never win a championship the way you drive. It is not only won on first places but on points." But Gilles was Gilles and Jody was right.' Gilles Villeneuve was killed in qualifying for the 1982 Belgian Grand Prix.

Il Commendatore's road cars remained the most desirable in the world. Faye Dunaway drove a 275GTB Spider in the scarlet colours of Ferrari for the 1968 Hollywood movie, *The Thomas Crown Affair* – one of Bernie Ecclestone's favourite films. Dressed all in white, she sits up on the rear of the Ferrari cabin to spy on Steve McQueen at a polo match. The car is the epitome of Ferrari glamour, low-slung and sleek, and was the first of only ten to be built. McQueen and co-star Jean-Paul Belmondo were enchanted, and both bought one in what was an endorsement of the mystique of the Italian marque.

Bernie Ecclestone never feared anyone and was rarely impressed, but he was charmed and awestruck when in the company of Enzo, even when trying his hardest to stitch up deals that would count against Ferrari. Ecclestone still speaks with reverence of a man he believes set the template for modern Formula One, with its glamour and passion, and he clearly admired the stylish façade that Enzo presented to the world, so much so that he produced a rare flourish when he convinced Dietrich Mateschitz, the Red Bull billionaire, to sign his first commercial deal in Formula One. Ecclestone produced a fountain pen given to him by Il Commendatore, filled with the same violet ink that he always used. Except the pen wasn't quite filled. 'Bernie made quite a thing of this pen as he produced it and sat Dietrich down in front of the agreement. Dietrich started to write his signature and the pen ran dry. He only just made it to the end,' Christian Horner, Mateschitz's team principal, remembers.

This was the myth: Enzo Ferrari in his dark glasses, even indoors, his pressed tailored suit with high waistband and white shirt and tie. In the later pictures, there is no trace of a smile, no hint of satisfaction. The scowl was part of the make-up, and the tempers could have come straight from the West End stage. 'He would suddenly go red in the face and explode and start shouting,' Brenda Vernor says. 'It was very noisy and a bit frightening at first. I got used to it and I knew it would be over soon. So, I would wait and then say, "Right, can we carry on now?", and we would get on with things.' But she believes the dark glasses were a shield, a device to protect him having to confront people with a direct gaze. 'I don't think he liked looking at people. He seemed to be embarrassed and I never saw him without dark glasses.'

There was also the softer side that Enzo Ferrari did not want to show. Despite demanding huge amounts from his workforce – like working long into the night to prepare cars at the last minute – he valued them, all drawn from Maranello and the surrounding villages. Just as his father's workforce in Modena had been, this was artisanal labour, comprising skilled metalworkers and mechanics and, in the road car division, people who could handle expensive and fragile materials, such as leather. From his five-windowed ground floor office at the front of his factory, Enzo watched with the eyes of a strict but benevolent schoolmaster, quick to chide and slow to praise, but always careful for the welfare of those who worked there, watching them come in and out and wondering at the outsiders beyond the gates who had come to stare as though paying homage at a shrine.

He built a school in Maranello – it is still there – and paid for hospitals and cared when it mattered. 'He was very kind-hearted,' Brenda adds. 'He once helped a young boy who had cancer of the brain. He got me to phone a specialist in Bologna and I got an appointment for him because the family hadn't been able to. The doctor operated, it was a success, and the boy is still here in Maranello. No one ever knew about it and it was never mentioned who paid. He cared about the local people. He only hired local people. If anyone needed anything, he would be there. He answered all of his letters, particularly to children, who he would send a present to sometimes. I think he was sensitive somewhere deep down. He had come from very little and became rich, but he was still that boy from Modena.'

Brenda says that there was such restraint in his emotions, it was as if a belt was taut around an inner fragility that would not even allow him to give thanks for a task completed. 'He was very strange because if you did something, he would never say thank you and he wouldn't say sorry.' The day after one row, there was a gift – a watch – on Brenda's desk, wrapped up with a note: '*Cordiali saluti, Ferrari*. Best wishes, Ferrari.'

His routines were set: he would pick up his mail after breakfast and go to his office at 11 a.m. where Brenda would be waiting. Then he would work on into the evening, week-ends, too. 'He couldn't understand why anyone wanted to go on holiday because he never did. He was at the factory every day into the evenings. Sometimes I would want a long week-end and he didn't say no, but because he never went anywhere, he couldn't understand why anyone would want time off.'

He never travelled and showed no interest in flying to the exotic locations where his teams would be racing. Instead, that daily routine of going to the office, eating lunch in the Ristorante Cavallino, directly across the road from his office, and working in his farmhouse in the centre of the team test track at Fiorano was immovable.

The only roving was in his eye for the ladies. Lina Lardi was his long-term lover and mother of his child Piero, but he appears to have had energy where the opposite sex was concerned, even late into life. A cache of more than 140 letters revealed his long-lasting passion for Fiamma Breschi, a former Miss Italy and mistress of Luigi Musso, Ferrari's driver killed at the 1958 French Grand Prix. Ferrari wrote a letter of condolence to Breschi, and then the letters kept coming, in the customary violet ink, with Ferrari becoming more passionate by the day. It is said that he adored her to the day he died.

Brenda Vernor found out early on that Ferrari enjoyed the company of the opposite sex, but managed to swerve anything more than banter, particularly one night when the Old Man gave her a lift home, but discovered that she lived in a top-floor apartment. His claustrophobia ruled out following her into the lift and the night was ended early. 'When you turned around to walk out of the office you could feel his eyes on you,' she told me. 'One day, I was wearing a white pencil skirt. I sat down and, as I bent, it split from calf to hip. I started pushing my seat back with my feet so I could get out with my dignity. He looked at me, wondering what was happening, and I had to say that I had a problem and my skirt had split. "Good," he said. "Let's see your bum."'

Ferrari's wife, Laura died in 1978, aged seventy-seven, a victim of the same strain of muscular dystrophy that had taken their son Dino twenty-two years before. It was an unhappy marriage, Ferrari torn between Laura and Lina and his second family with Piero. Ferrari mourned his wife, but he was soon making arrangements for Lina and Piero to move into his house and giving his lawyers the authority to draw up adoption papers for his illegitimate son.

Pope John Paul II travelled to Maranello in 1988, but Il Commendatore was not there, too ill to see the Holy Father driven around his test track in an open-top Ferrari Mondial and they spoke only by telephone. Maranello was the monument to one of Italy's most famous men and a life that had featured so many trials and tribulations as well as triumphs.

Enzo Ferrari died at 6 a.m. on Sunday 14 August 1988, in the bedroom of his house on the Largo Garibaldi in Modena, the city of his birth. He was ninety years old. The following day was a holiday in Italy, and Brenda Vernor's birthday. There was hardly any traffic and few people on the streets, which were clear when the small funeral cortege set off for the Ferrari family tomb in the cemetery of San Cataldo. Only those closest to him attended. Brenda Vernor was in the United States on holiday. 'It was all so quick. The Old Man didn't want any fuss, people of the streets crying and all that sort of thing. It was typical he wanted everything to be done quietly and with dignity.'

More than 3,000 letters, cards and telegrams of sympathy poured into Maranello, and Piero Lardi Ferrari answered each personally. Even today, flowers and cards arrive on 18 February, the anniversary of the birth of Il Commendatore. Ron Dennis's McLarens wiped the floor with Ferrari and Formula One that season of 1988, winning every grand prix – except for one. Almost a month after Enzo's death, and at Monza, Gerhard Berger won the Italian Grand Prix in a red Ferrari.

9

WHO GIVES A TOSS?

THE world's most famous driver and Formula One's toughest boss stared down at the cheap living room carpet. Nestling on its brown shagpile surface was a coin, just a common-or-garden bit of pocket change, but on its head – or tails – rested $1 million.

Ron Dennis was confronted with a resolute Ayrton Senna when they came to discuss a deal for his first three-year contract with the team in 1987. Senna was the hottest draw in Formula One, and he wanted paying as the biggest name, which meant McLaren finding the money from somewhere to keep his star happy. Dennis was the most successful team owner of the time, providing a succession of brilliant cars, sponsored by Philip Morris's Marlboro brand, and with vital Honda power, but the talks went on for days, with neither man willing to back down. They were like rutting stags, locking horns and refusing to disengage, both knowing that the man who backed down would lose face.

Dennis did some creative thinking and came up with a

resolution: they would simply toss a coin. 'I doubt whether anyone has tossed a coin for $1 million,' Dennis says.

Dennis went to Senna's rented house in Esher, about thirty minutes from the McLaren headquarters in Woking, to explain how the toss would work. Senna's English was still sketchy at the time, and Dennis drew a diagram to help the Brazilian understand – the coin in the air, the fall to earth and the head or tail option. Senna was perplexed and sceptical at first, but he was a devout Christian and believed that God's hand would provide; Dennis, by stark contrast, was a fatalist, and believed that the outcome from the flick of his fingers could go either way. The key was that neither man would be conceding defeat if he lost, preserving both his pride and his dignity. The coin was flipped and dropped into the brown shagpile and then bounced agonisingly under a curtain. They lifted the curtain together to peer down into the earth-coloured carpet. Senna had lost and the two parted, neither man completely satisfied with the outcome, for Dennis had offended his own intense sense of fairness, a sense that burned inside him as he rose to the top of Formula One.

Dennis was well aware of Senna's sensitivity and his fragile ego. Formula One had moved a long way from the gung-ho days when drivers raced for fun and glory. Enzo Ferrari had regarded drivers as part of the machinery, while Frank Williams believed they were employees, just like a mechanic or a cleaner. When David Coulthard went to race for Williams in 1994, he was paid a meagre £5,000 a race to replace Ayrton Senna in the most high-profile team of the era. 'It wasn't about the money because I just wanted to be in Formula One, and I guess Frank and Patrick knew that,' Coulthard told me ruefully. Williams was even happy to part company with Damon Hill and Nigel Mansell immediately after they won their world championships rather than bow to their demands for number one status and a pay rise, ignoring howls of protest from British fans.

There are great drivers in Formula One and great champions, but only a very few rise above the crowd to capture the imagination of a public not particularly interested in the sport, like Stirling Moss, James Hunt and Jackie Stewart. Dennis can boast of employing a plethora of champions – Mika Häkkinen, Niki Lauda and Alain Prost among them – but only two names would leap to the lips of casual observers of the sport today: Ayrton Senna and Lewis Hamilton. The symmetry is perfect, Hamilton looking up to Senna as his hero, even painting his crash helmet yellow, just like the Brazilian's. They came from opposite sides of the world and utterly different families – Senna from a wealthy background in São Paulo and Hamilton from a council house in Stevenage – yet their personalities seemed to have been prepared in the same blender.

Sublimely talented, but mercurial, obstinate, selfish and deeply religious they were also, according to Dennis, burdened with a mountainous chip on each shoulder. 'They both thought the world was against them,' he told me. They both calculated their worth, too.

When Senna's next contract came around, he wanted $1 million a race. This time there would be no coin-toss, for it was a straightforward demand. Dennis didn't have the money, nor did he want to haggle, so he passed the buck to John Hogan, Philip Morris's Marlboro Man and ace fixer. Hogie, as everyone knows him, agreed a deal, but got a shock when the San Marino Grand Prix, the fourth race of the season, rolled around. There was no Senna: he was still in São Paulo because no money had arrived in his bank account. Hogie recalled in an interview with *Motorsport* magazine in 2014: 'I hadn't allowed for how intransigent Senna could get. "When [the money] arrives, I'll get on the plane," Senna told me. Senna had made his Varig flight land in Rio and wait there until the money arrived, then they could take off – with the other 360 passengers on board.'

Dennis always maintained that Ayrton Senna would have driven for $100 a year, if that was the going rate – except that he'd have wanted $101, simply as a measure of him as the best. Dennis miscalculated because he would have driven for nothing. Claire Williams was just sixteen when she was dining in a restaurant with Patrick Head in Budapest, where Nigel Mansell would clinch the 1992 world championship with five races of the season remaining. Senna wanted that wondrous Williams car and sent a discreet note to Head. 'The message said that he would drive for Williams for free in

The nation celebrated a breakthrough when Stirling Moss became the first British driver to win a world championship grand prix, at Aintree in 1955.

One of the most formidable pairs in Formula One: Colin Chapman's design genius coupled with Jim Clark's driving genius won two world championships and an Indianapolis 500 victory.

The horrific reality of early Formula One. Brenda Vernor witnessed the fiery crash that killed her friend and Ferrari star Lorenzo Bandini at the 1967 Monaco Grand Prix.

Max Mosley, the racer, in March 1968 as he moved through the ranks, racing against Jim Clark and Graham Hill.

Jackie Stewart, the world's first $1 million driver, rests against his March Cosworth before the 1970 British Grand Prix.

Ken Tyrrell outside the famous woodshed in Surrey where he built cars that took Jackie Stewart to three world championships.

A youthful Luca di Montezemolo guides Niki Lauda through qualifying at the 1974 Italian Grand Prix at Ferrari's home track of Monza.

A severely burnt Niki Lauda chats to Ronnie Peterson before the championship-deciding 1976 Japanese Grand Prix, with James Hunt alongside.

Enzo Ferrari hugs his favourite driver. Enzo Ferrari said he loved Gilles Villeneuve 'like a son', but the Canadian was killed at the 1982 Belgian Grand Prix.

A pensive moment between Brenda Vernor and Gilles Villleneuve. He was killed shortly afterwards at the 1982 Belgian Grand Prix.

Frank Williams checks on Alan Jones in the 1978 Saudi Williams. Two years later, Jones would be Williams' first world champion.

The odd couple at work: Frank Williams and Ron Dennis deep in conversation before the 1998 French Grand Prix.

Luca di Montezemolo is all eyes and ears as he watches as Michael Schumacher wins the 1998 Italian Grand Prix for Ferrari in front of thousands of tifosi.

Sir Jackie Stewart with the author on the Suzuka grid for the 1999 Japanese Grand Prix, the last for Stewart's team.

When Formula One met Page Three: Eddie Jordan with a young lady called Katie Price, who became famous as the Page Three girl, Jordan.

Old Pals: Bernie Ecclestone shares a secret with Max Mosley when they ruled Formula One together.

Paul Stoddart breathes a sigh of relief after negotiating another tricky moment for his Minardi team in what he called F1's 'gory years'.

Ferrari's most successful driver with the man who guided Ferrari to the top. Luca di Montezemolo congratulates Michael Schumacher on yet another victory.

1993, he was so desperate. I remember seeing the message on Patrick's napkin and now looking back I wished I had kept that because it was such a slice of history.'

As Senna proved, the first thing in a driver's mind is a winning car – just as it was for Hamilton.

In 2012, Lewis Hamilton was close to quitting. As a lone black man in a sport that had always been the preserve of white, mainly middle-class men, Formula One had become too much for this young, immature talent. When Hamilton approached Ecclestone to pour out his unhappiness, four seasons had passed since he had won the world championship. He had watched Jenson Button steal his thunder and his world championship in 2009, and then Sebastian Vettel make Formula One his personal property, with consecutive titles in a car sponsored by what Hamilton scathingly referred to as 'a fizzy drinks company', Red Bull.

The body language was no longer that of the combative youngster who had exploded into the world of Formula One, coming within an ace of winning the championship in his first year of 2007. Hamilton was everything that Ecclestone and Formula One needed: he was young, exciting, edgy, controversial . . . and black.

Hamilton was nurtured by McLaren, a personal project for Ron Dennis that had echoes of the plot of *Pygmalion*, with Dennis cast as Henry Higgins tutoring Hamilton's head-strong but pliable Eliza Doolittle. Dennis had signed Hamilton when he was thirteen, the result of that now famous meeting at an awards dinner three years earlier when a tot, full of bravado, walked up to the imposing head of the most successful Formula One team in Britain and told him he would be driving for him one day, just like his hero Ayrton Senna. Dennis sanctioned the spending of £4 million on grooming this bright but sometimes wilful youngster, until he was ready to become world champion. It took less than a decade for Hamilton to be transformed from go-kart phenomenon to Formula One's brightest star. But it was a Faustian pact: in return for Dennis's patronage, Hamilton was expected to behave the Dennis way, his father Anthony recognising that falling into line would smooth his son's career. Hamilton had barely had a childhood, regularly missing lessons at the John Henry Newman School, which stands on a dual-carriageway in the anonymous Hertfordshire town of Stevenage, so that he could be at the track at every opportunity.

He found a girlfriend prepared to put up with the sacrifices, but Nicole Scherzinger was a pop star from Hollywood, a world away from Stevenage's blank apartment blocks and dreary 1960s shopping centre. Hamilton was introduced to rappers and film stars, and invitations to Hollywood premieres and red-carpet events poured in and soon stories of wild partying started to emerge, while his relationship with Scherzinger was on and off with bewildering regularity.

Dennis was pointed when he talked to the American Academy of Achievement: 'There are challenges because grand-prix drivers start so young, it is to the detriment of their education and as they mature as world champions, they are not as clever and worldly as they could be.'Who might he have been talking about? Who might that world champion be who wanted to spread his wings and walk the red carpets, choose where he wanted to live and who he spent his time with?

The cracks showed when Hamilton effectively sacked his father as manager immediately before the 2010 season, just when it seemed he would need a steadying hand on his shoulder. There was much shaking of heads when, late on the Friday after practice for the second race of the year, in Australia, police charged him with 'hooning' – spinning the wheels of his Mercedes – in front of fans outside the Albert Park circuit in Melbourne. His car was impounded and he was fined almost £300 – and his apology was abject.

Jenson Button had joined the team that year and was immediately popular with fans, the motorhome staff, the mechanics and engineers and the management, and Hamilton's mood was compounded when his new teammate won that race in Melbourne.

Button was not just five years older, he was five years wiser, and had put behind him his bad-boy days when he had flaunted his £1.2 million yacht, *Little Missy*, alongside the harbour at the Monaco Grand Prix and got into an embarrassing tangle over contract negotiations with Williams and BAR Honda that portrayed him as a spoilt child. McLaren was Hamilton's team, but soon it seemed to belong to Button. The matey videos they shot together in their first season of 2010 – when they were tagged Britain's 'Dream Team' – were over, and the following year turned into Hamilton's *annus horribilis*. While he floundered psychologically, Button thrived. The rift with his father was 'as wide as the Grand Canyon' and those dreamy days with Scherzinger, when he drove the beautiful black singer around his hometown in his Mercedes and took her secretly to the movies and then for a dinner of peri-peri chicken at his favourite Nando's restaurant, were long gone.

Hamilton was vilified when he moved to Switzerland, claiming that it was to escape the swirl of fame in Britain. It was nothing of the sort, and my chance encounter with Anthony Hamilton at the Laureus Awards in St Petersburg revealed the truth: Anthony had advised his son to move for tax reasons. Hamilton's first contract with McLaren was only £380,000 in salary plus bonuses, according to veteran Formula One journalist Mark Hughes, but he moved rapidly up the pay scale as he won in every season. Strangely, no one quibbled when David Coulthard and Jenson Button moved to Monaco, or even when Jackie Stewart upped sticks for Switzerland to escape punitive tax laws.

The culmination came when Hamilton suffered a crushing 2011 Monaco Grand Prix, in which the stewards seemed to penalise him every time his engine was switched on. He then blundered through the race collecting a twenty-second penalty for causing two accidents. On camera afterwards, he was asked why the stewards seemed to have it in for him. 'Maybe it's because I am black,' he answered with a rueful smile. It was an innocent remark, and he applied the context when he said it was a line from Ali G, a favourite comic. It was a weak joke, but no one in Finland or the USA or China or Brazil knew about Ali G, and the remark bounced around the globe as a direct accusation of racism against the stewards. Hamilton fled to the McLaren motorhome near to tears, but there was no sanctuary because tension was at fever pitch and Anthony Hamilton was left to talk his son down. Hamilton remained inconsolable, and had to apologise to the stewards in writing. Sebastian Vettel had won the championship the year before and victory in Monaco meant he had won five of the first six grands prix of this 2011 season. It was a Red Bull wipe-out, and Hamilton couldn't see a way to prevent it.

It was a full-time job for Dennis to try to control his young tyro. Gifted he might be, but his lifestyle was starting to impinge on his performances. Hamilton was used to being treated as top dog, the team number one, and the driver every-one had to admire, but Button's laid-back personality and his coterie of family and school friends unnerved him. His friends were thin on the ground, his father was absent and Scherzinger was rarely seen. Whenever Hamilton returned to McLaren's vast hospitality centre, he dived upstairs to his room, while Button was often at a table with his father John and manager and friend Richard Goddard, as well as his fiancée Jessica

Michibata, a Japanese lingerie model who turned heads and was photographed at every grand prix. John Button, Jenson's dad, nicknamed Papa Smurf for his shock of white hair, was a fixture in the paddock, loved by everyone, while Jenson and Jessica were the golden couple.

After the Monaco debacle came Canada, where Hamilton burst into the paddock office of Christian Horner, the team principal who had masterminded Red Bull's dominance. 'He wanted to leave McLaren for Red Bull,' Horner told me. 'I was taken aback to say the least but I had to tell him we didn't have a vacancy.' Horner had Vettel signed up and Mark Webber alongside and, privately, Horner didn't want a driver, no matter how talented, whose mercurial personality could cause ructions.

Vettel would be just as dominant in 2012, with the McLarens, powered by Mercedes engines, only third best and Hamilton ill at ease with his team and himself. Martin Whitmarsh, who had taken over from Dennis as team principal in 2009, was a calm, steady hand who had done everything he could to stabilise Hamilton's moods, but even he was furious when Hamilton tweeted the secret telemetry traces of Button's 2012 Belgian Grand Prix pole position. Actually, it was the wrong telemetry, but no employee should ever put team secrets in the public domain, right or wrong. For any other employee, it was an offence punishable by the sack, but Hamilton escaped because he was such a valuable commodity for McLaren. Either way, it didn't matter to Hamilton because his life at McLaren was over.

Ecclestone had to lever Hamilton out of McLaren to keep him in the sport. He knew the resistance from Dennis would be massive, but he also knew that Mercedes would be receptive to signing a driver who would bring international profile to the massive German carmaker and started to stoke up Niki Lauda, his old friend and now chairman of the Mercedes F1 team, to move in to replace Michael Schumacher, whose second stint in Formula One had been a failure. There was a deal there to be done.

Martin Whitmarsh seemed oblivious to the backstage manoeuvrings of Lauda and Ecclestone, and a visit to Hamilton by Ross Brawn, then the Mercedes team principal, who laid out his plans for a brilliant future over cups of tea around the kitchen table. The fateful day for McLaren, Hamilton and Whitmarsh was 23 September 2012, the date of the Singapore Grand Prix. Dennis flew in desperate to know whether his star driver had signed his new contract, worth a staggering $22 million a year. Whitmarsh said it was just a matter of putting pen to paper, but warned Dennis that his driver seemed depressed and distracted and 'his head isn't in the right place'. It was on the track: Hamilton took pole position and led from the start until lap 23 when a gearbox component, made by Mercedes, failed him. He was distraught – the world was against him again.

That night, Niki Lauda turned up at Hamilton's hotel, the Conrad Centennial overlooking the Marina Bay circuit and laid out his vision for the future – and offered $10 million on top of whatever McLaren had tabled. The temptation was not just the money, but a chance for Hamilton to redefine himself as his own man – and the chance of finding that winning car. Dennis was furious and rang Dr Dieter Zetsche, the moustachioed chairman of Daimler-Benz who would write the cheque, to complain that his own engine supplier was stealing his top driver. He warned him that Hamilton was a psychological handful and that hiring him would be no easy ride. Zetsche was wobbling, too, according to Ecclestone, because of the size of the deal.

'I phoned Zetsche and told him that if he wasn't careful, he would lose Lewis. "You need Lewis, I need Lewis and Formula One needs Lewis," I said. "I tell you what – if we have to go to $35 million, I will pay half." They didn't want to pay that, even though I warned them they would have to move their position. They only wanted to pay $30 million. I got Lewis to accept $32 million and then I could tell Zetsche he had his driver. The best bit was I ended up not having to pay the half, which was a relief.'

Hamilton was on the move, and to a career that even he, with all his dreams of emulating Ayrton Senna, could not have imagined.

Even then, the doubts remained. The 2014 season, his second with Mercedes, went to a championship-decider at Abu Dhabi. Hamilton was pitched against Nico Rosberg, his own teammate and a friend dating back to the days when they drove together in junior categories. Rosberg seemed like the Golden Boy of Formula One, the son of Keke, the 1982 world champion, with his home in Monaco, his fluency in five languages and his blond good looks.

Rosberg had proved to be a thorn in Hamilton's flesh all season, and, although Hamilton took a 17-point lead into the final race, there was plenty of capacity for disaster, thanks to a bizarre double-points system thought up by Ecclestone to spice up the season finale. The doubts that plagued Hamilton quietly in the back of his head sprang to life when Rosberg secured pole position on the Saturday before the race.

That night, Hamilton was restless. He couldn't sleep. He was alone with his thoughts. He walked out of his hotel to face the calm Gulf waters and phoned home to pour out his worries to his dad before padding back to his lonely room. Anthony recognised the symptoms and, like the old days, was ready to put his boy first. He rounded up the family and Scherzinger and got the first plane out. When Hamilton arrived at the circuit, he was surrounded by family and his girlfriend. He won the grand prix and his second world championship.

But that was it: Anthony wasn't required again and Hamilton split up with Scherzinger in 2015 after seven years together. In an interview with a magazine two years later, she seemed to complain that Hamilton had been selfish and too wrapped up in himself for their relationship to work. It was familiar territory.

Like Senna, Hamilton had to be the centre of attention

and his relationship with Rosberg, the friend he played table tennis with and went to live near in Monaco, disintegrated under the assault of their rivalry. They barely spoke and the mind games were constant, and the table tennis was abandoned (even though Hamilton reckoned he was so good that he had bought a 'racquet' [sic] because he regularly beat his teammate at that sport, too).

Like Senna, whose aggression and ruthlessness forced Alain Prost to abandon McLaren in 1989 after their relationship hit the wall, Hamilton would see off Rosberg, although not until the German had the last word.

In 2016, Rosberg – a talented and supremely fast driver but not as talented or supremely fast as Hamilton – devoted every ounce of his being to winning the title. He rode his luck, but turned to Zen meditation to work on his mental conditioning, dieted furiously and worked out, and separated himself from his wife Vivian and daughter Alaia to concentrate on his life's ambition to emulate his father. The championship came to a finale in Abu Dhabi again. The pair refused to shake hands before the race, and Hamilton, somewhat discourteously, refused to acknowledge his teammate's talent, insisting he was still the better man.

Hamilton won a bad-tempered grand prix, but Rosberg won his first championship, his only one as it turned out, for the pressure was so great, it sucked the lifeblood from him. His hand had trembled when we spoke on Saturday evening, and it was clear this was his moment or he would never be champion. 'I am giving it everything,' he said in a not very convincing statement of intent. We met a couple of hours after the race and Rosberg was ashen and looked a stone lighter, as though someone had removed the huge burden from his back. Less than a week after Abu Dhabi, Rosberg quit Formula One, openly admitting that competing against Hamilton had drained him. Hamilton lost that battle for the championship in Abu Dhabi, but won the war. Just like Senna.

Before the 2018 Monaco Grand Prix, Hamilton and I sat on the top deck of the dark grey Mercedes hospitality centre parked on the Monte Carlo waterfront, looking out at the packed harbour, the dome of the famous casino ahead of us and to the right the £120 million super-yacht belonging to Lawrence Stroll, the billionaire Canadian who had bankrolled the career of his son Lance at Williams to the tune of £50 million. Hamilton, now a four-times world champion, arrived in the paddock on the £55,000 MV Agusta motorcycle he helped to design and had worked his way through his media duties before meeting me. He was in uniform – team T-shirt and shorts, white socks and trainers, and a pink baseball cap carrying the Mercedes three-pointed star in white. Hamilton is the only driver who has his own team colour range. The bling was on full display, the chunky gold and diamond necklace and the earrings with their huge diamond studs; he must have been wearing $1 million, never mind earning it.

The irony was inescapable when Hamilton – worth £159 million, according to *The Sunday Times* in 2018 – spoke earnestly about how Formula One excluded kids from back-grounds like his, who would never be able to afford to pay tens of thousands of pounds for a season in karting, let alone the millions it costs to put a youngster through the system from karting to Formula One. Hamilton had slept on a sofa in his dad's flat in Stevenage, watching the dealers dispense their drugs across the road, and gone to a comprehensive school where he was bullied and almost expelled for fighting back. His kart mechanic was his dad in the early days, fettling engines supplied by John Button, and he felt the wealth gap keenly when he entered the bigger world of single-seater racing, where he mixed with teenage rivals whose careers were funded by wealthy parents. He never got over flying to a race in Keke Rosberg's helicopter when he competed along-side Nico as a teenager. Keke was a millionaire Formula One world champion with a home in Monaco and Anthony was a former railway worker from Stevenage. And Lewis was black, the only black kid in the sport. He was a boy apart from the start.

Hamilton was lucky to have Ron Dennis and Mercedes as a benefactor, lucky to be groomed for the stardom he now enjoys. He has endured years of criticism for his lifestyle, but it is hard to fathom what it is that gives such offence. The qualities so admired in Senna seem to be reviled by many in Hamilton. Thirty years before Hamilton, a McLaren driver drank, smoked, took drugs, and shacked up with any British Airways stewardess he could lay his hands on. He even had the motto, 'Sex, breakfast of champions' embroidered on his overalls, and they made a movie about him. James Hunt lived a life that would set social media ablaze with indignation today if it was Hamilton, whose crimes appear to be enjoying music, wearing clothes that might not go down well at the RAC Club or Wimbledon, and having his body festooned with tattoos, but he is polite, well mannered, and a clean-living vegetarian who likes dogs and has an endearing openness that sometimes gets him into trouble.

Formula One was tantalised when Hamilton went onto his Instagram account to apologise for crashing his £1.5 million Pagani Zonda supercar into three parked cars in the early hours in Monaco, just two days before he was due in São Paulo for the 2015 Brazilian Grand Prix. The Mercedes public relations crew warned the media not to ask questions about the incident and the television crews and journalists duly obeyed, but when he appeared in front of me in the Mercedes motorhome with his baseball cap pulled down to his eyebrows I couldn't resist asking what was happening. 'Man, I have been partying,' he said – and he looked like it. He had clinched his third world championship at the previous race in the USA and had obviously indulged his new liking for tequila. It is the only time I had seen anything comparable with Hunt, and there was something disarming about the abandon with which Hamilton had greeted that third title. Since then, Hamilton has given up booze and turned vegan. He is still self-centred, but he was rid of Rosberg and can get on with his racing, believing he was safe from a serious challenge from Valtteri Bottas, the placid Finn who took Rosberg's place in 2017.

And he is still box office. Hamilton's persona does not radiate a world of tyres and computer programs and pistons, he is a creature from the pop videos that youngsters watch on their iPhones, or the red carpet, where he is in a picture on Instagram alongside Kim Kardashian and Kanye West. He was in the middle of planning a fashion range in association with Tommy Hilfiger when we met in Monaco. As Anthony Hamilton told me: 'The other drivers should be grateful because he is the one who keeps Formula One in lights and keeps the interest going.'

When I left Hamilton, he went to the security fence around the Monaco paddock to talk to dozens of fans who were holding out their autograph books and programmes appealing for a signature. Hamilton signed every one before he left on his motorcycle, the cameras clicking furiously to keep up with him. Bernie Ecclestone got it right when he said that the driver is the star, and Lewis Hamilton – like Senna – is the biggest star of his era.

10

RANCOUR AND RESENTMENT

G INGER Spice couldn't resist the joke when she was introduced to David Coulthard. Geri Halliwell was performing at Alexandra Palace with the Spice Girls at the launch of the McLaren car for the 1997 season when she wondered who this tall Scottish lad might be. 'I'm one of the drivers,' Coulthard told her. 'Oooh, will you be taking us home later, then?' Geri asked.

Geri knew full well that the silver overalls indicated that Coulthard's job was slightly more than a cab driver, but she with her bandmates were the stars of the show. The Spice Girls were the biggest pop band in the world, famous from Tokyo to Texas, and topping the charts in dozens of countries. But McLaren could afford to hire the five girls, who came with a six-figure price tag, for the day – or, at least, their sponsors could. McLaren had lost Marlboro's title sponsorship to Ferrari, after an association lasting twenty-two years, and needed to announce a new name and a new livery: the classic red and white had gone and now the McLarens of Coulthard and Mika Häkkinen would be painted in the silver and black of West cigarettes.

The launch was massive, with hundreds filling the great Victorian 'People's Palace', while the show was filmed for MTV and broadcast worldwide. It cost a fortune, but these were the days of spend, spend, spend. Money was gushing into the Formula One paddock like water from a burst mains pipe, and the teams were awash with cash from the tobacco industry. 'We were like cowboys in the Wild West, chasing around finding money. It was like being Wild Bill Hickock going out on horseback and shooting prey,' according to Eddie Jordan.

Jordan had found his prey in 1996 in the form of Benson & Hedges. Jordan and Ian Phillips, his right-hand man, had come across Nigel Northridge, who was on his way up the executive ladder at Gallaher, the brand's owner. Northridge liked the cheek of his fellow Irishman and the fresh enthusiasm of the upstart squad trying to beat the biggest boys on the block. B & H had the cash and the marketing nous, while Northridge had the imagination to exploit a Formula One car as a global billboard. The paint job on the car became a bright golden yellow called Desert Storm, and Northridge pumped pizzazz into the team, while Giselle Davies – the daughter of Barry, the BBC football commentator, who would later become head of communications for the International Olympic Committee – was given the job of spreading the word to national and international newspapers.

Part of the appeal would be glamour in its most obvious form – Page Three girls. A young model called Katie Price renamed herself Jordan, jumping at the chance to become part of the Formula One scene, draping herself over the team's yellow cars at races for the cameras. Katie obviously caught on fast to Formula One's hustle: when Jordan's lawyers went to trademark the team's brand, they discovered they had been beaten to it. 'Being a Jordan girl was something big and Katie was Jordan,' Mark Gallagher, Jordan's commercial director, says. 'When Warburg Pincus, who bought into the team, wanted to register a number of trademarks for sunglasses and stuff, they couldn't because she had got there first and already registered under her name. Someone out there was very smart.'

Formula One was no longer a sport purely for the anoraks and geeks but an arm of show business.

The irony is that it was propelled onto the global stage by tragedy. Ayrton Senna had, like Stirling Moss before him, transcended the sports pages and become a sporting super-hero. He won his first title in 1988 in swashbuckling style, stalling on the grid at the penultimate grand prix in Japan, dropping to fourteenth and then working his way through the field to overtake his teammate Alain Prost for victory and the world championship. Senna was the driver who took an extraordinary pole position in Monaco, claiming to have had an out-of-body experience when he set a time 1.4 seconds faster than Prost, and he was the driver who had conquered atrocious conditions at the 1993 European Grand Prix at Donington for what many considered to be his greatest victory.

Senna was the sport's biggest name when he was killed on global television at the 1994 San Marino Grand Prix. Shockwaves rippled around the world as viewers watched Senna's Williams car spearing off the Imola track at the Tamburello corner and hitting a wall. The pictures were shocking, the prone body of the three-times world champion being worked on by medical crews led by Professor Sid Watkins. There was little that commentators like Murray Walker could say to mask the horror as the minutes ticked by and it became increasingly clear that viewers, from grandparents to youngsters, were watching what was clearly a fatal accident. Bernie Ecclestone said it was like watching Jesus Christ being crucified on live television. One nine-year-old was competing at a kart track, wearing his yellow helmet, just like Senna's, that day. When Anthony Hamilton told his son Lewis that Senna was dead, the youngster disappeared behind a car and cried.

Formula One faced a torrent of criticism and accusations from fans angry that the sport was a killer, reinforced by the death of Roland Ratzenberger during qualifying for the same race. There had not been a death at a Formula One grand prix in twelve years, and now here were two in one weekend. Ecclestone braced himself for a terrible backlash that could wipe out the sport he had spent years nurturing, yet the audience for the 1994 season grew by 30 per cent as viewers indulged in an almost ghoulish interest in what might happen next. The season was sustained by the battle between Michael Schumacher and Damon Hill for the championship. It was

Schumacher, the pantomime villain against Hill, the house-wives' favourite, and it ended with what appeared to be a dastardly deed when the German seemed to drive his Benetton into Hill's Williams. He got away with it – and with the world championship. And Ecclestone got his money-machine working.

Just like the 1976 season, interest in Formula One had been ignited by the most grisly of circumstances. Ecclestone soon became a face on television known for his pronouncements, which included his thoughts on why there was such a low number of new drivers into the sport – because tighter safety meant there was no 'culling'. It sounded like insensitivity of the highest order, but no one who knew Ecclestone's back-ground and his personal losses could think that. He was, in his usual way, stating the unadulterated fact that drivers were occupying their places on the grid longer than ever because Formula One was safer than ever.

Newspapers were taking notice, because they had found a new and engaging character with a hint of the scurrilous about him, and rumours of criminal connections – even though he was never convicted of any crime – only added to his air of mystery. Ecclestone appeared to love the notoriety and was happy to play up his image as the south London wide boy. A rumour did the rounds that he was the 'Mr Big' behind the Great Train Robbery of 1963, one of the most sensational crimes in British legal history, during which fifteen men robbed the Glasgow-to-London mail train and fled with £2.6

million. The getaway car driver was an occasional racer called Roy James, who had shown promise in junior series but decided to put his talent to more lucrative use by driving for a gang headed by Bruce Reynolds, one of the masterminds behind the robbery. James served twelve years and, on his release, started to hang around the Formula One paddocks, setting tongues wagging. The most famous of the robbers was, of course, Ronnie Biggs, who escaped over the wall of Wandsworth Prison after serving just a year. Biggs had a facelift and fled to Brazil where he remained a fugitive for thirty-six years.

Biggs became quite the paddock celebrity at the Brazilian Grand Prix, although he knew nothing about it. Mosley says: 'When we were in Brazil Bernie would have the promoters announce over the loudspeaker, "Would Mr Biggs come to reception to collect his passes." Bernie loved to do it just to wind people up. This went on for years until a journalist plucked up the courage to ask Bernie whether he was the boss of the robbery and Bernie looked him up and down and said: "What me? Rob a train for £2.6 million? Not enough to bother." Bernie loved all that mystique.'

The japes were to come under serious scrutiny when Ecclestone's name suddenly emerged at the top of the *Sunday Times Rich List* as the highest-paid executive in Britain. In 1993 alone, he was paid £45 million at a time when chief executives of the biggest companies would be lucky to take home £1 million.

Now everyone was interested in the little 'Mr Big', who ruled his gang behind the fences of the paddock and was getting rich at Formula One speed.

Ecclestone sold Brabham in 1987 for $5 million – a healthy profit over the purchase price of £100,000 – and started to take serious charge of Formula One, unlocking television contracts held by the European Broadcasting Union, which allowed him to negotiate country by country, signing lucrative contracts and channelling money into his company, Formula One Promotions and Administration (FOPA). According to authoritative estimates compiled by Tom Bower for his biography of Ecclestone, in the three years to 1995, Ecclestone had $341 million paid into his personal account. Ecclestone was rewarding himself for transforming Formula One from a rabble of enthusiasts to a sport to rival football with global audiences second only to the World Cup and the Olympics and attracting some of the biggest corporate names as sponsors.

Soon, Ecclestone had organised Formula One so that it took all of the money from circuit advertising and sponsorship, plus a substantial fee from the promoters at each track, the television money, and the rake-off from the Paddock Club, the £1,000-a-plate executive club where businessmen could wine and dine their friends and associates while enjoying access to the teams and the best seats in the house.

The ringmaster had his circus and his acts lined up to perform, but the audience was unaware of the mounting bitterness backstage: the promoters were squealing because they had to pay huge fees to stage a grand prix, and their only income was whatever they made at the turnstiles: one rainy day and they were in the red. Meanwhile, the teams were now on the warpath and wanted a bigger share of the profits.

Dennis, the most forceful character in the group, decided he would stand up to Ecclestone, particularly when it came to signing a new Concorde Agreement – the commercial deal named after the Place de la Concorde in Paris where the FIA has its headquarters. The agreement was the cornerstone deal that bound the teams to Ecclestone's companies and the FIA.

The contract, a secret outside the confines of Ecclestone, Mosley and the teams, was open on Ecclestone's huge glass desk in his Princes Gate office, awaiting signatures, but Dennis, as clever as any tycoon in British industry, was adamant that no one would sign a deal that appeared to Ecclestone's advantage. 'I'll bet they do,' Ecclestone said, looking up at Dennis, a broad-shouldered, commanding figure towering above him. 'I am telling you, Bernie, that no one will sign that agreement,' Dennis came back. 'Yes, they will. Bet you.' The bet was taken and the amount quickly escalated until it reached £5,000, when Ecclestone said finally: 'Someone will sign. Look.' With that, he picked up a pen and scribbled his signature at the bottom of the document. 'Told you,' he grinned. Dennis had been outfoxed, but there was revenge. 'I knew Ron would pay up, but he sent the five grand round in 50p pieces,' Ecclestone chuckled.

Dennis would have to reserve his ire for the forum of team owners' meetings at the Heathrow Hilton Terminal 4, where they were supposed to plan their future in concert with Ecclestone and Mosley. The meetings were already rancorous, but the tensions between them and Mosley and Ecclestone were out in the open, and discussions were somewhere between a shambles and a fiasco. No one kept minutes, and no one seemed to know what was being agreed. It was perfect for Ecclestone, who could keep everyone distracted and off balance, sowing the seeds of confusion at every opportunity and then wielding his ultimate weapon – divide and rule. He understood where the weaknesses and strengths were: Ron Dennis's arrogance; Frank Williams's gratitude for past aid; Eddie Jordan's desire for cash; Flavio Briatore's friendship, and Montezemolo's insistence that Ferrari was pre-eminent in any settlement.

It was a technique perfected by Ecclestone and Mosley when they made their grab for power. Mosley left March in 1977, seeing his future in FOCA as a leading light in the battle for the upper hand against the authoritarian and pompous Jean-Marie Balestre, who ran FISA, and ruled Formula One like a latter-day emperor.

Ecclestone had picked out Mosley early on, needing an intellect beside him, a lawyer with a forensic mind and an obstinate character who would back him up in the hottest of fights. They took Balestre on with a combination of cheek, ruthlessness and humour. They spoke Cockney rhyming slang to confuse the self-important Frenchman when they wanted to secure a list of Balestre supporters, resorting to a conversation that went something like, 'You do the Cain and Abel', meaning you turn over the table, and 'I'll hoist it', as in steal the list. It sounded unlikely even today from the lips of Mosley with his received pronunciation when he retold the story over lunch, but it worked. He tipped up the table and, in the confusion, Ecclestone secured the list.

Balestre was convinced he was odds-on to win the 1991 presidential election, after making sure that the key FIA members were onside with lavish food and accommodation before the crucial vote in Paris, but Balestre was an ego waiting to be punctured. He had controversial associations with the Nazis during the war, and there were some accusations that he was a collaborator, although he claimed to be a double agent. John Hogan says that at one FIA meeting, where Balestre's bluster was at peak volume, Mosley leaned over and whispered: 'I have a very incriminating photograph of Jean-Marie making a Nazi salute. Is this a good moment to show it?' Balestre had been in office more than twelve years and had more than his fair share of rows with both teams and drivers, most notoriously being seen to favour Alain Prost, a fellow Frenchman, over Ayrton Senna at the climax of the 1989 season. Senna was disqualified after he collided with his McLaren teammate and Prost became champion before leaving for Ferrari.

On the day of the vote, Balestre collared Ecclestone and

commiserated, telling him it was a shame for Max because he was about to be the easy winner. 'Balestre had done what they all do, fixing up first-class flights and the nice hotels so they would vote for him,' Ecclestone told me. 'I told Balestre that he could forget that and the best thing he could do was to stand up and say that Max would succeed him, then he could leave with dignity. He wouldn't have it.' Balestre took Ecclestone into a back room to show him the list of his potential backers, but Ecclestone had got to them all the night before – and swung their votes to Mosley. Balestre lost his election.

Two years later and Mosley was president of the entire FIA, a federation of motoring associations and motor-racing groups in 145 countries. Their grip was complete, and together Mosley and Ecclestone swept away the old ruling class, with Mosley writing the regulations, while Ecclestone set about adding lustre to the grands prix and his finances. This was the powerful alliance against which the team owners gathered to air their grievances and disquiet.

When Paul Stoddart walked in for the first time at one of the Heathrow summits after buying the Minardi team, he was shocked at the atmosphere. A successful entrepreneur dealing in the aircraft business, he was expecting the calm of the boardroom but found a bear pit. 'What scared me the most was the forcefulness of the way everyone talked. I left the first meeting thinking, "How the hell do these people get anything done?" Individually, they were very, very successful, but, collectively, they needed to park their egos at the door. In most meetings, Bernie knew the outcome before we started and would have already done all the deals he needed to do. The personal falling out between team principals was something I saw to the detriment of F1. Too many grudges.'

Oliver Weingarten left football's English Premier League to become secretary general of the Formula One Teams' Association (FOTA) and could barely believe his eyes. 'The degree of self-interest was incredible. You could sit around a table and agree something and the minute they left they were railroaded into something else. There were so many things wrong for the sport, but people were railroaded because they were too scared to stick up for themselves.'

David Richards has one image in his mind from his time as BAR team principal: Eddie Jordan standing on the table cursing his fellow team owners. 'When we were talking about the distribution of income from the computer games' rights, we had the debate with Eddie Jordan standing on the table. One day, we were packing up, putting stuff in briefcases and ready to go. As I reached the door, Tom Walkinshaw [then owner of the Arrows team] put a hand on my arm and said, "Don't go yet. This is when all the big decisions are made." With that, Bernie suddenly said, "Come back. There's something we've forgotten," and we sat down and started again.

'The intellect of Max coupled with the streetwise manner of Bernie and the way he understands people was a formidable combination we will never see again.'

Jackie Stewart hopes not. Stewart was among the bravest, cleverest and most successful drivers in the history of Formula One, with three world championships. Severely hampered by dyslexia, he watched his father, a garage owner in their small hometown of Milton in Dunbartonshire, fuss over customers, making sure they were so satisfied that they would bring their Austin or Jaguar back a second and third time.

When he made the decision to run his own team with his son Paul, a successful team owner in junior formulas, it would be on the correct business terms – just like his father – or not at all. When I asked Stewart why he quit Stewart Grand Prix and sold to Ford after just three years on the grid, Stewart shot back: 'Those meetings at Terminal 4.' He didn't need a moment to think.

'It was appalling. I walked out of one meeting and said to Paul, "Paul, we shouldn't be here. This isn't my type of business." All of my other relationships in business were blue chip, integrity and care. You had to present yourself and show what you were doing and where you were going. You would have dialogue. We had nothing like that. It was very unhealthy. It was a bad atmosphere. Max and Bernie wanted everyone to feel threatened. That was empire building and most of those empires have now collapsed because it wasn't right. We were not made welcome.'

So unwelcome that at the team's first Monaco Grand Prix in 1997, Ecclestone arranged for their motorhome to be parked at the top of the steep hill overlooking the harbour.

When asked why, Ecclestone made reference to Stewart's boasts of his royal connections: 'I thought he would prefer to be nearer the palace.'

The ultimate insult was served when Stewart Grand Prix's name appeared with an asterix against it on the FIA entry list for 1998, denoting the team was only a possible entry. Stewart was asked to provide guarantees that he had the funding to compete for a second season, even though there had never been any financial problems. Stewart remembers bitterly the embarrassment as he had to call each of his blue-chip sponsors to reassure them that all was well and his team would be competing. The damage was done and laid the foundations for a feud with Mosley that has lasted years.

You could understand that Ecclestone, a man of connections but who keeps them to himself, would weary of Stewart, a good man but a good self-publicist, too. A conversation with Sir Jackie Stewart is littered with famous names — George Harrison and Sean Connery mixed with Princess Anne and the Crown Prince of Bahrain and King Hussein of Jordan, the greatest man he ever met. We are sitting in the office of his apartment complex outside Geneva and there is a phone call: it is from Prince Albert's secretary in Monaco making some final arrangements. I tell him that at every Monaco Grand Prix, I walk along the cliffs from Beaulieu-sur-Mer towards Cap Ferrat, passing the gorgeous, dusky-pink villa, La Fleur du Cap, cheerfully nicknamed 'Cirrhosis-by-the-Sea' by David Niven when the popular raconteur and

British film star owned the house and threw hedonistic parties for his Hollywood pals. There is a small boat jetty in front of the house where stars like Cary Grant, Brigitte Bardot and Sophia Loren would sunbathe and swim, often joined by Prince Rainier, Monaco's ruler, and his Hollywood wife Princess Grace. Among the guests would be the little Scotsman with his pretty young wife. 'Oh, it's a beautiful house,' Stewart says, his eyes misting with memories of gloriously sunny days with Rainier and Grace before the scent of jasmine gave way to the smell of oil and petrol on the Monte Carlo waterfront.

Stewart's Swiss apartment is not far from Michael Schumacher's huge estate, on a hillside yards from the front entrance of a Swiss clinic. Lady Helen, the love of Stewart's life and mother of his sons, Paul and Mark, suffers from dementia and needs round-the-clock care. She still smiles and enjoys conversation as we discuss the old times over lunch of asparagus and chicken, washed down with some Swiss white wine, in their dining room, which looks out towards Lake Geneva. Even in his late seventies, Stewart is a bundle of restless energy and needs a team of staff in Switzerland and at Clayton House, his home in Buckinghamshire, to keep up with his commitments around the world.

As much as Stewart is remembered for his driving, his short spell as founder of a Formula One team is burnished into his memory. Stewart cajoled Ford into supplying engines, alongside £100 million worth of support over five years, in exchange for the famous blue oval on the car. Then Stewart set about raiding his contacts book to bring in some of the biggest sponsor names, like HSBC bank. Stewart didn't have to bother with phoning agents and middle-ranking executives – he went straight to Sir William Purves, the chairman and a friend. Then there was the MCI phone business: Stewart understood quickly that putting a sticker on a 200 mph billboard wasn't enough, so he put them in touch with Ford and, in the first year, the company was supplying 10 per cent of the carmaker's worldwide telephone business. Stewart brought in Texaco to supply the team's fuel, but also negotiated a deal for every new Ford car to be filled with their petrol. 'You can't keep taking money without offering benefit,' Stewart says. 'The balance has always been completely wrong.'

The Stewarts built a new factory on an industrial complex on one of Milton Keynes's many roundabouts. Each corridor was lined with carpets patterned with the Stewart Racing tartan weave that used to adorn Stewart's helmet in his racing days – a rare extravagance, for Stewart ran a tight ship in a way that was alien to some of the hustlers who were always passing money from hand to hand.

'We paid everyone on the right date, at a time when some teams like Arrows weren't paying their bills,' Stewart says. 'So, the suppliers were always with us and we got everything done immediately. Stewart Grand Prix never had an overdraft. The most important man in the team was the chief financial officer.'

There was no phone call that Stewart couldn't make and no contact that he wouldn't approach – even the most famous businessman in the world. Stewart was a feature of television coverage of motor racing in the USA, appearing for years on the popular ABC Wide World of Sports as a commentator and pundit so that he seemed like a home-grown American star. Years before he launched his own team, Stewart called Steve Jobs at Apple to invite him to a grand prix. His name was readily recognised.

'I phoned Steve Jobs and a girl answers the phone. I told her I was calling from Switzerland and wanted to arrange a call with Steve. She recognised the voice immediately and told me her daddy loved me. She put me right through.'

Jobs, intrigued by the call and this sport called Formula One, turned up at Milan Airport in sneakers, black jeans and T-shirt and carrying a knapsack for the Italian Grand Prix at Monza. Stewart booked him into the Villa d'Este on Lake Como, one of Italy's most exclusive hotels, which meant that the maître d' had to find a jacket and tie so that the whizz-kid of American technology could eat in the plush dining room.

At the track, Jobs was fascinated by everything, from the colour and noise, to the banks of computers where Benetton were cheekily trying to spy on transmissions from Honda, the leading engine supplier at this time in the 1980s, but couldn't discover the frequency on which they operated. 'We left the garage and I am telling Steve about this. He goes into the toilets for a pee followed by a Japanese engineer. There they are, this Japanese engineer and Steve Jobs, the God of the computer world and as imposing as he is tall. They start talking and after fifteen minutes Steve emerges and has the frequency to pass on to Benetton.'

The anecdote is clearly a Stewart favourite and he smiles broadly, bending down to pet his little Norfolk terriers, Pimm's and Whisky, who have waddled into the office behind us.

I spoil the moment by raising the decision to quit. Stewart Racing had its successes – second in 1997 in Monaco with Rubens Barrichello at the team's fifth race, and a victory for Johnny Herbert at the Nürburgring at the 1999 European Grand Prix. Stewart was candid: he couldn't fulfil his ambitions. He couldn't be, as he was a driver and a safety campaigner, a leader. He had been cold-shouldered by the Formula One establishment and, despite the impressive roster of sponsors, costs were soaring in the paddock, too high for a team with an annual budget not much more than £16 million.

'I couldn't see myself being able to get as high as Ferrari, Williams and McLaren and we had turned down £40 million in tobacco money. In the end, we couldn't see where we were going. A lot of teams were losing money and I didn't want to be involved in that.'

When Stewart's son Paul was diagnosed with cancer of the colon late in 1999, Stewart knew he had made the right decision to sell to Ford. Jac Nasser, the pugnacious chief executive of Ford, had big ideas when he took over the carmaker and was equally ambitious in Formula One. His idea was to buy out the Stewarts and put Jaguar, one of the most famous marques in world motoring, into Formula One. Stewart won't confirm the sale price, but has never denied that it was £100 million – perhaps reward for a savage test of nerve and endurance.

The green Jaguars looked fabulous, and the launch at the start of 2000 at Lord's Cricket Ground spoke of ambition, of a grand name that would climb to the lofty perch of the great Formula One teams. Johnny Herbert was retained as team-mate to Eddie Irvine, who had been runner-up in the world championship the previous year, and was said to have clinched a deal worth as much as £18 million over three years – a figure that stunned Luca di Montezemolo, the Ferrari president, who had only hired the Irishman as a compliant second-string to Michael Schumacher and rated him no more than a middle-ranking driver.

Nasser brought in Wolfgang Reitzle, an executive from the Ford division that owned Jaguar, to run the team, but he was a corporate man out of his depth in Formula One. Reitzle left and Bobby Rahal, a legend in the world of IndyCar racing, was appointed team principal for 2001. Within months, Niki Lauda was needlessly brought in as Rahal's partner, and the friction was too much for the American and Rahal walked out. And still it got worse, until Lauda was shown the door along with seventy staff at the Milton Keynes factory at the end of 2002. The tartan carpets had gone, too. John Hogan, the wily executive who had guided Marlboro to McLaren and

Ferrari and was Jaguar's commercial director, steadied the ship until he handed over to Tony Purnell, a tech entrepreneur who had sold his business to Ford, and David Pitchforth, an engineer. They looked as though they could get a grip, but Ford never really understood the politics of Formula One and, as with all corporations, they tired of being bit players when the glory went elsewhere. The huge green motorhome was impressive, but little else was. Ford decided enough was enough. It was time for someone else to take over the team that Jackie built.

11

THE HUSTLERS

EDDIE Jordan is giggling long before he reveals the details of the ruse he has perpetrated on the world's airlines for years. We met a few days before the 2018 Azerbaijan Grand Prix, when he passed through London on his way to join up with the Channel 4 Formula One television crew headed by David Coulthard. It was Coulthard who alerted me he was on his way.

'I know he is coming because I am sharing a hotel room with him in Baku,' Coulthard chuckled half-heartedly. Why would two multimillionaires share a hotel room? I wondered. 'Because he is so bloody disorganised. He just turns up and wings it. He probably hasn't even got a flight booked.'

True enough, Jordan – known to everyone in Formula One as EJ – wasn't sure if he had a flight or not. He had, but he didn't know if it was economy or business class. He wasn't worried, though, because he has a trick: he gets on the plane full of confidence, a famous face, well dressed and carrying a briefcase, waving and smiling before turning left into the business class section ... even if the ticket says economy.

Jordan then hopes no one notices. 'I get on almost last, they check the ticket and send me right, but I turn left and put my briefcase on an empty seat and then vanish to the loo or walk about. One time, I put the briefcase down, no one comes so I sit down and fasten my seatbelt. Then I realise someone was in the toilet, he comes out and says, "That's my seat." I was caught. I still do it, though. It's an adventure. I hate boredom. I can't read a book. I have read ten books in my life – I haven't even read my own autobiography.'

I tell him he is definitely in his autobiography, but now his ruse is public, he may struggle to wangle his way into business class again. Jordan is one of the most recognisable faces in Formula One, even though he left the sport as a team owner at the end of 2004. His transition to Formula One pundit was simple: if he doesn't have an opinion, he can make one up.

Life now is divided between his homes in London, Monaco and South Africa, and his many business interests include co-ownership of the Jazz FM radio station and the posh people's bible, Debrett's. He is tickled by the idea of owning a slice of the British high-life, after being brought up in Bray, a nowhere little seaside town south of Dublin – like Blackpool without the trams, the tower or the glitter, he says in that autobiography he has never read. He started his working life as a bank clerk, but soon tired of the formality and struck out on his own, ending with a fortune estimated at as much as £85 million.

'I had to be a hustler every day in Formula One. We were all hustlers. I always had belief. That is the most powerful asset. Sometimes that belief can become an obsession and boring for other people, but you have to believe and not be afraid to raise the target as you go along.'

EJ was forever raising targets, from the days when he arranged car loans for customers in his Bank of Ireland branch and then tried to sell them the car, too. The Dublin bank clerk only discovered motor racing because a strike closed his branch and he went on a trip to Jersey where he watched a kart race. Within a year, he was Irish kart champion and progressing through the single-seater ranks. His career could have been finished early by an appalling crash at Mallory Park in Leicestershire where, he says, he discovered that driving fast wasn't enough: you had to brake, too. He suffered compound fractures to both legs, injuries serious enough to keep him out of a 1976 season in which he would have figured prominently. There were not just injuries to his legs, but a disfigurement that has had millions of fans guessing for years. The trauma made his hair fall out and he has lived with alopecia ever since, wearing wigs so convincing that few who have seen him on television have any idea. Although he seems unembarrassed, he rarely mentions it, not even in his autobiography.

EJ recovered to establish a reputation as a driver, even testing for McLaren, and moved to Silverstone with his wife Marie. There he set up home, buying second-hand furniture from an auctioneer for a few pounds, and eventually a team that would rip through the lower series. He freely admits he was not much of an engineer – once forgetting to tighten the wheel nuts on a car that came back to the pits with three instead of one at each corner – but he was a genius at convincing sponsors to get on board.

He could also spot talent and ran good drivers like Johnny Herbert and Martin Donnelly in Formula 3000. As a part-time manager, he sent drivers out to race in Japan, collecting 10 per cent of their earnings, until he had a gang of about twenty, including a fellow Irishman called Eddie Irvine, who was so well known in Japan that he was a millionaire before he came back to drive for Jordan in 1993, and then was hired as teammate to Michael Schumacher at Ferrari three years later.

At home in Silverstone, the Jordans took in lodgers to help pay their way, mainly young drivers, like Martin Brundle, who remembers sitting in the kitchen pouring his cornflakes into a bowl among the bustle of family life, while Marie did the washing and cleaning for her brood of up-and-coming stars. It was fun and the Jordan team was successful, but it was not enough.

For Eddie Jordan, being top of the pile in Formula 3000 was one thing, but Formula One was the Everest of motor racing, waiting to be conquered by a garrulous Irishman with ambition beyond his knowledge and his budgets. As the saying goes: how do you make a small fortune in Formula

One? Start with a big one. Jordan conquered the problem by starting with a bank account splashed with red. 'You need to start with nothing because if you start with money, you will lose it. Me, I was always starting from the back, always in danger of losing my arse. You can't call me clever, but I am very good at making two plus two make five and making money out of it.'

Not enough money for Formula One, though. Mark Gallagher, who worked side by side with Jordan for fifteen years in F1, remembers: 'People have no idea the pressure Eddie put himself under to create his team. In 1991, he had £1.5 million in the bank and he put all of that into designing and building that first Jordan F1 car. He personally flew to Japan to tie up a sponsor deal with Fujifilm; he browbeat 7 UP into sponsoring the team when they didn't want to. He pulled it all together.'

Problems came thick and fast: his driver Bertrand Gachot was on his way to speak to executives at 7 UP when he was arrested for spraying a taxi driver with a CS gas canister he kept in his car for emergencies. A London court didn't see a row with a taxi driver as an emergency, and Jordan was left with an empty seat for the upcoming 1991 Belgian Grand Prix.

Willi Weber, a German businessman, was managing a promising youngster making a name for himself with the Sauber Mercedes sports car team. The substantial upside to the deal was that Weber would pay Jordan £150,000 a race to put Michael Schumacher in his car, but a maiden grand prix at Spa-Francorchamps – a long and fearsomely fast track featuring the famous Eau Rouge hill taken flat out into the blind crest called Le Raidillon would be daunting in any series, never mind Formula One. Jordan was worried. As an ex-driver, he thought it might be too much to ask of a debutant being pitched onto a grid that would include some of the greatest of all time, like Ayrton Senna, Alain Prost and Nigel Mansell – and in a humble Jordan car in its first season. Jordan asked Schumacher if he had been round Spa; Schumacher was exact in his answer when he said he had; in fact, he had cycled it.

If Schumacher was expecting to enter the glossy world of Formula One, with its huge salaries and gorgeous girls, he was to get a rude awakening as soon as he arrived for the Belgian Grand Prix weekend. The 'hotel' was more like a hostel. This was bargain-basement Formula One, Jordan-style. 'We had to share a girls' dormitory with Ian Phillips [Jordan's right-hand man] and Michael and Willi Weber. We had two bunks separated by a chipboard wall,' Jordan says. There was another unpleasant surprise for the young driver. He arrived with Jordan at the circuit on Friday morning for practice, only to discover the garages had been locked by bailiffs. There was a moment of panic before Jordan did the only thing he could think of and turned to Ecclestone for help. Practice went ahead without the Jordan cars, but as soon as the gates to the Spa circuit closed, Ecclestone commandeered a motorcycle for Pasquale Lattuneddu, his paddock fixer, and set him to work.

'Bernie sent Pasquale off on a motorbike around all the entry gates to collect ticket money on the Friday night. We got that, which wasn't enough, and then Bernie topped it up so we could go to the bailiffs and get the cars out,' Jordan says.

The rest is history: Schumacher impressed at the Belgian Grand Prix and set himself on the path to becoming the most successful driver of all time, as well as the richest, with a fortune calculated at more than £600 million. But for Jordan, there was a rude awakening as he realised Ecclestone was the ringmaster and he was merely an act in the show.

Ecclestone had finally found the German he needed to bring back the fans from Europe's industrial heartland and decided that he had to get Schumacher out of Jordan's strugglers and into Benetton under Flavio Briatore, a well-funded team where there was a chance of him achieving success and fame.

Jordan dug his heels in, and there was a messy night of negotiations when Ecclestone brought the factions together at the Villa d'Este, the beautiful hotel on Lake Como, before the Italian Grand Prix that followed Belgium. Attentive waiters passed along the quiet corridors with cocktails for guests baffled by the goings-on down the hall where Ecclestone buzzed from room to room into the early hours, trying to iron out the contractual problems the move had triggered – not helped by phone calls every hour from an anxious Schumacher wanting to know where his future would be. The talks went on for so long that at one point the cleaners arrived.

'The first time I ever saw Bernie drunk was that night at the Villa d'Este,' Briatore laughs now. 'He was going backwards and forwards talking to everyone as we were trying to get Michael. Luciano Benetton [Benetton's owner] called me from New York because he had read in the press about this guy Michael Schumacher. "Who is Michael Schumacher?" he wanted to know. I said, "Luciano, I promise this guy will be world champion. In three weeks, everyone will forget this mess, but this guy will be world champion."'

That didn't help Eddie Jordan, who needed a driver – and he needed the money that Schumacher would have brought. The compromise came when Roberto Moreno, who was being replaced by Schumacher, dropped his threat of legal action and decided to go with Jordan, bringing with him a fee worth £300,000. It was better than a poke in the eye with a blunt stick, even though Jordan had lost Schumacher. In Monza, the two drivers simply swapped seats – Schumacher in the Benetton and Moreno in the Jordan. More important, Ecclestone got what he wanted – box office.

'I realise now that Bernie was the man pulling all of the strings,' Jordan told me. 'He says to me: "Listen, Jordan. I have waited for a German driver for years. I got 24,000 extra [fans] on the gate [at Spa] because of Michael Schumacher. You wouldn't even have got the car out of the garage if it hadn't been for me. I have prayed for a German all of my life, so what am I going to do? Let him stay with you when you are skint. I gave you the money to stay alive, so he's going to Benetton.'"

Jordan's telling of the story is as animated and hilarious today as it must have been stressful, and he laughs off Briatore's suggestions that he was him who pulled off the swap deal.

The Italian was new to Formula One and had come with a reputation as an aggressive businessman rather than a pure racer like Jordan, Frank Williams or Ron Dennis. Born in northern Italy, Briatore flunked school, spent time as a ski instructor and then worked for an Italian businessman who was blown up by a car bomb, which may or may not have been planted by the Mafia. Whoever was responsible, the story adds lustre to Briatore's colourful background, littered with brushes with the law and narrow squeaks with authority. When we meet in London, Italian courts have just sentenced him to eighteen months in jail on appeal for his part in an alleged tax fraud worth 3.6 million euros, impounding *Force Blue*, the impressive yacht that used to be a feature of the Monte Carlo waterfront during the Monaco Grand Prix where he would entertain Naomi Campbell, a one-time girl-friend. He showed little concern over the sentence because his answer to the court is simple: it's not his yacht. Briatore, like Jordan and the gang that ruled Formula One for so long, shrugs off adversity.

He set up a chain of stores for the Benetton fashion brand across the United States, making a small fortune as he took a percentage from each franchise deal he completed, until

Benetton was a major name and Luciano Benetton, the head of the family, was impressed enough with this flamboyant Italian to send him to England to run his Formula One team. In her autobiography, *I Just Made the Tea*, Di Spires, who ran Benetton's hospitality, remembered Briatore turning up at a test at Rio de Janeiro at the start of the 1989 season and settling into the motorhome with his newspaper. The cars started their test and Briatore looked up, seemingly puzzled. 'What's that noise, Di?' he asked. She told him they were testing. 'What are they testing?' When she told him it was to shake down the cars, Briatore shrugged. 'All they do is go round and round. Seems stupid,' he said and returned to his newspaper. He didn't much approve of testing when he was team principal either, but he did understand what sold.

'My image was me,' he tells me across the table at Sumosan Twiga, the restaurant where he staged the farewell party for his old mate Ecclestone. The grey hair is long and curly as usual as he peers through blue-tinted spectacles, and he is wearing a black jacket with gold embroidered lettering spelling out 'Billionaire', the not very understated brand he founded, from fashion shops to nightclubs. 'I was treated differently by Ron Dennis, Frank Williams and the rest. They didn't really respect me, and when we started winning they wondered what was happening. People decided I was a bad guy because I am not a mechanic and didn't have motor racing deep inside me. But Eddie Jordan copied my style and so did Red Bull when they came into F1.'

Briatore helped changed the landscape of Formula One, from its addiction to mechanics and technology to fun and fashion, dating supermodels like Heidi Klum and marrying Elisabetta Gregoraci, the Wonderbra model thirty years his junior. 'I understood there was potential and I started to bring in fashion people, like *GQ* instead of *Autosprint* or *Autosport*. For the first time, we decided to be strong with the media, inviting Heidi Klum, Naomi Campbell or Beyoncé. Think about it, if you are a sponsor – do you want a photograph with Beyoncé or with 350 mechanics and engineers? We put glitz into it because that is what the sponsors wanted.'

Ecclestone and Briatore became the most unlikely of best friends – the down-to-earth car-salesman-turned-racer with the understated lifestyle, and a flash Italian sweater salesman with an eye for the ladies, big spending and rumours of his Mafia connection. Christian Horner says they are like minds and Ecclestone enjoys Briatore's bravado and business sense. Whatever the connection, Ecclestone made sure that Briatore was looked after, handing him the television rights in Spain, which became worth millions when Fernando Alonso joined the grid, while Briatore was active across the spectrum of Formula One, taking shares in the Ligier and Minardi teams before selling them on. He also managed Mark Webber and Alonso.

Sometimes it seemed Ecclestone and Briatore worked hand-in-glove, as when they went into partnership when they jointly bought Queens Park Rangers football club. The team had an entertaining past but not much of a future, languishing mid-table in the English Championship, the second tier of the national professional game. The deal was billed at £14 million, but Ecclestone was reported to have paid only £150,000 cash for his stake, hardly money to keep the multi-billionaire awake at night, while Briatore put in £540,000.

'I only did it because Flavio wanted it,' says Ecclestone, who had toyed with the idea of buying Chelsea and Arsenal in years past. Briatore, though, loved it. He couldn't tell a Formula One mechanic how to change a wheel nut, but he could yell at an under-performing manager and make the team selection. He liked to give team talks, unlike Ecclestone, who only spoke to the team once. 'I told them to be nice to the referee,' Ecclestone said. 'If he thinks you are polite and obedient, he will think better of you if you commit a foul or have a chance of a penalty. Made sense to me.'

Christian Horner discovered that QPR was part of the bargain when he was negotiating with Briatore to get Renault engines, which Briatore then controlled through his Supertec business. 'I had to keep going down to Shepherd's Bush to matches for meetings in the directors' box. Flavio was really into it. Then he would be ranting at the goalkeeper at the very moment I was trying to convince him to give us the engines. He did give us the engines eventually, but I had to report back to Red Bull the good news that we had a supply of Renault engines, the bad news was that we had a box at QPR and we were sponsoring Flavio's Billionaire Club in Sardinia for the summer.'

By 2011, the fad for football was over, and they sold up for a handy £35 million to Tony Fernandes, owner of the Caterham F1 team. It's a small world.

Briatore rarely attends grands prix now, but misses the action, like that night when he and Ecclestone prised Schumacher from Eddie Jordan. EJ remembers that period with affection, too, despite the fractious atmosphere and the fear of another knock on the door from the bailiffs. By the end of 1991, Jordan had made a remarkable debut season for a team with a workforce of forty people and a budget the fraction of the dominant McLaren squad or the famous Ferrari Scuderia. But he lost the 7 UP sponsorship and faced a winding-up petition filed by his Ford Cosworth engine supplier. According to Mark Gallagher: 'In December at the end of that season, Eddie was sitting in a café in Silverstone with a team that was fifth in the championship and he couldn't pay the VAT bill.' Debts had hit £4 million and were rising.

Jordan refused to give up, ducking and diving wherever he sensed a deal, performing an unlikely double act with Ian Phillips, a former motor-racing journalist, as they struggled to keep the Jordan ship afloat. Sponsors would be confronted with an Irishman who couldn't stop talking, mangling every sentence and waving his arms around, and his laid-back partner, an Englishman, cricket lover and chain-smoker, who could translate the wild ramblings. 'We were like Bill and Ben. We would come up with some awful scams and I would ask, "Can we pull this off?" And he would say, "Of course we can." We didn't need to rehearse what we did.'

It didn't always work: Max Mosley tells a funny story about how Jarno Trulli's Jordan was excluded from the 2001 United States Grand Prix and Jordan insisted on protesting the decision, although that meant lodging a deposit. He paid in dollar bills so old that they were no longer legal tender.

When the Benson & Hedges money kicked in – real money, unlike the dodgy dollars – so did the fun, and a dinner in Malaysia particularly sticks in the memory. Jordan invited me and the *Daily Express*'s Bob McKenzie to join him, Katie Price (aka Jordan), his driver Heinz-Harald Frentzen and his attractive wife Tanja for dinner at the grandly named Palace of the Golden Horses, where the team were staying in Kuala Lumpur. Frentzen comes from a family of undertakers and his slightly mournful air was only an indication of his shyness. His wife was bright and clever, but clearly not used to the knockabout conversation that warmed up substantially when Jordan – the female one – opened up after a few glasses. Meantime, Jordan – the real one – had become obsessed with a watch I was wearing. We had been to Chinatown in KL earlier in the day, where I bought a fake Omega; it was extraordinarily realistic – and it actually worked. Jordan spent ages admiring it and I strung him along, telling him it was worth thousands of pounds until I finally admitted it was a fake. 'How much?' he shouted across the table. 'About twenty quid,' I said. Ten minutes later, Jordan had disappeared – in fact, both Jordans had. She was in the bar carousing with the team, and he returned after about an hour clutching a plastic bag crammed with fake watches. He had grabbed a taxi to Chinatown for a rapid purchase of everything he could find. He could easily afford the real thing, but here was an irresistible deal for a hustler. For years afterwards, Jordan would want to know if I was wearing 'a moody', his term for a fake.

The breakthrough came in 1998, at the circuit where Jordan had almost sunk without trace when the bailiffs impounded his cars seven years earlier: Spa-Francorchamps. Jordan won his first grand prix, but the race had to be dramatic to fit the Jordan story. The weather was awful, the dense forest of the Ardennes covered in a heavy fog as the rain lashed the circuit. There were crashes galore, starting with a thirteen-car smash after the first corner. Damon Hill emerged from the melee as winner of an astonishing grand prix and Jordan was ecstatic. 'I can still see him now, leaping about like a madman,' Max Mosley smiled. The following year, Frentzen came within an ace of the world championship after winning two grands prix to keep up the pressure on Schumacher and McLaren's Mika Häkkinen, who took the title at the final race of the season.

But the effort of maintaining the attack was debilitating for such a small squad on such a small budget. Realising that money would always be a problem, and that he would personally go down with the team if there was a catastrophe, Jordan looked for investors. He refused an offer from Honda to buy the team when he discovered that he would be thrown out as part of the deal, so he turned to bankers Warburg Pincus to secure his own future as well as the team's. Twenty years on, Mark Gallagher was not so sure it was a good deal.

'The decline of Jordan Grand Prix started when Warburg Pincus bought half of the team in November 1998. Fair play to Eddie, who put everything he had into that team and risked everything he had, but when the banks took over, the dynamic in the team changed because the management were suddenly answerable to a board that wanted profitability and growth. I remember sitting in a meeting and Warburg asking if we had the budget for next season. This was November and Ian, Eddie and I were out looking for sponsors and pay drivers. They wanted a budget ready of $120 million and we had $40 million and Eddie was telling them not to worry. But they were worried because, as far as they were concerned, we were insolvent. They had no concept of how a race team worked. In their world you can't operate that way.'

There was an image of a hornet on the nose of the Jordan cars – another cunning ruse as cigarette advertising became toxic and the 'Buzzin' Hornets' became code for the forbidden Benson & Hedges brand – but the buzz was diminishing for Jordan. He had to make staff redundant and the continual quest for money was grinding as the tobacco cash machine was shut down by European legislation banning cigarette sponsorship. Big manufacturers – such as BMW, Toyota and Honda – were moving in with huge budgets and ambitious plans to take over the sport, and there was no place in their reckoning for a tiny independent team that was long on hope and short on cash. Jordan was playing with the big boys, like Ron Dennis and Sir Frank Williams. The difference was that they had won multiple titles and kept finding the biggest money and hiring the best drivers.

There was one more Jordan win, for Giancarlo Fisichella at a chaotic Brazilian Grand Prix in 2003, but there was also one last, arguably reckless, act in the August of that year, when Jordan took Vodafone to the High Court, claiming they had reneged on a £100 million deal to sponsor the team. Mark Gallagher is Jordan's greatest supporter, but he could see the writing on the wall and didn't hold back on his feelings. 'Everyone warned him – Ron, Max, Bernie – just don't do this.'

Jordan not only lost, but the judgement was humiliating. Mr Justice Langley found that Jordan's claim was 'wholly without foundation and false', and effectively trashed the reputations of Jordan and Ian Phillips. He added: 'On occasions, even Mr Jordan was unable to offer an explanation and was reduced to an embarrassed silence by the exposure of blatant inaccuracies in what he was saying.' The blarney, so convincing in front of gullible sponsors, had failed under the forensic examination of legal counsel. This time, Bill and Ben couldn't swing one of their 'scams'. The legal costs were horrendous – £5 million – and now Jordan was apprehensive about his future.

Jordan was torn, but he knew the game was up by 2004, especially after a deal with Mercedes to sponsor his team with the Smart brand of small car fell through. 'When you are at the centre of it and ploughing on, you don't see stuff. Bernie said to me, "Jordan, I think you need to pull the shutters down because I don't want to see you becoming a bankrupt." By then, I knew every bailiff in Northamptonshire by their first name. It was almost funny because the factory would ring me on a Friday morning and tell me not to come in. I am the luckiest guy on earth. Every win was lucky, but I didn't want it to end in tears.'

Jordan became close to Ecclestone, who liked his cheek and the publicity he brought, even though he was often first in line for his generosity. Ecclestone sometimes kept struggling teams afloat through a curious sort of largesse, dispensing what Sir Jackie Stewart called 'rain cheques', money to get a team through a short-term crisis like paying for their tyres or engines.

Ecclestone, inevitably, was at the centre of the deal to sell Jordan Grand Prix. He called Jordan to Princes Gate to introduce him to Alex Shnaider, a Russian-born Canadian businessman, who wanted to buy and set up the unimaginatively named Midland team. Behind Schnaider was Colin Kolles, the Romanian former dentist, who would turn up in Formula One again when attempts were made to sell the bankrupt Caterham team. Formula One was finished for Eddie Jordan. Well, almost.

There was small print in the sale contract that neither Shnaider nor Kolles had spotted: they bought the factory, which sits on land opposite the Silverstone circuit, and the cars and were getting set for the 2005 season, but Midland had not bought the wind tunnel, nor the transporters, nor the land around the factory, nor even the driveway to the front doors.

'They thought they had a cheap deal. I got a truck and a crane and put big concrete blocks across the drive. They couldn't get in, so what were they going to do? Miss the next race? If the Tsar of Russia turned up, he wasn't getting in. They had to pay,' Jordan crowed, his delight at having pulled off one of his favourite career stunts, the sort of wind-up that was the perfect send-off from Formula One. 'I didn't give a fuck. I made them pay for the wind tunnel, the trucks, everything. The devil is in the detail. I learned from the master.' Ecclestone would have been proud.

We are in a pub around the corner from Grosvenor Square, where Jordan is clearly a regular and pints of Guinness are being dispensed with frequency to the smart-suited business types crowded around the bar. Jordan has taken me to meet his chums and the chatter swings between classic cars and music, Jordan's passion. He still plays the drums with his own band, and combos sometimes featuring some of the world's greatest musicians and tells me he will be playing three gigs at the upcoming Monaco Grand Prix, but only after a mammoth charity bike ride. He is fitter than at any time in his life, carries no excess weight, and David Coulthard and Mark Webber one day watched open-mouthed as this seventy-year-old former team owner completed seventy press-ups.

As we drink and chat, another pal arrives to tell us he has just spotted Bernie Ecclestone leaving a restaurant with one of China's richest businessmen. It is meat and drink, the kind of gossip that has always enthused Jordan, and he sets off on one of his monologues, all fun and cheek and blarney. The Irish bank clerk has moved on from Formula One, but it is still deep in his soul.

Paul Stoddart warms to Eddie Jordan's theme when he hears his old pal has described them both as 'hustlers'. While Bernie Ecclestone dealt in second-hand cars, Stoddart does the same with aircraft. We are in his headquarters office, in the little town of Ledbury in England's picturesque West Country, when he takes a call. There is a brief chat and then Stoddart puts the phone down. He has just acquired ten Airbus A340s from the Etihad airline; around the corner in the factory, he has 10,000 aircraft seats awaiting dispatch. But the pictures around his office and in the corridors are mainly of racing cars, almost a life pictured in Formula Three, Formula 3000 and Formula One machines. 'Aircraft are my business,' he tells me between long drags on his cigarette, 'but Formula One is my passion.'

He has no team now but lays on the ultimate Formula One experience with rides in two-seater Formula One cars, constructed and maintained at his Ledbury factory, at each grand prix. Stoddart calls his outfit Formula One's 'unofficial eleventh team' but he is first to admit it is nothing like the real thing.

Stoddart is an entrepreneur with a keen eye for a gag and a torrent of gossip about his short time at the top, what he calls 'the gory years'. Well, not quite the top, for Stoddart bought the Minardi team, the Italian squad anchored firmly at the bottom of Formula One's league table for years. He knew what he was up against when he acquired the team and he also realised the struggle was unequal for a small independent up against the multimillions of the manufacturers bent on dominating the sport.

With his European Aviation business based in England and enough money to indulge his fantasy, Stoddart started looking for a team to buy in the late 1990s and made an offer for Ken Tyrrell's ailing team. Tyrrell was in failing health and fast realising that an operation based in a woodshed in Surrey was past its sell-by date. He hadn't won a grand prix since 1983, and memories of those glorious days when he and Jackie Stewart had dominated Formula One, winning three world championships, were fading. Tyrrell had seen Jim Clark and Moss and Surtees in the days when the *garagistes* started to impose themselves on the traditions of grand-prix racing, but he could see the wheel turning away from independents like him, who raced for the love of it, towards corporations who wanted their names plastered on cars that the world could see.

Tyrrell looked uncomfortable at his final car launch at the trendy Bluebird Club on the King's Road in London in 1998. He was out of place among the cool surroundings inhabited by fashionistas from Chelsea, and was facing a season of handover to Craig Pollock, a former ski instructor and manager of Jacques Villeneuve, the 1997 world champion with Williams. Pollock had manoeuvred British American Tobacco into position to buy the team, with the prospect of a £120 million budget for 1999 and a handsome pay cheque for his driver. The last Tyrrell season was a sad farewell, perhaps exemplified by events at the Monaco Grand Prix, where Ricardo Rosset, a pay driver from Brazil, whose budget substantially outpaced his talent, spun his car and then ploughed into a gap in the safety barriers, scattering safety marshals. Rosset failed to qualify for the most prestigious grand prix and, his race weekend over, he returned to his scooter to head for the sanctuary of his hotel. On the windscreen, which bore his surname, mechanics had reversed the first and last letters.

Pollock bought the Tyrrell entry on the grid, but didn't want the assets housed in the famous Surrey woodshed. The new British American Racing team built a factory in Brackley in Northamptonshire, but it was an unhappy ship from the start: Pollock resigned to be replaced in 2002 by David Richards, who found a team that was 'shambolic'.

'They wanted to spend £27 million on a wind tunnel because they reckoned that was why they weren't winning, but we went without a wind tunnel and chose CFD [computational fluid dynamics] because that was the new thing. We had a lovely little CFD department with absolutely no resources, so

I asked them what they needed. They said they wanted 200 PlayStations. I said, "What on earth do you want 200 PlayStations for?" And they said they would put them in an air-conditioned room and link them together – and that would be our supercomputer. So that's what we did. We started with 200 PlayStations, which was considerably cheaper than a £27 million wind tunnel.'

Richards guided BAR to a high in 2004, when Jenson Button finished third in the drivers' championship behind the dominant twin Ferraris of Rubens Barrichello and Michael Schumacher. A year later, the tobacco giant sold out to Honda, a motor giant wanting to flex its muscles in Formula One, and Richards was gone.

It was a shift in the Formula One power base that Giancarlo Minardi had understood for years as his factory in Faenza in northern Italy, almost neighbours with Ferrari at Maranello, did little more than tick over as he searched for a buyer. He found a brash Australian with a smoking habit, tons of confidence and a lot of business nous. But Formula One was an unknown for Stoddart, and the effort to get Minardi onto the grid for 2001 was epic. 'I bought Minardi in December 2000, not knowing what it was going to cost, which was probably for the best because no one sane would have bought it. I turned up at the Faenza factory on December the ninth to find a wooden mock-up of the car in the race bay and only thirty or forty people. I had six weeks and three days before the freight went to Australia.'

Stoddart shipped thirty-five people from the Ledbury headquarters to Faenza, where he booked an entire hotel, including a room for his teenage driver, Fernando Alonso.

'Fernando will remember there were times when he and I were helping to build the car, working until midnight. The hotel didn't have enough rooms, so we had to "hot bed" with people going into the factory, working until they dropped and then going back to the hotel to push the next guy out so they could get some sleep. It was a twenty-four-hour operation. One day I sent a BAC 1-11 aircraft back from Faenza to Coventry Airport to sit on the ground to wait for a company in the north of England who were making two titanium brackets for the exhaust. The car couldn't run without them, so we had to have them. That BAC 1-11 waited until three a.m. and then flew back. It was that stupid. The second car for Tarso Marques didn't even get built until we got to the opening grand prix in Australia. We had done only a single day of testing in a straight line at Fiorano. That was all we had.'

There was nothing but admiration for this curious, ragtag outfit with a headquarters in England, a home in Italy and a heart in Australia. There was a civic reception on the steps of the Victoria Parliament, and MPs stopped work for the day to revel in the first Australian constructor entry in Formula One since Sir Jack Brabham had brought pride to the nation thirty years before.

Tiny Minardi was suddenly the 'Everyman' team, and even the hard-bitten team owners and principals in the paddock were prepared to tip their caps to Stoddart, who was not just a folk hero in his homeland but also winning plaudits from those who knew just how hard it was even to make it to the grid. In his first race, Stoddart's Minardi would be up against the likes of Jaguar, which had backing from its Ford parent, plus Renault, the French manufacturer that had taken over Benetton, and BAR. It was David and Goliath but with wheels and engines. The costs seem puny now but were eye-watering then for an entrepreneur funding the entire operation from his own pockets. Stoddart spent £35 million just to get Minardi up and running and lost £18 million on that first season – but it was worth it. A nineteen-year-old Fernando Alonso finished twelfth at that maiden Australian Grand Prix, and on the final timesheet below him were two Benetton-Renaults, two Williams-BMWs, a Jordan-Honda and a McLaren-Mercedes. This was the magic of Formula One. 'When I got off the pit wall in Melbourne, there were grown men crying. That was the stress and the joy all at once,' Stoddart says fondly.

Like a second album, the second season is the toughest. Stoddart had found the Malaysia government as a sponsor, got a supply of free engines from the now defunct Asiatech outfit, brought in Mark Webber, a fellow Aussie, as his number one driver – and, while he was at it, acquired a fleet of 747 Jumbo jets. The maiden flight for one of the Minardi Jumbos would be to the first grand prix, in Stoddart's home city of Melbourne.

'Going to Melbourne in your own 747 with the team, to be met by a government reception, the red carpet and a brass band is as good as it gets. I remember getting off the plane and then thinking, the dream's over – we have the slowest car in the pack. On Saturday night, I got back to my apartment and lay awake thinking how we would get slaughtered in the race.'

The dream wasn't over at all. The 2002 Australian Grand Prix was a race of extraordinary attrition: eight cars went out at the first corner and only eight survived to the finish. In fifth place was Mark Webber, an Australian driving a car owned by an Australian on home turf in Australia. It was a minor miracle that sent Melbourne into paroxysms of delight. Michael Schumacher, the winner, called Webber and Stoddart into Ferrari to congratulate them, while the Minardi motorhome, usually a desert of disinterest, was mobbed.

'We didn't have champagne in the motorhome,' Stoddart remembers. 'Our motorhome people thought they might be able to borrow some, but they didn't have to because staff from other teams were marching towards us with dozens of bottles to give us to celebrate. It was a magical moment. That night Murray Walker was on the phone – he had retired the year before and it was the first race he hadn't commentated on – and he was in tears.'

Times were changing quickly, though: Toyota entered that 2002 season with $1 billion to spend and a year's testing behind them. They still finished behind Minardi – budget $28 million – but Stoddart could see the writing on the pit wall in capital letters. Internal politics were turbulent, with the big corporations vying with each other and with Ecclestone and Max Mosley. Even Stoddart's enthusiasm was being sapped as the finances became an annual slog and every meeting of the team owners was conducted from the trenches.

Alain Prost, a four-times world champion, had given up the fight in 2001 after just five seasons running his own team. Tom Walkinshaw was the *Autocar Man of the Year* in 1997 after a career that included championships as a driver and as a team owner with Jaguar, winning Le Mans, and then taking on Arrows in Formula One. At the height of his powers, Walkinshaw's TWR business employed 1,500 people around the world, but the money ran out and the Arrows team collapsed embarrassingly in 2002, taking the TWR group with it. Formula One's finances were no respecter of past successes, it seemed.

The failure of Prost and Arrows made 2003 a critical season for the two independents – Jordan and Minardi – struggling to stay alive. The magic number for Ecclestone was ten. He needed ten teams on the grid because that was the guaranteed minimum in contracts with race promoters around the world. It also meant that Formula One had to find a way of propping up its stragglers and keeping Jordan and Minardi on the grid, if only to make up the numbers. After all, if they disappeared, one of the big teams would replace them as the embarrassed backmarkers.

But the numbers were grim, and eventually it was agreed there would be a fighting fund set up worth $3 million each for Jordan and Minardi. The money never turned up, though. Stoddart felt betrayed, his budgets were at breaking point and he expected the worst when Ecclestone called him on Saturday morning before qualifying at the Canadian Grand Prix. Ecclestone cut to the chase. 'Stoddart, how much do you need?' Stoddart told him and Ecclestone agreed on the spot to become a 50 per cent shareholder in Minardi. 'As soon as I announced this to the press, our worries and all our creditors went away. The people pressuring me disappeared after threatening to do all sorts to us. I couldn't give people money, they wouldn't take it because Bernie's word carried such weight. By the time I went to Bernie's office to sign the papers, we were in much better shape. Bernie realised I didn't need him any more and we forgot about the whole deal. Bernie is Bernie and only he could sort things like that.'

Stoddart had one more card to play in his quest for his fighting fund: he was tipped off that almost every car on the grid was technically illegal. Electronic driver aids had been outlawed, but lax policing meant that most teams had been pushing the boundaries, so they were infringing the rules and liable to be thrown out if someone raised the issue – and that someone was Stoddart. At a team owners' meeting before the French Grand Prix, the race after Canada, Stoddart drily informed the participants that he had two legal Minardis ready to race and might lodge a protest to have every other car excluded. There was uproar, with accusations of blackmail and skulduggery, but Stoddart stood his ground, and when the meeting broke up, Ron Dennis came and put his arm around the Australian. 'You have big balls,' Dennis said. 'I never realised, and I will make sure that McLaren pays its share first thing in the morning.' Dennis alone kept his word and a cheque for his share of the fighting fund – £282,000 – duly arrived the next day. 'I respected Ron for that ever since,' Stoddart says.

With Ecclestone's help, Minardi stayed afloat, but Stoddart knew that perilous waters were ahead. It was time to get out and Ecclestone was there yet again. He brought Stoddart into his motorhome at the 2005 Belgian Grand Prix to introduce him to a tall Austrian called Dietrich Mateschitz, who manufactured an energy drink called Red Bull.

'I had lots of offers for the team. On the wall there is a $10 million cheque sent as a deposit for Minardi – it bounced from here to kingdom come,' Stoddart says. 'It was a fraud and became a standing joke. At the time, we had Eddie Irvine and a consortium doing due diligence and they were number forty-six in the line of people inquiring to buy the team. I shook hands with Dietrich in Spa, but they told me that Mateschitz didn't celebrate with champagne and I would have to toast the deal with Red Bull. I couldn't stand the stuff, but someone said: "For the amount of money you are being paid, just drink it." I did, we signed, and I have been a loyal Red Bull drinker ever since.'

The deal was worth £75 million: Stoddart, airline magnate, Formula One fan and ace hustler, is said to have got away with £45 million in cash.

12

WHISKY AND SOUR

WE are flying between the tops of the Styrian mountains, the four propeller engines droning music-
ally. The leather seats are like armchairs and the wood finish
is the finest veneer, running the length of the carpeted cockpit, which has hostesses serving drinks – no champagne,
or wine, or beer, though: water or Red Bull is all that is on
offer.

This Douglas DC-6 was the last to be built, in about 1958,
and has been restored to shining glory. It has history, too, as
the previous owner was Marshal Tito, the authoritarian
ruler of Yugoslavia. The engine tone changes as we start our
descent over Salzburg, the mountains giving way to fields
and then buildings until the runway comes into view.
Alongside the tarmac is our final destination – Hangar-7. It
is not so much a storage building for aircraft as high-tech
lair, built to order for Dietrich Mateschitz, the Austrian
billionaire and co-owner of the Red Bull drinks brand. The
building has a high glass dome with a luxurious office
suspended from its centre, and you could almost imagine the

tanned, white-haired Mateschitz sitting in his armchair stroking a white cat surveying all of his passions paid for by a fizzy concoction of sugar and caffeine and packed into a distinctive, slender silver and blue can. At one end of the vast hangar, there are aircraft of every vintage, from Second World War bombers to dinky little stunt planes, while at the other there are Formula One cars in their familiar dark blue, red and yellow livery – all world-championship winners.

Red Bull were the fun team, the new kids on the block, when Mateschitz ordered the purchase of the struggling Jaguar team at the end of 2004. He then acquired lowly Minardi, which became Toro Rosso, a year later, to turn them into his twin entrants into Formula One. He was a godsend for Ecclestone, who needed a big spender to keep his ten teams on the grid. And then Red Bull rampaged through the sport, winning four consecutive drivers' world championships with Sebastian Vettel to become just as powerful as teams who had been in Formula One for decades. The transformation was startling, but perhaps not surprising: if Dietrich Mateschitz could make a fortune out of a sour-tasting fizzy drink, then anything was possible.

Born among the mountains and forests of Styria in Austria, not far from the A1 grand-prix circuit he now owns and has renamed the Red Bull Ring, Mateschitz started his business life marketing detergents for Unilever. It was a chance discovery on a trip to Thailand that changed his life and fortune. He found Krating Daeng, an energy drink devised by Chaleo

Yoovidhya, who came up with a formula to energise workers in the steamy fields of his homeland. Mateschitz went into partnership with the Thai businessman and applied his marketing skills, advertising Red Bull as the pick-me-up for anyone needing a quick caffeine boost, from droopy-eyed businessmen to sweaty sportsmen. He pushed the label into sponsoring adventure sports, from skiing to dramatic air races, and now has a portfolio that stretches into soccer, ice hockey and even canoeing.

Formula One is the ultimate adventure, a sport that combines danger, speed, technology and glamour. It was a perfect billboard, and Mateschitz had dipped his toe in the water with the Swiss team owned by Peter Sauber. Based in Hinwil, southeast of Zurich, Sauber had been a plucky make-weight for years under the aegis of one of the most respected men in motor racing. Peter Sauber decided against joining the family business making traffic lights, and set up his own race team, culminating in a successful partnership with Mercedes in the World Sportscar Prototype Championship, winning the title twice as well as the Le Mans 24 hours Endurance race.

The jump to Formula One was a big one, though. Mercedes ended their partnership and a team based in the German-speaking region of Switzerland was too far out of the loop of British domination to make inroads into the highest level of motor racing. BMW bought the team in 2006 and then sold it back to Sauber after only three trying years, when even their huge investment, thought to be around £1 billion, could not break the stranglehold of Britain and Italy. For a brand based on youth and excitement like Red Bull, Sauber was too staid, too solid and too middle of the field, and cigar-chomping Peter Sauber preferred to leave the antics and noise to more extrovert characters like Eddie Jordan and Flavio Briatore.

Mateschitz needed a bigger stage, which would be provided by an Englishman new to the corridors of Formula One power. Christian Horner was young, but one of the most successful team owners in Formula 3000. He already had a reputation as a smart and savvy operator with a good eye for drivers and a talent for organisation, and he was looking for a Formula One team to buy.

Motoring was in the Horner family. His father Garry owned an automotive components business, so the young Christian understood simple mechanics, put to the test by making a soapbox with old pram wheels. The turning point came when he was eleven years old and his parents went to view a house they were thinking of buying.

'There was an old kart in the garage and my parents agreed to have this kart as part of the sale, but, unfortunately, they didn't, so I pestered and plagued them until we found an advert in the local paper for a go-kart that was about sixty quid in Leamington Spa and my mother bought it for my birthday. It turned out to be some 1970s racing kart with a crack in it and an engine that packed up constantly. I couldn't drive it on grass or the drive, so my father took me to a track at Sheddington. Then – boom! – I discovered the world of racing.'

His progress through the ranks was rapid, winning a Renault scholarship aged seventeen and then racing against drivers like David Coulthard, Jan Magnussen and Dario Franchitti. He bought a Lola racing car and a trailer from an Austrian, a former racing driver whose career was ended early at the 1972 French Grand Prix when a stone flew into his helmet and blinded him in one eye. Helmut Marko is from Graz and would become chief advisor to Mateschitz, who was born a few miles down the road.

Horner was good, but he admits to a revelation one day, following Juan Pablo Montoya, the talented Colombian who was driving ahead of him. 'I watched him and realised he was in a different league. Having seen what Montoya was capable of, I knew it was over. So, I decided to start a team.'

While Montoya plotted a career that would bring victory at the fabled Indianapolis 500 and drives at Williams and McLaren in F1, Horner was winning three consecutive Formula 3000 championships as a team owner. It was time to move up.

'I had backing from Hutchison Whampoa and I knew I wanted to try Formula One, so I did the obvious thing and spoke to Bernie about it. He was encouraging me to call Eddie Jordan, so I started due diligence, but the deal became typical EJ. It was more and more complicated and I backed out. By then, Red Bull had bought Jaguar. Helmut remembered me and asked me to go to see Dietrich at the end of 2004 where he offered me a two-year contract to take over.'

Horner was now in the direct line of descent from Jackie Stewart. The team had gone from tartan to British Racing Green to the yellow, blue and red of Red Bull, and this was Horner's team to mould with Dietrich Mateschitz's blessing – and hard cash. 'When I walked into Milton Keynes for the first time, it was announced to the staff that Tony Purnell and Dave Pitchforth would be leaving – in fact, they left thirty minutes earlier – and I was their new team principal. I was probably one of the youngest guys in the room. I was thirty-one. There were a couple of faces I recognised, but I arrived at the desk in my new office with some unopened Christmas cards, a half-drunk cup of coffee and a secretary weeping outside. I thought, "Okay, where do I start?"'

David Coulthard was McLaren's longest-serving driver, a winner of thirteen grands prix, but the nearly man of Formula One, forced to look on as his teammate Mika Häkkinen won two world championships with the Scotsman as the support act. Coulthard, like Horner, was clever, a good networker, articulate and ready for a new challenge in 2005 – and he came relatively cheaply at just £1.8 million. Coulthard knew McLaren inside out and could transmit their organisational structures to Horner as well as drive to the highest level.

At first, Red Bull were just Formula One's entertainers. They brought a gigantic hospitality centre over three floors into the paddock where the music blared, the drinks were free and the guests were all A-listers. It was not about the racing but Mateschitz's brand. A party team with party people.

Not for Horner. He was assiduously working his way into Formula One, first with Ecclestone, the boss. In spite of the gap in their ages, they became firm friends and allies in the back-room battles. Horner plugged into Coulthard's experience, and they both knew they needed one key component to soar from midfield to winners. Adrian Newey was Formula One's most wanted, which makes him sound terribly glamorous when, in fact, he is a slender, bald and quietly spoken man of gentle humour and great dedication to a paper drawing board and a 2B pencil. Newey might seem like a throwback, but he has drawn more winning racing cars than anyone: by 2013 he had won ten constructors' world championships with three different teams, and F1 world titles with six drivers.

Educated at Repton public school, Newey gained a first-class degree in aeronautics and astronautics at Southampton University before moving into the world of motor racing. After spells in junior teams and the United States, where he worked with Bobby Rahal's CART team, he returned to Britain to work at March in Formula One. He was soon snapped up by Patrick Head at Williams, where his talent flourished, and he created winning cars for Alain Prost and Nigel Mansell. But Newey felt excluded from the team he was making a success because of the tight bond between Frank Williams and Head, who ran the team through their contrasting personalities – Williams controlled and cutting and Head bombastic and loud. It worked, but not for Newey, who wanted more control as technical director. Ron Dennis wasted no time in making the call, and Newey was on gardening leave when his final Williams incarnation, the FW18, was driven to the world championship by Damon Hill in 1996.

Clearly, Newey spent little time on his roses, and when he returned to Formula One and McLaren it was with a bang: the McLaren MP4/13 scared the living daylights out of the competition at the first grand prix of the 1998 season in Australia, lapping the entire field. Two world championships for Mika Häkkinen followed, but Newey was already struggling with Dennis's austere working environment. It was claustrophobic for a free spirit like Newey, who favoured jeans over uniforms and found it difficult to fit into the increasingly complex management structures set up by Dennis.

After only three years with McLaren, Newey was anxious to break out, and a call from Bobby Rahal, the man he'd worked for in the USA and who was running Jaguar, looked like the chance to get over the McLaren fence. Newey signed a contract to join Jaguar for a salary of £3 million but hadn't reckoned on the ferocity of Dennis's determination to keep him. Dennis used every tool available, even his wife Lisa, when the couple turned up at the Newey home together to convince him to stay. Lisa was friends with Marigold Newey and the two wives could often be seen together at grands prix, enjoying a glass of wine in the McLaren hospitality centre. The assault worked, and Newey pulled back – to the dismay of Jaguar executives, who had already issued a press release announcing his arrival. Niki Lauda, supposedly working alongside Rahal, was apoplectic, and Jaguar issued an injunction to prevent Newey staying at McLaren. It was a useless gesture and Jaguar backed down, accepting an apology from Newey and Dennis, while McLaren picked up the legal bill of £30,000.

It didn't help. Newey remained restless, while McLaren's form dipped and Ferrari's star rose, and rumours flew that he wanted to flee Formula One to design an America's Cup yacht. There was someone Newey needed to meet, and he found him staring up at the steel and glass edifice of McLaren's huge hospitality centre in the paddock at Imola before the 2005 San Marino Grand Prix. Horner was the new kid on the block and planned to be a disrupter – and he needed Newey. 'We hit it off immediately,' says Horner. 'We came from the same area of Warwickshire and he even went to school up the road from me. It was clear to me he felt stifled at McLaren and wanted a new challenge and I wanted to provide it.' Horner had his man.

Newey's entry was a slow burn, trying to turn around a midfield team with shaky foundations, but he and Horner started to recruit the best talent from around the paddock, people curious to join this laid-back outfit with none of the strictures or formality of McLaren, Williams or Ferrari. By 2009, Red Bull were winning races, by 2010, they were world champions and on a run of four years dominating Formula

One. The fun team had become the dream team, and Horner and Newey were the instigators.

In the summer of 2011, I popped my head around the door of Newey's office in Red Bull's factory on the outskirts of Milton Keynes, a city better known for roundabouts and concrete cows than the £1 million speed machines that were conquering Formula One. Sebastian Vettel already had one world championship to his name at the time, and Red Bull a maiden constructors' title, and the new season had started at pace with Vettel taking six victories in the first eight grands prix. Newey, in white open-neck shirt and blue jeans, barely noticed my presence, his concentration was so intense. The room was filled with sunlight, but he frowned at the white sheet of paper on which, stroke by stroke, he was creating a Formula One car.

His margin for error, he told me, was 0.2 millimetres – the width of his 2B pencil point, in fact. Outside his open office door, there was an open-plan space where more than 120 designers were gazing at their computer screens, busy translating Newey's artwork into the fastest hardware on the Formula One track. From one extraordinary mind through the medium of a humble pencil came tens of millions of calculations. It has made Newey the most expensive designer in the history of Formula One, paid more than £7 million a year. He has remained loyal to the squad, which offers him freedom and fun, so that even an astonishing offer of £20 million a year from Ferrari was not enough to prise him from

Milton Keynes. He is happier than ever, with his own design team also putting together a Ferrari-rivalling supercar for the road for Aston Martin, the Valkyrie, a futuristic 200 mph monster. In addition, he gets the chance to race his stable of historic cars – although he appears as adept at crashing them as he is at driving.

Horner's achievement was to elevate Red Bull's position to the elite in less than a decade. Along the way, he has become the most recognisable of team principals, his family life now a subject for gossip magazines where he features almost as often as he does in *Autosport*, thanks to his new wife, Geri. She, of course, is the former Geri Halliwell, better known to a generation as Ginger Spice, one of the five Spice Girls who ruled the world of pop music in the 1990s. She has moulded and changed the lad from Leamington Spa, who was once comfortable in a tweed jacket, jeans and brown brogues into a sharp-dressing socialite, while he is building his own motor-racing dynasty with the backing of Dietrich Mateschitz, something he would never have had if he had taken the plunge and bought Jordan. He left that to someone else.

Vijay Mallya lives a couple of streets along from Sherlock Holmes's famous address in Baker Street. He parks his gold Range Rover – number plate VJM – outside his beautiful mews house, where the security man and the butler have already clocked my arrival and the door opens before I reach for the buzzer. I am directed up the ornate staircase to a drawing room that could come straight from *Downton Abbey*:

at one end, a group of sofas and chairs are turned to the floor-to-ceiling picture windows looking onto Regent's Park; in the middle, there is a group of more formal gilt chairs with plush red velvet seats, which is obviously where business takes place, and then at the opposite end is another relaxation area, complete with a bar resplendent with a couple of dozen of the world's finest whiskies.

I am studying a bottle of Singleton Special Reserve, which I reckon costs upwards of £250, when Vijay Mallya enters. He has been meeting his lawyers all afternoon, still battling the extradition order issued by the Indian Government, which wants him to face charges of fraud and money-laundering after the collapse of his Kingfisher airline business. The Indian authorities allege he left behind debts of almost £1 billion and diverted millions through his Formula One team, and the pursuit of Vijay Mallya, the billionaire whom Indians once revered as the 'King of Good Times', has become one of the greatest political *causes célèbres* in his homeland. As a result, Mallya cannot leave Britain for fear of arrest. But if this is prison, it is a gilded cage.

This ornate room was a long way from the courtrooms of India, where motor racing is a fringe sport for the rich and the majority of the population, consumed by cricket, would barely have heard of Formula One. Anyone travelling down a dusty road in India will witness a game between barefoot children, with a makeshift bat, imagining themselves as a national hero like Sachin Tendulkar or Virat Kohli, hitting the winning runs for their country. They will have heard of Lord's, but the name of Silverstone would be completely unknown to the mass of the Indian population outside the tiny coterie of Formula One enthusiasts. Which is why Mallya wanted a Formula One team, named Force India, for the country that now shuns him. 'We couldn't turn on the television to watch Formula One because we only had one channel. Access to Formula One didn't exist. We had one racetrack, a disused airstrip, in what is now Chennai. It had bamboo stands and hay bales, but we got 75,000 people for events.'

He started building his own cars as a student, stripping them down and then trusting in his own mechanical ability by going racing when at college. He left his home city of Kolkata to come to Britain to buy two Ensign Formula One cars to take back to India, meeting a young engineer called Bob Fernley, who had made a name for himself in motor racing in the United States, and was later to become Mallya's most trusted advisor.

He was 'blasting everyone off the track' in India but couldn't spread his wings to race elsewhere and his driving career stalled. The bug didn't leave him, though, and when he was installed as chairman of United Breweries at the age of just twenty-eight after the death of his father in 1983, he started to explore new ways of expanding the family's brewing empire. Kingfisher was the most popular beer in India, but he wanted to push into new markets, and Formula One was his chosen advertising vehicle. Mallya put Kingfisher on Briatore's Benetton cars in 1993 and

1994, good years when Michael Schumacher was becoming a big name and this new Indian sponsor in the paddock was able to absorb the intricacies of a sport he had only watched from afar. 'Flavio treated me as one of the team and we became really good friends. He gave me a team uniform, I was on the pit wall and took part in briefings. Whatever I know about being a team principal, I owe to Flavio. I could sit down with Johnny Herbert and I became very good friends with Michael Schumacher. It was a great experience for me. Once you are immersed like that, your adrenalin pumps so hard, you can't get Formula One out of your system.'

Toyota came next as Kingfisher went global, but Mallya was already toying with the idea of owning a team. Midland had been a failure after buying Jordan, and Colin Kolles had found Spyker, a Dutch supercar manufacturer, to take over the team. That didn't fare any better, and Jan Mol, the chief investor, was looking for an exit. Mallya opened the door by taking over and creating the first Indian team – albeit one headquartered in England at Silverstone.

'The reaction was disbelief and shock. Everyone thought an Indian owning a Formula One team was a fantasy. I realised this could create nationwide excitement and, given that the Indian demographic has 50 per cent of the population under eighteen, I wanted to excite young minds and spark something big.'

Mallya was a demanding owner. The Spyker team was the worst on the grid, with fourteen retirements from twenty-eight starts with both cars in 2007. He had inherited Kolles as team principal, Ian Phillips in charge of commercial, and technical director Mike Gascoyne, known as Pitbull in the paddock for his nightclub bouncer appearance and combative manner. Gascoyne had taken the credit for Jordan's successful 1999 season and then moved to Toyota on a salary of about £3.7 million, but fell out with them, which made Spyker his next destination. But Mallya wanted results for the big money he was paying and 2008 passed without a single point on the board. Mallya's solution was radical: he got rid of all of his executives.

'It was one shot – gone – and now I am sat there alone in the factory with no one around me, not one senior manager. I phoned Bob [Fernley] and appealed for help.' Mallya went to McLaren for technical assistance and Mercedes for engines, alliances that have lasted ever since. Every year after that was marked by improvement, until Force India were the best of the rest, in fourth place in the constructors' table behind Mercedes, Ferrari and Red Bull in both 2016 and 2017.

If only he could have enjoyed it on the pit wall where he, with Fernley, had directed operations for so long. The Indian authorities put paid to that. Apart from the British Grand Prix, Mallya had to live his passion for Formula One by remote and, thanks to modern technology, he did it from his second home in Hertfordshire, where he installed a personal pit wall, wired direct to the team. He watched on a big screen television, while listening to the pit-wall conversations at races all over the globe with his own communications button to join the debate with the engineers. 'It was better than being on the pit wall. I always watched the race live wherever it was in the world. I had my console with all the data, just the same as the pit wall, and the headphones so that I could talk to the drivers, the race engineers, whoever I wanted. I was missing nothing.'

Nothing except the smell, the sound and the camaraderie of the sport that took a boy from India and planted him in the heady world of Formula One.

Fighting legal challenges on all fronts at home in India, as the government chases him over the mess left behind by the collapse of his Kingfisher Airlines, became all-consuming. The brewing business his family founded and owned has gone, too, now belonging to Diageo, the Guinness to Johnnie Walker whisky conglomerate. Subrata Roy, his co-owner in Force India, has also been a target for the Indian authorities: the chairman of the Sahara Group, one of India's biggest employers, was named one of India's most powerful men in 2012, but two years later was the subject of a series of legal probes.

Mallya believes he is the victim of a witch-hunt, just a high-profile celebrity target because of his money and his flamboyant image, the millionaire with the long hair, diamond earrings and flashy jewellery. 'Kingfisher grew to be the biggest airline in India, but the government killed it,' he says. 'The government of India is saying I am personally responsible for the entire debt of a public company. How can you hold the chairman responsible for a plc? Because India has a very bad debt record where Indian banks have folded without any recourse, they decided here is someone we can use as a poster boy.'

Mallya sold homes around the world, from an island off the Côte d'Azur to his $2.4 million apartment in Trump Tower in New York. The *Indian Empress*, the fabulous £70 million yacht that used to be 'party central' during the Monaco Grand Prix weekend, was impounded in Malta where it was moored.

By the summer of 2018, Mallya was trapped between the rock of his legal troubles in India and the hard place of a team that demanded millions. The decision was made for him when Sergio Pérez, his lead driver, triggered a request to put Force India into administration over $4 million in unpaid salary. The team also owed Mercedes more than $15 million. The bad news for India is that it lost its only link to Formula One, but the good news for the Force India team of 400 people at Silverstone was that another billionaire, Lawrence Stroll, was waiting to move in. Stroll, the mastermind behind brands like Tommy Hilfiger and Ralph Lauren, bankrolled the career of his son Lance to the tune of £50 million to get him into the Williams team and created a consortium to run the fifth incarnation – Jordan, Midland, Spyker, Force India and now an outfit called Racing Point – of the team at Silverstone in just thirteen years.

India is in the past now for Mallya. He has been living in

England since 1992 with his family, and the only interests in India are his charity projects, such as his hospital in Bangalore, which has a ward for the poor, and his school in the same city, which is rated one of the best in India. He has also started a project to educate more girls, who are neglected under the Indian education system, and is behind plans to supply drinking water to hundreds of villages. Everything has to be administered from Britain, where he splits his days between his home in London and the estate in Hertfordshire, which belonged to Lewis Hamilton's father, Anthony, a good friend who lives just down the tree-lined avenue. Even though he is selling an estimated $2 billion worth of assets, Mallya still owns a couple of dozen exotic cars of every marque, from Ferrari to Jaguar, reminders of his passion for speed, and they will remain his pride and joy even if the thrill of Formula One fades.

13

YOU STOLE
OUR MONEY

KEN Tyrrell was a big man, six feet something before he pulled on his shoes. He had big hands and a long face with tombstone teeth. It was a formidable sight when he clambered onto a table to confront Bernie Ecclestone. 'You stole our money,' he shouted at the top of his lungs.

Ecclestone, at 5 feet 3 inches, looked him up and down and, according to some, threatened to throw him out of the window. If it was physically unlikely, Ecclestone had already completed the ejection metaphorically. The teams now realised it – and that much of it was their own fault. 'Stole' was an emotive word, but their internecine squabbling had made it easy for Ecclestone to collect his riches, and those who fell for the fast buck rolled over easily when a cheque was waved.

Divide, rule and control were the ways Ecclestone worked. He was rarely wrong-footed, but his new-found notoriety had positioned him firmly in the sights of politicians and newspapers. After being named on the *Sunday Times Rich List*, he was catapulted into a new crisis – the cash-for-ash scandal, when he was found to have donated £1 million to

Tony Blair's Labour Party. When Blair came to power in 1997, governments were moving to end tobacco sponsorship, and Ecclestone had threatened to cancel the Belgian Grand Prix after the authorities there said they would implement a ban. Formula One's biggest teams were in hock to the tune of hundreds of millions of pounds to the cigarette manufacturers – Williams with Rothmans; McLaren with West; Benetton with Mild Seven; Ferrari with Marlboro; Jordan with Benson & Hedges, while BAR was British American Tobacco's team. One study for the British Medical Journal claimed that the annual spend by tobacco giants on Formula One was as much as $250 million.

Mosley and Ecclestone were looking to delay the inevitable before a blanket ban was imposed, using the threat that Formula One would up sticks and leave Britain for Asia where the rules on tobacco sponsorship were relaxed. It was smoke and mirrors, because the teams based in Britain were entrenched, and moving factories lock, stock, and barrel to faraway locations in China or Thailand would be nigh on impossible. According to Mosley and Ecclestone, the tobacco story was fake news anyway. Tobacco advertising was already banned in Britain and on its way out across Europe, and Mosley's FIA governing body was gradually securing agreement with the teams for a voluntary sponsorship ban in Formula One. They wanted time for transition, though, otherwise teams might be bankrupted by their loss of sponsorship.

Ecclestone says he believed that the £1 million was a one-off donation to the bright new prime minister, who was promising to hold down taxes for the rich, as well as supporting thrusting, innovative industries like Formula One. Whichever story you believe, Ecclestone was unimpressed by the entire farrago, and by Britain's new prime minister. He forcibly made the point that Blair had asked for the money and there was no question of trying to buy the prime minister's acquiescence in the tobacco debate.

It didn't matter what Ecclestone believed, because an unwelcome storm erupted around the man who, up until then, had been used to keeping his business and his money private. Now he found himself being scrutinised at the highest level of government, and in the news pages of the papers. Ecclestone never forgave Blair or his government and his disdain for politicians remains. The Labour Party returned the cheque and Blair apologised, but Ecclestone didn't bother to cash it for four months. 'Too busy,' he sniffed.

Mosley remembers: 'They behaved appallingly. I wanted access to Number 10 because of the road-safety stuff we were doing, and Bernie needed access to protect Formula One. If we had a massive accident, as we did at Imola [when Ayrton Senna was killed during the 1994 San Marino Grand Prix], it is no good ringing round the politicians on Monday morning. They have to be onside from the start.'

It was agitation that Ecclestone could well do without, for the man who was always two steps ahead had been suddenly confronted with a future that might not include him. Surgeons discovered he had heart problems, and he realised he could control Formula One but not his own mortality. He was propelled into finding ways of offloading the sport, while making enough to put into trust for his wife Slavica and daughters Petra and Tamara. Here was the genesis of years of disputes and splits and millions of pounds of legal actions. Ecclestone was warned that, if he died before her, his wife would be liable for 40 per cent tax, so he heeded the advice from Stephen Mullens, a specialist lawyer, to set up an offshore trust in Jersey, which eventually became Bambino Holdings, into which some of Formula One's profits would pour. He then set about organising a flotation of Formula One that would reap as much as £2.5 billion by turning the sport into a public company.

But business didn't stop, even for an operating theatre. On the Friday of the French Grand Prix, in June 1999, I found ITV's anchorman Jim Rosenthal and pundit Tony Jardine looking glum as they leaned on a balcony rail outside the press room. It was apparent something was wrong at a time when they should have been setting up interviews and features for the Saturday qualifying show for British television. 'There is no qualifying show,' Rosenthal said starkly. 'Bernie pulled the plug.' I couldn't talk to Ecclestone because he had undergone a triple heart bypass about forty-eight hours earlier, although few people knew because he had said nothing publicly about an operation that would shake a sport so reliant on his leadership, triggering fears that the seemingly indestructible Bernie might be mortal after all.

The story of ITV's plight – paying £12 million a year for the television rights but left with a one-hour hole in their Saturday afternoon schedule where Formula One qualifying should be – appeared in *The Times* that morning. At about 11 a.m., I was in my seat in the press room when I got what I would come to recognise over many years as the dreaded tap on the shoulder. It was Pasquale Lattuneddu, Ecclestone's eyes and ears in the paddock. 'Bernie wants to speak to you,' he whispered. 'But he's in hospital,' I said, wondering how this would work. We marched down to the headquarters office in the paddock, where Ecclestone was at the other end of a speakerphone in his private hospital room in London. I mumbled hopes that he was recovering well, imagining the scene with him in his hospital gown, attached to a drip and with a couple of anxious nurses listening as he gave the man from *The Times* chapter and verse. Ecclestone sounded as fit and combative as ever as he told me with his deadpan delivery: 'There is good news. I have one, apparently . . . a heart, that is.' And he also – it turned out – had a head start on ITV. They didn't appear to have read the small print, but he had, and he reckoned ITV had got live qualifying free for almost two years. Like everything calculated by Ecclestone, this was the moment to turn the financial screw: the race at Magny-Cours came before the British Grand Prix at Silverstone, ITV's showpiece race of the year. Ecclestone's timing was perfect, and ITV were over a barrel if they wanted complete coverage of their biggest sporting event of the year. They had to pay up.

Ecclestone was back on his feet in no time, and the famous 'Kremlin', his grey battle bus in the Formula One paddock, was soon receiving a line of team owners furious over how much the flotation could be worth to Ecclestone and his family.

To outsiders, it seemed a bizarre argument, as Ron Dennis broadsided Ecclestone for his greed. Dennis and Williams had personal fortunes worth tens of millions, while Formula One's drivers had become a new breed of multimillionaire. The motorhomes were no longer caravans with awnings, but vast complexes with offices and communication systems, bars and restaurants; meanwhile team owners and their drivers went everywhere by private plane or helicopter – not that it always helped.

The 2000 British Grand Prix was held in April, a sure-fire recipe for disaster. Ecclestone had been wrangling with the British Racing Drivers' Club for months about the future of the circuit that staged the first world championship grand prix in 1950. The stalemate led to what amounted to a punish-ment, holding a grand prix at a time when the weather was likely to be awful instead of the traditional July date. So it turned out to be, and helicopters were grounded because of a heavy fog around the circuit. Ron Dennis and his driver Mika Häkkinen were staying near Oxford at Le Manoir aux Quat'

Saisons, owned by celebrity chef Raymond Blanc, and had planned to take a helicopter to the track, but they were quickly herded into the back of a limousine for the thirty-mile journey to Silverstone. It was hopeless, as they were locked into huge tailbacks of cars all heading for the track, and it became clear that Häkkinen would not make the grid in time without urgent action. A motorcycle pulled alongside the Mercedes limousine and Dennis jumped out, pulled the passenger off his pillion, put Häkkinen on it and sent the bemused rider away with his famous driver, while the pillion passenger arrived at the paddock in luxury with the McLaren team principal.

Häkkinen was always prompt, but one British Grand Prix saw Ayrton Senna holding everyone up. The helicopter blades were whirring and Dennis and Gerhard Berger, then Senna's teammate, were growing restless as they waited and waited. The helicopter was in a field next to Le Manoir, which had been populated by sheep. Dennis saw the opportunity for punishment and amusement. He jumped down and picked up a ball of sheep excrement and pushed it into Senna's headphones. When the Brazilian arrived and put them on, he was the only one who noticed the strange smell. Senna and helicopters were a regular location for pranks: he once bought a carbon-fibre briefcase that was smart but unbreakable, so Berger decided to test its strength by throwing it out of the window of their helicopter. No one ever found out if it broke.

The pranks were in stark contrast to the tense atmosphere

of mistrust over Ecclestone's plan to float. The senior team owners were angry that the Ecclestone family should walk away with so much of the sport's profits, and now this bonanza from the Stock Market, when they were the ones putting on the show.

By 1999, Formula One was at its zenith, with viewing figures of almost 41 million people in 202 countries, and broadcasting contracts worth more than $200 million a year, plus another $150 million from circuit promoters. This truly was the sporting Klondike, constantly yielding riches, and Dennis wasn't going to let it escape him or his fellow team owners. He presented a detailed submission to the European Union competition authorities, claiming that Ecclestone had a conflict of interest, representing the teams, yet taking a large slice of the profits and sitting on the decision-making FIA governing body.

The EU authorities stepped in and demanded that the FIA's regulatory position was separated from Ecclestone's commercial interests. To ensure fairness, Mosley set up a four-man tribunal to organise a sale and to decide the final amount of $313 million for Formula One's commercial rights for 100 years.

No one was more surprised than Ecclestone that he was being charged for what he thought were already his rights. He had driven F1CA and then FOCA, signing broadcasting contracts and rounding up circuits to banish the haphazard deals of old. Ecclestone had transformed Formula One single-handedly to its pre-eminent position as the world's leading motor-racing series and created a Formula One eco-system that had made plenty of people rich and created thousands of jobs.

But the settlement seemed paltry compared with the amounts changing hands in football, where Sky Television was paying the English Premier League £670 million for a four-year deal from 1997, and there were howls of discontent from the paddock, now suspicious that, far from being fair, Mosley was in cahoots with his old friend, saying one thing in public but dealing for his pal in private. Mosley brushed it away at the time and says now that it was the only way to secure the FIA's precarious finances and he channelled the money into a road safety foundation responsible for saving tens of thousands of lives.

Formula One was in disarray. No one trusted anyone, least of all Ecclestone. There were claims and counter-claims and the big carmakers in Formula One – Ford, Toyota, Honda, Mercedes and BMW – were ganging up with a threat to start their own racing series outside the control of Ecclestone and Mosley's FIA. The Grand Prix World Championship (GPWC) was a potent weapon as teams fought for better terms, but Ecclestone knew the way out – divide and rule. He went to Luca di Montezemolo with the offer of $100 million to abandon the GPWC and return to his fold. Montezemolo grabbed the money, which meant that resistance from Fiat, Ferrari's owner and a leading light in the GPWC, was over.

The GPWC was finished and Ecclestone had restored his rule.

Ecclestone was still hemmed in after it became clear that Dennis and the European Union would head off his plans for a flotation. He decided the best way out was to sell and found a willing buyer at a price of $1.1 billion in a German television company called EM.TV, which owned the rights to programmes like *The Muppet Show*. EM.TV was owned by Thomas Haffa, an entrepreneur with ambition, but apparently more show than business: he was accused of falsifying the company accounts, the share price nose-dived and the company collapsed. Leo Kirch, another German television magnate, stepped in to save the deal, paying $2 billion, further enraging the teams, who now wanted to know who really did own their sport. Even Mosley was now fearing for the future as the merry-go-round of owners never seemed to stop.

Ecclestone was now a constant in the headlines, his methods and his obsessive secrecy arousing distrust. The dynamics of Formula One were changing, and big carmakers were returning to Formula One to cash in on its global television appeal, but they operated a conventional business model that was forced to be transparent, with boards of directors, statements of account and shareholders, and they couldn't handle Ecclestone's clandestine activities and refusal to reveal any of the inner workings of his empire.

Even Ecclestone was taken aback when Leo Kirch's

business also collapsed in 2002, which meant that Formula One devolved into the hands of Kirch's lenders – Bayerische Landesbank, the Bavarian bank based in Munich and now known as BayernLB, J.P. Morgan and Lehman Brothers.

The atmosphere in the paddock remained febrile, and not a day seemed to pass without an argument. One face became a fixture, though. Gerhard Gribkowsky, the chief risk officer of BayernLB, was looking after Formula One on behalf of the banks. He was jolly, enjoyed a large cigar and the fine wines he was served by Karl-Heinz Zimmermann in Ecclestone's motorhomes, and he clearly loved being at the hub of the action at races, beaming as Ecclestone introduced him to the major personalities in the sport and passing celebrities and royalty. Gribkowsky was a banker and, although he dealt in tens of millions of dollars every day, it wasn't his. From a desk in Munich, he was suddenly catapulted into this exotic world created by Ecclestone. Like so many before and so many to come, he was seduced by the glamour, the smell and the sound of Formula One.

Just occasionally, though, there would be an awkward customer, a potential sponsor or investor who resisted the champagne and the glamour and started deploying the most hated weapon in Formula One finances – logic. Eddie Jordan had a cunning plan for them: a few minutes before the start of a grand prix, Jordan would wheel his vacillating money-man down to the front of the garage. And then he would wait. As the clock ticked down to the start, twenty engines fired up, screaming steadily to 16,000 rpm to produce an ear-bleeding noise, like Concorde taking off. The ground vibrated as though an earthquake was about to hit, rippling through the feet and legs and into the torso, while a shock-wave blasted into the chest. It was a sensory overload beyond the comprehension of a company boss used to being cosseted at the wheel of his executive Jaguar or lounging in a comfy office chair. This was raw, terrifying ... wondrous. And EJ knew it.

Gribkowsky loved that same visceral thrill, too, but the more pressing duty of the banks was to get their money back. Gribkowsky attempted to sell to the carmakers, but they were too fractured and self-interested to put together a deal, and the teams didn't want to know. Gribkowsky failed to find a buyer, but Ecclestone didn't when he was introduced to Donald Mackenzie, the chairman of CVC Capital Partners, in late 2005. From its office in the Strand in London, the private equity group co-founded by Mackenzie had gobbled up some of the most familiar names in business, from the Automobile Association and the RAC to Samsonite luggage, Kwik-Fit, Halfords, Moto service stations and Breitling watches to compile a $50 billion portfolio.

CVC wanted Formula One but were searching for finance to help them buy. Ecclestone solved that, too, with his prodigious contacts book. One phone call to Fred Goodwin, chief executive of the Royal Bank of Scotland – Fred the Shred as he became known before he was disgraced during the 2007 banking crisis – and the money was in place. CVC paid $2.5 billion in total.

Ecclestone had sold Formula One again, and the Bambino family coffers were overflowing. His personal fortune has been calculated at almost £2.5 billion, but who really knows? Possibly not even him. There is the cash at the bank, the property from Biggin Hill Airport to his hotel in Gstaad, his homes, investments – the list goes on. The only certainty was that this complex process of sales, which needed expert accountants and lawyers to fathom, made Bernard Charles Ecclestone, son of a Lowestoft trawlerman, staggeringly rich, and put at least £3 billion into the family trust for his wife and daughters to spend.

But, from now on, he was a CVC employee on a £2.5 million salary, plus bonus of up to £1 million, while CVC promised to pay for the fuel for his £25 million Falcon private jet that carried him between grands prix and the new locations that would help make Formula One a heady investment for CVC.

Ecclestone wasn't used to being an employee, and the new directors appointed to Formula One's main board – including Sir Martin Sorrell, then head of WPP, the world's biggest marketing and public relations company, and Peter Brabeck-Letmathe, the former chairman of Nestlé – weren't sure what to make of this quietly spoken, mischievous character with a glint in his eye and joke for every occasion. Ecclestone hadn't answered to anyone before, let alone a board, and when at the first board meeting the new directors wanted to know what was happening in Formula One, his response was to the point: 'Nothing to report.' They would soon plug into Ecclestone's business methods, though, as the television money continued to roll in and he expanded Formula One away from its European heartlands.

Formula One was born in Europe and for almost a century remained the home of grand-prix racing. In the 1998 season, only five of sixteen races were held outside Europe, but there were two in each of Italy and Germany, alongside the traditional roster of France, Britain, Austria, Monaco, Spain, Belgium and Hungary. In 2018, only nine of the twenty-one scheduled grands prix were in Europe, with the rest scattered from Shanghai in the east to Austin, Texas, in the west. The world had been welcomed. At least, its money had.

Ecclestone uncovered a rich seam of income when he was introduced to Mahathir bin Mohamad, the Prime Minister of Malaysia, by Sir Jackie Stewart. Malaysia was a young country and wanted to advertise its modern outlook to the world. Sport was to be the billboard. In 1998, Kuala Lumpur staged the Commonwealth Games, and a year later came the first Malaysian Grand Prix on a grand circuit that made Silverstone or Spa-Francorchamps look positively dowdy. Better still, they were paying four times more for the privilege of staging a grand prix than the traditional European circuits.

It was nirvana for Ecclestone – bright, shiny, new tracks built to his specifications. This was a model for the future and these 'super-circuits' started to spring up around the world, with the racetracks constructed by Hermann Tilke, Ecclestone's favourite designer. Europe was 'Third World' now, proclaimed Ecclestone, and the money was with ambitious governments in the Far East, like Malaysia and China, who were prepared to pay over the odds – as much as $40 million for a single grand prix – to push themselves onto the world stage. Formula One was all the rage as promoters decided the sport grabbed global attention. Turkey, India, China and Korea followed, with huge temples to Formula One – but they looked alike, they felt alike and, unlike the European heartlands, most were not destined to enter legend like Monza or Silverstone.

The phone call came at 9 a.m. UK time. It was 2011, and I was in a hotel in Seoul, the Millennium Hilton, perched high above South Korea's exciting capital, but it was only a stopover because next morning I would be on a train to Mokpo. I knew what was coming. Ecclestone would have been given a cutting from *The Times* and hit the phone immediately after reading my devastating preview of the second Korean Grand Prix in Mokpo, a seaport about four hours south of Seoul by train, and so remote that not even the Koreans appeared to know where it was. The third paragraph of my story said: *The trains and planes will be full of Formula One personnel today, heading for a grand prix ghost town. Welcome to Mokpo – and, as far as almost everyone in the sport is concerned, you are welcome to it.* That obviously hit home in London, where Ecclestone, his spectacles held to one side and one eye shut while he focused, would have read the offending piece.

'Where are you?' was the first question. 'In a lovely hotel in Seoul, Bernie,' I said, waiting to see what was coming next. 'So, you haven't gone to that Mokopoko place yet, then?'

'Putting it off to the last minute, Bernie. It's not a place I want to spend much time in – and it's Mokpo.' Then silence before Ecclestone came back. 'Yeah. It's a shithole, isn't it?'

Ecclestone is nothing if not candid and, in this case, perfectly happy to accept the blame for landing Formula One in what many would argue was its most disastrous location. The circuit, perched on a southern tip of South Korea, had been constructed on reclaimed marshland facing the Yellow Sea. An entrepreneur had convinced Ecclestone that Formula One would be the centrepiece of a new city in Yeongam, with the circuit becoming a street track through a glamorous new resort with homes, casinos and nightlife. The only thing missing from this fabulous development was the resort.

At the first race in 2010, alarm bells rang at the entrance to my hotel, described disturbingly as a 'Love Motel' with its black doors with smoky windows set back from a side street. At reception, I was handed a welcome pack – comb, shampoo, soap, toothbrush and, er, condoms and lubricating cream. The room was like a set for a porn movie, with huge mirrors and a widescreen television with any number of channels showing enthusiastic sexual action. Apparently, it was very difficult for young Koreans to find somewhere to do what they needed to do when hormones surged, so they hired rooms in love motels, like mine, by the hour.

When we returned a year later, the Yeongam circuit had been locked and sealed since we left, like motor racing's version of Miss Havisham's cobwebbed, dusty house in Charles Dickens's *Great Expectations*. The trappings of Formula One were still there, but so were the mouldy sandwiches in hospitality centre fridges, left behind from 2010, and dead flowers still in vases, their petals layered onto grimy tables. Spectators were scarcer than the insects that left the nearby marshes to invade the paddock after dark, and the race was losing money hand over fist, even after the deal with Ecclestone was renegotiated. Little wonder my preview of the 2011 race was damning.

Each race was knocking up a loss of about £20 million, and 2013 was to be the last Korean Grand Prix. No one cared, except in Mokpo, which now has a huge Formula One circuit, which will probably never see a Formula One race again. India and Turkey followed Korea into history, while Valencia's efforts to race around the docks that had been revamped for the America's Cup failed, too.

Indianapolis was, like Silverstone, one of the foundation stones of motor racing and Ecclestone had tried for years to revive a US Grand Prix in a nation that regarded Formula One as like cricket, only even more incomprehensible. When the George family, the Indianapolis Motor Speedway's owners, took on the US Grand Prix after a gap of eight years in 2000, it was a breakthrough. Unfortunately, the cultural and commercial differences were huge and Ecclestone didn't help when he was asked at the inaugural press conference what the prize money was.

'None of your business,' Ecclestone said without raising his eyes to his questioner. There was enough open hostility as it was, with one newspaper deciding that Formula One people dressed entirely in black, swilled champagne and lived the high-life. At least the bars, restaurants and hotels were grateful for the trade, although even the scions of Indianapolis were to discover that they were only guests in their own home. When Mari Hulman George, chair of the Indianapolis board and mother of Speedway president Tony George, tried to enter her private suite for the grand prix, she was turned away because she didn't have a pass issued by Ecclestone. 'I own this place,' she reportedly told the doorman. 'Not today you don't,' he said.

If the dress code was baffling and the racing mystifying, the 2005 US Grand Prix was a disaster. In the run-up, Ecclestone was asked how he rated Danica Patrick, the rookie woman who had finished fourth in that year's Indianapolis 500, one of the world's toughest races. His reply was to become notorious. 'You know, I've got one of these wonderful ideas that women should all be dressed in white like all the other domestic appliances.' Ouch. That guaranteed headlines, but nothing like what followed, for the race was arguably the greatest embarrassment in the history of Formula One.

Indianapolis had constructed a circuit inside the famous Indianapolis bowl, with the run to the start-finish straight in the reverse direction to the Indy course around a steeply banked right-handed turn. But the speeds were so great that the Michelin tyres used by seven of the teams were over-loaded, while Bridgestone tyres – used only by Ferrari, Jordan and Minardi – were coping. There was a stark warning during Friday practice when the left rear Michelin on Ralf Schumacher's Toyota blew at 180 mph in the final turn and he crashed heavily, which put him out of the race.

By Saturday night after qualifying, it was evident that the Michelins wouldn't complete a race at competitive speeds, and the phone line to Max Mosley in London was hot. Ecclestone rounded up the teams to agree a compromise by putting in a chicane to slow the cars and run a non-championship event if it fell outside the FIA's rules. But Jean Todt, Ferrari's sporting director, was implacable and refused to take part in the negotiations, and Mosley warned Indianapolis that the insurance implications were too great and that the circuit would be thrown out of Formula One if they went ahead. It was an extraordinary stalemate.

I had never seen Ecclestone so rattled, as he sped from garage to garage, his mobile phone glued to his ear as he pleaded with Mosley to relent and let the Michelin teams race with a chicane, if only to placate the tens of thousands of American fans filling the Indianapolis grandstands. There would be no 'old pal's act' this time and, in the hour before the race, rumours circulated that the Michelin-shod teams would not race. It seemed unbelievable. The grandstands were packed and television sets around the world were being switched on for the biggest sporting event of the day. Jarno Trulli led the field of twenty cars in his Toyota from pole position, followed by McLaren's Kimi Räikkönen and the BAR Honda of Jenson Button. Michael Schumacher was the lead Ferrari in fifth. As they came slowly into the final corner, where Ralf Schumacher had crashed, Trulli peeled off into the pit lane, followed by Räikkönen and then Button, Giancarlo Fisichella, Fernando Alonso and the rest of the Michelin runners. Spectators jumped to their feet as it dawned on them what was happening and started howling with anger. Only six cars lined up – two Ferraris, two Jordans and two Minardis. Schumacher and Rubens Barrichello finished one and two for Ferrari. It was Schumacher's only victory of the season . . . and it stunk.

Few spectators stayed to watch as fans marched to the paddock entry to vent their fury. It was wise not to speak out loud because an English accent was incendiary. With the help of the police, the teams got out in one piece, but Formula One's name hit the dirt that day in the USA. There were only two more grands prix at the Speedway after Tony George – and, perhaps, his mother – complained that it was not commercially viable, never mind the angst that came with it.

The failure of the US didn't perturb others, though, and just when you thought Formula One could stop digging for gold, Ecclestone, the master panhandler, turned up more. European races that were once charged hosting fees of as little as $10 million were now facing competition from governments prepared to sanction fees four times higher and spend tens of millions more on building lavish circuits or transforming city streets into racetracks.

Peter Brabeck-Letmathe may not have been one of Ecclestone's most enthusiastic supporters when he joined the Formula One board of directors, but his mind was changed on his first visit to the Bahrain Grand Prix. As his car drew up, the outline of the Sakhir circuit, built on the lines of an Arab fort on desert outside the capital of Manama, came into view. 'Now I know why Bernie Ecclestone is a genius,' he muttered. The Bahrainis had spent more than $150 million building the circuit, the first bricks in a $2 billion project to develop an entertainment and business district.

If only it was as easy as that. Ecclestone had dealt with rebellious teams, worried bankers, aggressive lawyers, European investigations – and now he had human rights activists on his case.

The Bahrain Grand Prix of 2011 was cancelled as the Arab Spring swept through the island nation. Protestors claimed that as many as ninety-three people died as nonviolent protests ran out of control and police used tear gas to quell the crowds. A year on and the Arab Spring was a memory, but the protests went on as the date of the Bahrain Grand Prix came closer. Protestors declared a 'Day of Rage' against Formula One, which was seen as the puppet of the ruling royal family, and it was a difficult one to argue against, given that the race was the pet project of Crown Prince Salman, the king's son, and was being run under the banner of 'UniF1ed' a title that was surely a contravention of Article 1 of the FIA statutes, which decrees: 'The FIA shall refrain from manifesting political discrimination in the course of its activities.'

Teams were nervous about whether they would be safe in a country where tear gas and petrol bombs were common currency, and the Sakhir circuit was a fortress, surrounded by heavily armed troops, personnel carriers and tanks. VIPs were driven into the track by military personnel, and a SWAT team had practised their drills in case of attack. This was a grand prix being run under martial law.

Five days before the race, in a village called Al Dair, in the shadow of the barbed wire of Bahrain International Airport, I watched as women, dressed in the black abaya, the traditional garment of Islam, led a quiet procession through the streets. A phalanx of police looked on, rifles at the ready, while the women and their children shouted, 'Down with Hamad', a call to overthrow their king, and, 'Freedom not Formula One'. Ecclestone had told me at length that 'Formula One does not do politics' before we set off for Bahrain, but politics was inescapable now. I met women who told me that their husbands and sons had disappeared, and one little girl who said her father, a blogger, had been returned to his doorstep dead. There were drawings of faces on white walls, makeshift shrines to the dead, and an old man came to me, pointing into the gutter where we picked up rubber bullets and tear-gas canisters. I still have them on my desk. The people were calm and kind, offering cold juice to ease the heat and dust, but then we waited for prayers to end in the mosque at the entrance to the village, for the villagers said that was when the police would come in the night to lay down a carpet of tear gas that would leave their children wheezing and their eyes weeping.

It was difficult not to be affected by their stories, to suddenly realise that sport and politics cannot be separated. There was no glitz and glamour of Formula One for these villagers because the Bahrain Grand Prix would be staged behind a ring of steel and guns and armour, yet Ecclestone was right – if Mercedes could sell cars and Coca-Cola bottles of pop in Bahrain, why couldn't Formula One sell its wares like them?

Our driver Mohammed, a jolly chap with a permanent smile, took us to a coffee shop where we waited with about fifty demonstrators waiting to take to the streets. In the distance, we could hear tear-gas canisters popping and the acrid smell started to seep into the alleyways. My deadline for *The Times* was fast approaching. I hunkered down in the back of our tiny hatchback – our getaway car if everything went wrong – and typed. When it came to filing, though, there was disaster; my 3G transmitter refused to work and I was running out of time. As I pressed keys on the laptop frantically, about 100 youths ran past. One stopped and asked if I had a problem. I explained and he grabbed his iPhone from his pocket, gave me his access code and I filed successfully through his phone. The strangest things . . .

We ran to a safe house while the police swept the streets and watched from a balcony until the soldiers had gone and we could race down the alleys into the clear. The next day, a young woman led a protest in the centre of Manama, facing lines of police alone to demand the return of her elderly father, who had been jailed. She was joined by a handful of women until a crowd of their menfolk came out from a side street. Suddenly, there was a loud crack as police fired stun grenades and the crowds scattered. It was frightening, frantic, and a slice of daily life in Bahrain.

The teams were not immune, and Force India's mechanics were terrified after a Molotov cocktail narrowly missed their bus on the way back to Manama from the circuit. Bob Fernley, the deputy team principal, decided to withdraw his team from the afternoon Friday practice session to head back to the capital in daylight. Ecclestone turned the screw to make them stay, but Fernley was adamant, and Formula One was on red alert as Force India packed their bags and went back to their hotel.

Ecclestone bore the brunt of the criticism, but he had quietly met Dr Ala'a Shehabi, a leading human rights activist, in London before the race, and listened to her complaints, and his outward bluster was at odds with his private concerns. He knew it was a risk, but he and Formula One got away with it. No one in the sport was hurt . . . but the sport's image was shattered.

Dealing with governments whose reputations were high on the hit list of human rights organisations had become a hazard of the business because they paid big, and Ecclestone walked into the trap when he decided he would praise Vladimir Putin as Europe's potential saviour. Like his admiration for Adolf Hitler, it was a view universally condemned. I wasn't surprised, though. In 2008, I was at the Laureus Sports Awards in St Petersburg and, after the ceremony, waited in the small press conference room for the Russian president to address journalists. The doors opened and there was Bernie Ecclestone. 'What are you doing here?' he blinked at me. 'More to the point, what are you doing here?' I asked. The answer was that he was attempting to arrange a Russian Grand Prix. Putin originally wanted a race on the streets of St Petersburg, his home city, but when Sochi won the rights to the 2014 Winter Olympics, the focus switched to the Black Sea resort, where the government had pumped about $40 billion into the infrastructure and needed something new to justify the investment.

Human rights activists were scornful when it was announced that Formula One would follow the Olympics into Sochi, but Ecclestone was unrepentant, and Ecclestone and Putin seemed to form a mutual admiration society. Putin refuses to speak English in public, but Ecclestone says he chats to him quite happily in private and their relationship even extended to an invitation to the 2018 World Cup in Russia for the former owner of Queens Park Rangers. There was a touching scene at the 2015 Russian Grand Prix when the evening was closing in and became chilly as Ecclestone sat next to the Russian president in his private box. Putin motioned to his bodyguard, who produced a jacket to drape over the white shirt of the man who was about twenty years past pension age. Ecclestone was so touched by the photographs of the moment, he asked me for a copy for his office.

There was no deference, though, even for one of the most powerful men in the world. Ecclestone had a room full of the state hierarchy in the hospitality suite above the Sochi racetrack when he started ruminating about a new grand prix he was thinking of setting up. It had lots of potential, he said, but the location was a bit of a problem – somewhere called Damascus in Syria. 'Trouble is,' he said, as he turned to the top man, 'you seem to have blown all the roads up, so how would we get in?' And then he grinned. The top man chuckling throughout this wind-up was president of all Russia, Vladimir Putin.

14

TURMOIL

THE biggest espionage scandal in the history of Formula One hinged on two young men consumed by their rivalry. Fernando Alonso and Lewis Hamilton seemed like a perfect match when Ron Dennis placed them side by side in his McLaren team for the 2007 season, a blend of experience and youth.

There had been too many lean years, and although McLaren were still a front-rank team winning grands prix, there had been no world championship driver since Mika Häkkinen in 1999. Alonso joined the team as a two-times champion with Renault: he was young, smart and ambitious. Hamilton was Dennis's prodigy: he had won everything in the junior categories and was desperate to break through into Formula One. Dennis was reluctant at first because his tyro was just twenty-two, but his father Anthony was pushing hard and there was always the chance that he would move his son elsewhere. Dennis had no choice but to put him into the Formula One team.

Dennis unleashed a whirlwind. Hamilton was brilliant, and Alonso was unnerved by the extraordinary talent and ruthlessness of his young teammate, but a world championship still beckoned for McLaren – the only question was with which driver.

A thousand miles away from the optimism in McLaren's Woking headquarters in Surrey, Spygate was born when a print-shop owner, Gary Monteith, called Ferrari's Maranello headquarters to report that a woman had come into his shop and copied what appeared to be the 780-page manual for their 2007 car onto a hard disk. The woman was called Coughlan and Mike Coughlan was chief designer at McLaren. The source of the manual turned out to be Nigel Stepney, Ferrari's chief mechanic, and right-hand man to Ross Brawn, the team's technical director, who had left Maranello at the end of 2006, along with Michael Schumacher, ostensibly to take a year's sabbatical.

Jean Todt wasted no time in setting the wheels in motion by passing his evidence to Mosley at the FIA, for the revelation was sensational, and there was a high chance that it would devastate the Scuderia's main rivals if the allegations of industrial espionage were true. Dennis sensed that this was not the ordinary type of information exchange that went on between teams and realised that it had the potential to ruin a season in which one of his McLaren drivers would be world champion. More important, the credibility of his team would be blown, and any hopes he harboured of becoming a knight of the realm, to follow Sir Frank Williams and Sir Jackie Stewart, would go down the pan.

The embarrassment was already bad enough, heightened during Dennis's speech at the British Grand Prix, where the cold, tart sauvignon blanc from New Zealand in the McLaren motorhome was served: it was from Spy Valley. Bottles were swiftly removed and replaced.

Four days after Fernando Alonso won the European Grand Prix on 22 July at Germany's Nürburgring to reduce the deficit in the world championship to Hamilton to two points, Mosley convened his FIA World Motorsport Council to investigate Dennis's assurances that no intellectual property belonging to Ferrari had gone further than Coughlan. The council found in McLaren's favour, but Ferrari were furious and Mosley was under massive pressure from Montezemolo and Sergio Marchionne, then chief executive of Fiat, Ferrari's owner, to find Dennis and McLaren guilty. Montezemolo said this to me of Dennis: 'In McLaren, it was impossible to move without Ron knowing – that was his strength on one side, but his weakness on the other. I don't know the truth, but I would bet he was aware, particularly knowing the way he handled his business.'

Dennis's reputation was as a manager who managed everything to the finest detail, and that fuelled suspicions that he knew everything. However, it seemed that the episode was closed ... and it was, until the next grand prix in Hungary where Dennis was attempting to juggle two fractious egos, with Hamilton leading the championship from his supposedly more illustrious teammate. In qualifying, all hell broke loose: in the arcane world of Formula One, teammates are rivals and colleagues, which means there has to be order. Hamilton, looking odds-on for pole position, was due into the pits for tyres for his final flying lap but stayed out, coming in just behind Alonso and disrupting the schedule. The Spaniard saw Hamilton stacked behind him and refused to drive away. By the time Alonso was on his way to pole position, Hamilton was out of time to set a faster lap. Dennis was incandescent, flinging his headphones onto the pit wall and seeking out Alonso's people for a frank exchange of views, although he later admitted Hamilton caused the fracas by ignoring team orders. Worse still, Alonso was penalised for lingering in the pits and relegated to start sixth on the grid.

Just hours before the start of the grand prix the next morning, Alonso appeared in front of Dennis warning that he had an incriminating email on his laptop that he would show to Mosley unless there was action taken against Hamilton. As far as Dennis was concerned, it was blackmail, although he couldn't see anything dangerous in the message from Pedro de la Rosa, his test driver, which seemed to be about how Ferrari used nitrogen to fill their tyres and other irrelevant material. Dennis called Mosley immediately, his trust in Alonso so broken that he wanted to take him out of his car immediately and sideline his world champion. Mosley advised caution and Alonso raced, but to fourth place, while Hamilton won again.

The email might have been innocuous in Dennis's eyes, but

it was enough for Mosley to trigger a massive trawl of McLaren's databases and then set a date for a new hearing. Dennis produced statements from both his drivers and more than 140 engineers as well as himself and executives to guarantee that they had not seen the offending material from Stepney. But the FIA hit McLaren with a world record $100 million fine and disqualified them from the 2007 constructors' championship. It was a bitter – and expensive – blow for Dennis and McLaren. There was the humiliation, but also the cost, for McLaren would earn nothing from the teams' prize-money pot because of the disqualification, even though they were the champion constructor.

At the Belgian Grand Prix, days after the judgement, Mosley and Dennis took part in a staged photo-shoot, shaking hands on the steps of the McLaren motorhome. The body language was excruciating, Mosley smiling at a tight-lipped Dennis, seemingly repeating the reason for the fine: '$5 million for the offence and $95 million for being a twat.' Mosley later told me: 'It was only when Ron pissed off Alonso that we got the evidence, and even then he was still denying it.'

A season of hope exploded in Dennis's face. His drivers spent so much time sniping at each other on the track that Kimi Räikkönen, who had left McLaren for Ferrari for the 2007 season, sneaked the championship at the final race.

It was also the end for Alonso at McLaren and he was gone at the end of the season after a tense meeting at Woking with Dennis. Humiliated and hurt the Spaniard went back to

Renault. Dennis believed the punishment went further than supposed espionage and that he was paying the price for opposing Ecclestone's plans to float Formula One on the Stock Exchange, and his constant attempts to disrupt the favourable status handed to Ferrari and win bigger payments for the rest of Formula One's teams. While payments to McLaren, Williams and Tyrrell were held back when they refused to sign the 1997 and 1998 Concorde Agreements and Dennis continued his campaign against the flotation of the sport, there were rewards for Flavio Briatore, Tom Walkinshaw, Alain Prost and Eddie Jordan, who each received $10 million. Dennis told friends: 'I know what this was for. All those times in the past when I have stood up to Max and Bernie. This was payback.'

Dennis had travelled through Formula One from mechanic to leader of one of the most successful teams in the history of sport. He was independently powerful and unafraid to speak out, and had spent a lifetime in Formula One making himself unpopular with his peers for his forthrightness and his insistence on doing everything by the book, even though he had to suffer what he describes as 'a few poison pills' along the way, but he misjudged Mosley, according to Paul Stoddart, the former Minardi owner, who knew well the cast list of characters.

'Ron was robbed when the championship was taken away and that $100 million fine imposed. That was Max at his worst,' Stoddart said. 'If Ron had said at any point that he was going to step back, that whole thing would have gone away, McLaren would have been 2007 champions and the $100 million would have gone. It was so obviously personal. It was a dark day for Formula One.'

The decision left Formula One reeling. The record fine was not just humiliating, but a potential threat to a business employing hundreds of innocent people. Sir Jackie Stewart, who found out the hard way as a team owner what it feels like to be an outsider, decried the punishment. He regarded Dennis as one of the few straight players in the sport, but viewed the FIA president with suspicion. For their part, Mosley and Ecclestone tolerated Stewart and his publicity-seeking, turning up in the paddock in full tartan regalia plastered with the name of his next sponsor. At a small media lunch in London, Mosley turned resentment into a grudge with some spicy words. 'There's one particular ex-driver who, because he never stops talking, never has the chance to listen, so he doesn't know what's going on. Then he starts saying this is personal between me and Ron Dennis, at great length, because everything he does is at extreme length. He's a figure of fun among drivers. He goes around dressed up as a 1930s music hall man. He's a certified halfwit.' Stewart was incandescent and threatened legal action.

Mosley denies the punishment was personal, yet there appeared to be an element of glee in the way he brought Dennis – a proud, even arrogant man – to his knees. Knowing Dennis, I found it hard to believe he would lie or that he would cheat so blatantly and the pain of the episode is etched on his soul. Dennis refuses to talk about Spygate even now, though he promises he will write a book to clear his name and explain events to his grandchildren.

Bernie Ecclestone always liked to say that his job was to put out fires – and if there weren't any, start one. But Formula One had become an arsonists' paradise. Cheating – or pushing the boundaries, as the engineers would say – was always a factor in Formula One, right from the earliest days of the sport, and Spygate seemed to have been the ultimate inferno. Or so Ecclestone thought, for another wildfire was about to break out.

Flavio Briatore had become outspoken and even more flamboyant as he talked up his role in Formula One, but he was under pressure as Renault, the team he returned to when the French carmaker bought the Benetton operation, were squeezed out of the prizes by Ferrari and McLaren. Results were thin on the ground, and it seemed Briatore was spending more time on the politics of the sport than finding a way to win. Ecclestone was in his late seventies and Mosley believed that the Italian was moving into position to try to succeed his friend.

Hamilton and Ferrari's Felipe Massa dominated 2008 and after fourteen rounds of the season, Fernando Alonso's best finish was a meagre fourth. The fifteenth grand prix of the year was under the floodlights of Singapore, a glittering Far Eastern rival to Monaco, with its street circuit around the harbour in the shadow of the huge Marina Bay Sands Hotel.

The track is narrow and confined by walls on either side, so that one error means a shattered car. Massa led from pole position, followed by Hamilton and Kimi Räikkönen giving chase in the second Ferrari. Fernando Alonso pitted his Renault early and, soon after he reappeared on the track, his teammate Nelson Piquet Junior crashed. Piquet was the son of the three-times world champion, but was struggling to impose himself on Formula One at the Renault team, where Briatore was cold and condemning of poor results, just as he had been with Jenson Button six years earlier when he kicked him out to bring in Alonso. The debris from Piquet's Renault forced a safety car out onto the track and a dash to the pits for the main contenders. When the race unwound, Alonso led to the finish and a first victory for Renault in a year. The pressure on Briatore and his team was relieved and Alonso won again at the next grand prix in Japan. But 'Crashgate' was about to shatter the brief peace of Formula One.

Briatore's hubris meant that he thought he could do anything. He cut Piquet Junior's salary by $500,000 to $1 million for 2009 and, when the youngster failed to score a point by the Hungarian Grand Prix, he was fired. Piquet was furious, calling Briatore his 'executioner'. His career in Formula One was over and there was no longer any need to maintain the steadfast silence that he had kept since Singapore. It was then that the story of Crashgate started to pour out – how Piquet had allegedly been ordered to crash deliberately to orchestrate Alonso's victory.

Mosley was among the first to hear the full story. 'When Flavio fired Nelson Junior, Nelson Senior then came to tell me. He started crying because it affected him so much. I already knew because we had been alerted. I couldn't see him because it had to be impersonal, so I sent Nelson Junior off to see a lawyer to give a sworn statement to a very senior policeman.'

Briatore had invited Mosley to lunch at Rampoldi, a chic restaurant on the road down to the Monte Carlo casino, before the 2009 Belgian Grand Prix. 'He kept stressing that none of this was personal and we would remain friends and all the while I was patting my briefcase which had in it Nelson Junior's sworn statement.'

At the race in Belgium, Mosley smuggled a lawyer and a former Metropolitan Police superintendent from the Quest investigation company into the paddock to start digging. The race stewards were asked to summon team members one by one for interview and, according to Mosley, it was Pat Symonds, the long-serving technical director, and one of the most respected people in Formula One, who gave the game away. 'When Pat, who is completely honest, was asked if he did it, he said, "I can't answer that question."'

The Renault team principal, one of the most colourful figures in Formula One's history, who had won world championships, was banned from the sport for life. Even Ecclestone, used to the cut and thrust of Formula One politics, was taken aback. He suggested a lighter sentence, but Mosley refused.

'[Briatore] probably thinks I [punished him] out of vengeance but I didn't,' Mosley told me. He was right because that is exactly what Briatore thought. The Italian went to the French civil courts to clear his name and won. His ban was overturned and he was awarded €15,000 in compensation, while Symonds, also banned, was allowed to return to the paddock and was awarded €5,000. The FIA appealed but a settlement was agreed: Briatore's ban from Formula One was reduced to three years and both men agreed not to work in Formula One until 2013. Briatore never returned, though.

'Winning in a French court against a French federation should be impossible,' Briatore told me bitterly. 'All the reports were manipulated. Everything you tell Max is manipulated. The judgement was not from the FIA, it was Max. This was a Max vendetta, simple as that. When Max said everyone had to jump at the FIA, they jumped.'

There was one more 'gate' – 'Liegate'. Crashgate was yet to be revealed in its complete and awful glory when Lewis Hamilton went to the 2009 Australian Grand Prix. During a safety car period, Hamilton was told to allow Jarno Trulli to pass him. Cars are not allowed to overtake during safety car periods and the race stewards penalised Trulli and promoted Hamilton to his third place after the McLaren driver denied he was told to let Trulli pass him. Unfortunately, recorded radio transmissions told a different story. Hamilton was beside himself. He had witnessed the trauma of Spygate in his first season and called his father to ask for advice.

Anthony wasted no time and rang Max Mosley. 'I remember like yesterday Anthony calling me and it was so blindingly obvious what to do and there was poor little Lewis in the team with all that pressure on him. Lewis got a gentler handling by the press after that. Lewis was caught in the middle.'

Hamilton was disqualified and Dave Ryan, the long-serving team manager at McLaren who had issued the instruction to Hamilton, was sacked. The confession and apology from Hamilton, prompted by his father and Mosley, in front of the world's cameras was heartfelt and difficult to watch, but the reputational damage to McLaren just months after Spygate was huge, another crushing blow to Dennis and his proud team.

Formula One was exhausted by scandal, but the infighting was not over as the 2009 season wore on. There were so many scores to settle and so many battles to be fought – and Max Mosley was to be the biggest casualty.

15

THE OUTSIDER

MAX Mosley loved a fight. His rule at the FIA was outwardly democratic, but often mischievous and autocratic. 'Machiavellian,' according to Ron Dennis.

But then, Mosley was used to a fight. He had little choice, as the son of a far-right fascist leader and a mother devoted to Adolf Hitler. He fought to defend his father in brawls when he was a young man and he had fought for his place in Formula One, first as a driver then a team owner and finally as the sport's regulator. He was independently wealthy, reminding Andrew Neill, the political journalist, in an interview on the BBC, that his family once owned most of Manchester; there is still a Mosley Street that runs through the centre of Manchester up to the city's St Peter's Square.

Mosley never feared fighting alone. In 2005, during one of his many spats with the teams, Mosley called a meeting at the Heathrow Hilton. Only Ferrari turned up and my report in *The Times* the next day said that Mosley looked like 'Johnny No Mates'. Mosley was so delighted with that description, he adopted it as his email address. Unlike Bernie Ecclestone,

Mosley wasn't trained on the streets, he was trained at the Bar to use forensic examination and outfox his opponents intellectually. His enemies thought him haughty, aloof and sneering, ready to slide the verbal stiletto into their ribs when he wanted to humiliate them. Along the way he had lit the desire for revenge among too many.

Mosley could see that Formula One was spiralling out of control. Teams were spending enough to launch rockets to the moon, devising complex aerodynamics and technology that brought nothing useful to Formula One except to bloat their organisations and justify obscene budgets of as much as £300 million a year. The result was that the biggest teams with the biggest budgets were winning the biggest prizes, while the smallest teams were struggling to survive. Mosley devised plans to restrict spending to as little as £40 million annually, to help create a level playing field that might put an end to the era when a handful of teams passed the parcel of world championships between each other.

The plans were greeted with intense opposition, led by Luca di Montezemolo, the grandest and most charismatic of the team principals, who had always been able to negotiate hugely advantageous deals with Bernie Ecclestone. His ace card was that Formula One without Ferrari was a dinner without wine, and his argument was convincing enough to force Ecclestone's hand to give the Scuderia preferential treatment.

Montezemolo prepared the fightback, by laying the groundwork for the Formula One Teams' Association (FOTA), a trades union, to fight for their multimillion-pound rights – and to oppose Mosley. They were digging in for a long battle, but little did they realise what would explode around them.

One Sunday morning in March 2008, the *News of the World*, then Britain's biggest newspaper, landed on the doormats of hundreds of thousands of homes. The front-page headline was startling: 'F1 Boss has Sick Nazi Orgy with Five Hookers', and the inside pages carried pictures of the president of the FIA bent over waiting for a girl in a corset, boots and military cap to whip his bare backside. It was jaw-dropping stuff, and the immediate expectation was that Mosley would be so ashamed of the pictures that he would resign his presidency of the FIA and go into hiding. But that was not Max. Astonishingly, Mosley held firm as the furore gathered pace and calls for him to resign came from all sides, particularly from Jewish groups inflamed by the 'Nazi' element of the allegations.

This was the moment when Mosley's long and largely distinguished motor-racing career started to unravel and his personal life took its most tragic turn. Barely a year later, his son Alexander, a young man with a brilliant life ahead of him, died of an overdose at the age of thirty-nine. This was a blow more crushing than any that the *News of the World* could land on him and may have done more than anything to propel Max Mosley out of Formula One.

Bernie Ecclestone, a friend and ally of Mosley for four decades, had been lukewarm in his support, but had done his best to deflect questions. 'Knowing Max, it might all be a bit of a joke rather than anything against Jewish people,' Ecclestone had said, but his outwardly phlegmatic dismissal of an event that had 'done nothing' to damage Formula One evaporated as the pressure became unbearable. The publicity was toxic and strengthened the hand of teams threatening yet again to break away from the FIA's and Ecclestone's Formula One series. If they did that, CVC's investment in the sport would be trashed, broadcasting contracts would be torn up and chaos would reign. The clamour was huge: Formula One director Sir Martin Sorrell, a leading Jewish businessman, was appalled at the implications of the 'Nazi' theme, and the Bahrain royal family warned that the FIA president would not be welcome at the country's grand prix. King Juan Carlos of Spain, a keen supporter of Formula One, also distanced himself and, suddenly, even those closest to Mosley were wobbling. Team owners were in a state of near panic, as well as nervous excitement, as they realised that the autocratic reign they had come to despise was drawing to a spectacular conclusion.

At the Monaco Grand Prix two months later, Mosley was a pariah in his own sport. The Formula One paddock was haunted by the scandal, and barely a conversation passed without some joke or other about the FIA president and his predilection for a leather basque and a whip. The moral argument for him resigning was a powerful one and the practical one overwhelming. Mosley contended that what he did behind closed doors – like paying a prostitute a reported £2,500 for a sex session in a London apartment as the *News of the World* alleged – was his business and had no bearing on his duties as a regulator of motor racing.

But the teams were looking at their wallets. They sensed the nervousness among sponsors and high-rolling clients, whose private lives might well be just as murky, but who could not afford for their companies to be associated with such a high-profile humiliation. 'This is no moral issue,' Eddie Jordan, who had switched from team owner to pundit, told the BBC, 'It's a practical one. [Business and team leaders] no longer wish to deal with Max Mosley.'

No team principal would be seen dead with him, no sponsors wanted to shake hands with someone who in one picture could taint their brand, and no journalist was allowed to speak to the man who ran the sport. Mosley was in charge in Monaco, but it was a hollow reign of a man without a friend in a sport that had been his life for more than fifty years. The race ran beneath the window of Mosley's grand suite at the Hôtel de Paris, where he had taken to living, but that was as close as he would get that weekend.

By chance, I stayed on in Monaco following the race, and took my wife Jacqueline to Pulcinella, a favourite of the Monte Carlo in-crowd, an Italian restaurant not so much known for its food as its location. Tucked down a narrow side street, it opens out onto the Rue du Portier, just metres from the barriers that form the boundary of the most famous grand-prix circuit in the world. Just twenty-four hours before, the air around these streets had been filled with the sound of screaming Formula One engines, as cars dropped down through the famous Loew's hairpin corner before tearing off into one of the most familiar sights in sport – the Monte Carlo tunnel.

On this warm May evening, we spotted a lone figure walking by, head down, staring at the pavement. As he passed, I leaned over the pavement balcony and called out. Mosley looked up, briefly startled, and I thought he would walk on. Instead, he beamed a 100-watt smile and walked around into the entrance to pull up a chair. Within seconds, Pulcinella's proprietor had sent over his best bottle of Barolo. 'Monsieur Mosley, one of my best customers. A great man,' he told me. Tables stirred and autograph-hunters emerged from every corner, holding out notebooks and napkins for Mosley to sign. Someone still liked him, it seemed.

It turned out he had dined alone, as he often did. In Monte Carlo, where people crowd into Casino Square and wish for a lottery win, Max Mosley, who could buy any car and any apartment at any price, could not find someone to sit opposite him at dinner. Despite the high intelligence, fluency in three languages and vast inherited wealth, there is a sense of isolation about Max Mosley. Now back in London, he lives in one mews house in Chelsea while Jean, his wife of almost sixty years, lives around the corner. He says she gets irritated by him, so they remain largely apart, living their own lives.

He has been called an outsider, a loner condemned by his family background. He went into motor racing because it was the only place where the Mosley name was not toxic and he could get on with his life like anyone else. In Britain, there is no place for him in public life, in spite of long-harboured ambitions to go into politics; whereas in France, he is a Chevalier of the Légion d'Honneur, the highest honour the country can bestow, and Italy elevated him to the status of Grande Ufficiale dell'Ordine al Merito. He also holds high orders from Bulgaria, Romania, Armenia and Ecuador. In Britain, there has been nothing for the nation's most effective road-safety campaigner, who helped devise the Euro New Car Assessment (NCAP) programme, now used by every major carmaker, which is calculated to have saved 78,000 lives in Europe. Mosley also pushed through reforms in Formula One that have banished the fear of death from the racetrack – but it will never be enough. 'Because my family are outside the establishment and regarded as beyond the pale, I would be astonished if I was offered anything. I know what the establishment here think,' he said ruefully.

On that evening in Monte Carlo, Mosley seemed to appreciate having company after weeks of enforced silence and no one to speak to apart from his lawyers. Jacqueline, a primary school teacher, was fascinated. She knew the name but was about to put a face to the backside she had seen in *The News of the World* and she wasn't spared any detail – the girls, corsets, whips and all, and how a harmless personal peccadillo was no matter for public consumption. 'I cannot allow myself to be driven out by something which was wholly a private matter and which some people chose to make public,' he said. 'What I do in my personal life does not affect my ability to run the FIA. It is ridiculous. I won't back down.'

It was typical Max. His dogged intransigence meant he would fight to the finish. A few days later, he had to face his peers in the General Assembly of the FIA. Everyone thought he would be thrown out of the ornate doors to the organisation's headquarters in the Place de la Concorde in Paris, but Mosley was typically combative and at his persuasive best, his lawyer's language put to great use as he convinced the FIA members that this was not a resigning matter, no matter what the insiders in Formula One believed.

Next, he took on Britain's biggest newspaper. Mosley's appearance in his privacy action was more attack than defence and he proved that he was not taking part in a 'Nazi' orgy, winning damages against the *News of the World* of £60,000, thought to be the highest for a breach of privacy in British legal history at the time. The judgement found that exposing Mosley's private life was not in the public interest, a view Mosley had expounded on at length that night in Monte Carlo. 'When it came to the court case, my only preoccupation when giving evidence was not to take the piss out of their QC,' Mosley told me. 'I was asked which period of British history do these clothes [the leather uniform and corsets worn by the prostitutes] put you in mind of? I told him I knew of no period in British history where soldiers wore thigh-length boots and costumes with nothing underneath. I was determined and I wasn't holding back.'

In spite of these victories, this would never go away. Every Google search and every newspaper and magazine article would start by recounting the story of the sex orgy. It was a label almost as permanent as the Mosley name. He had failed to escape one burden and gathered a new one.

The storm had blown over by the end of the year, when Mosley intimated that he would stand down at the end of his term of office in October 2009, but that seemed to add urgency to his plan to curb the excesses of the teams. The infighting became entrenched, and the FOTA teams threatened their breakaway series yet again. Unlike all of the previous threats, this one carried weight because the teams were intent on sticking together for once.

The climax came at the British Grand Prix in the June of 2009. Mosley looked rattled. He arrived at the Silverstone circuit with Ecclestone and Flavio Briatore, the Renault team principal and one of the ringleaders of the teams' defiance, which seemed to point to peace in our time. In reality Mosley was alone.

Mosley insisted that the 2009 breakaway threat could never work because the FIA's official series held all of the key circuits, organisation and commercial deals. Perhaps he forgot that he and Ecclestone had been busy arranging their own series when they attempted to break the stranglehold the FIA

Master and pupil: Ron Dennis with Lewis Hamilton, the youngster he nurtured from teenage karter to F1 world champion.

If looks could kill: Ron Dennis shakes Max Mosley's hand after the FIA had hit his McLaren team with a world record $100 million fine for Spygate.

A star is born: Lewis Hamilton celebrates his first world championship in 2008. He would become Britain's most successful driver.

Flavio Briatore, the man who claims to have brought La Dolce Vita to Formula One, with a collection of his supermodels.

A delightful drenching from Red Bull's Sebastian Vettel and Mark Webber for Jenson Button after winning a dramatic 2011 Canadian Grand Prix for McLaren.

Protestors took to the streets in the run-up to a turbulent 2012 Bahrain Grand Prix demanding that Formula One stayed away from the island Kingdom.

Father and daughter – boss and deputy: Claire Williams shares an intimate moment with her father during the 2014 Austrian Grand Prix.

Ecstasy: Graeme Lowdon, sporting director of Marussia Manor, hugs Jules Bianchi who scored the team's only points at the 2014 Monaco Grand Prix.

Formation flying for the Ferraris of Kimi Raikkonen and Sebastian Vettel. They spent four seasons as teammates at the Scuderia.

Lewis Hamilton makes it a hat-trick of world championships at the 2015 US Grand Prix, equalling Sir Jackie Stewart.

Kevin Eason bumps into Christian Horner, the Red Bull team principal, and his wife Geri – better known as Ginger Spice.

Roscoe joins his master's meeting with the man from The Times. He snored throughout the interview in the Mercedes motorhome.

Getting the lowdown from the boss: Eason interviewing Bernie Ecclestone before the 2015 Brazilian Grand Prix.

Ron Dennis meets Chase Carey at the 2016 Singapore Grand Prix, days after Liberty Media bought Formula One and installed the American as chief executive.

Above: Not even a Formula One car can disturb a girl topping up her tan. The impossible glamour of the 2017 Monaco Grand Prix.

Left: Christian Horner goes for the full Lederhosen look before his Red Bull cars competed at the Austrian Grand Prix. He was very embarrassed.

Below: The invitation to the most exclusive leaving party in Formula One went out to fifty high-rollers – and the author.

Save the Date

Tuesday 7th March 2017 / 8PM

A tribute to
BERNIE ECCLESTONE
THE MAN WHO MADE FORMULA ONE GREAT

[AND A LOT OF PEOPLE RICH]

Sumosan Twiga London
165 Sloane Street London SW1X 9QB

DRESS CODE   RSVP
Tenue de Ville   laura@officefa.com

had on the sport more than twenty years earlier, boycotting grands prix to get their way. Mosley called a small gathering of journalists but was clearly ill at ease as he mounted a spluttering attack on the teams, culminating in his judgement that they were 'loonies' for thinking they could defy the rule-makers and go their own way. It was a less elegant description than the one he had applied to Montezemolo, the ringleader he had dismissed as nothing more than a *bella figura* – a beautiful figure of no substance. If Mosley was trying to inflame the situation, he succeeded. The teams had met in secret at the Renault factory at Enstone, about twenty-five miles from Silverstone, and discussed their options late into the night. The breakaway was confirmed, with Montezemolo retaliating by calling Mosley a dictator.

Something had to give, and it wasn't going to be the teams, who for the first time in memory were united. Crucially, they also had the support of Ecclestone. The end game was played out at the FIA's headquarters just three days after the British Grand Prix, at a meeting between the FIA and FOTA where the teams would demand Mosley drop his budget cap or they would leave to form their own racing series. Ecclestone and Montezemolo moved to an anteroom for a private discussion with Mosley. Montezemolo sensed it was over, remembering the scene at the Place de la Concorde, a huge square that was the site of many a beheading at the guillotine during the French Revolution. This was to be another execution.

'In that room, Max was very, very afraid. He was a man who

walked alone,' Montezemolo said. 'I told him that unless he gave us an assurance that he would change his position, we were together – all of the teams – and we would leave. Bernie encouraged me the night before not to change my mind. I ~~member that Max suddenly sighed. He understood at that ~~oment that he was very, very weak. Sometimes he was not flexible enough to understand that not everything was black or white – it was his way or no way.'

Mosley chose not to stand for re-election and he left in October 2009. His reign was over. Jean Todt, the former sporting director of Ferrari and Montezemolo employee, was elected in his place.

The last act was with Montezemolo, who underlined his purpose in rounding up the teams into FOTA. Within days, Ferrari quit the organisation it started, followed quickly by Red Bull. The breakaway was finished. Jonathan McEvoy, the *Daily Mail* journalist covering Formula One at the time, has an incisive view of the relationship between Mosley and Montezemolo. 'Luca was behind FOTA only because he saw it as a vehicle that he could use to bring down Max. There was no other object. Once that was achieved, Luca had no use for FOTA or anything like it and he and Ferrari were out.' So much for that much-vaunted unity. Montezemolo had wielded the stiletto and Mosley was finished. There was something else: Ecclestone rewarded Ferrari's departure from FOTA with an $80 million sweetener.

Although Mosley seemed to have put the *News of the World*

revelations behind him, he had been significantly weakened, not just in public, but where it counted – at home. He says his wife Jean thought it was some sort of elaborate joke at first when he showed her the newspaper with its graphic pictures. 'It wasn't a happy conversation,' he said with breathtaking understatement. The effects may have rippled deeper, though. Friends say that Mosley worried that the gory details of the sadomasochistic sex in a basement had affected Alexander, and Mosley acknowledges that the death of his son – a popular restaurateur said to have been a maths genius – from a heroin overdose destabilised him at a time when he needed to be at his sharpest. Alexander Mosley died on 5 May 2009, just weeks before that crucial British Grand Prix and the face-to-face with Montezemolo. Friends said that living with the Mosley name had been a burden, just as it had been for his father.

After the *News of the World* story broke, the Mosley family were hounded by the paparazzi, with photographers in the usually quiet streets outside their homes, while a steady stream of stories emanated from the Formula One paddock as shock-waves reverberated through the sport. The privacy case at the High Court simply opened old wounds as lawyers picked over the details of the story. Over lunch at a restaurant around the corner from his home in Chelsea, Mosley analysed the effects of that turbulent year, culminating in the death of his beloved son. Like his father and, I suspect, his mother, Mosley doesn't do public displays of emotion. He is stiff upper lip, matter of fact and to the point, but the language heated up as he recalled this most tempestuous period of his life.

'When the *News of the World* story broke, I was clear what I had to do. You had Bernie and Flavio running around getting the teams to vote for me to go. I didn't give a fuck what they voted for because my constituency was the FIA. I called the General Assembly and put it to the vote. Bernie called me up and warned me not to do that because it would be so humiliating to lose. If you lose, you lose and I wasn't going without a fight.

'I was undoubtedly weakened by my son dying because it was unrelenting all the way. The court case was painful for my family, but my attitude was always, "For fuck's sake, it is only sex."

'I was in touch with a German doctor from time to time and after she heard about my son, she wrote to me warning that it would have a big effect on me. I thought nothing of it. Alexander died on the fifth of May, and then we had a hostile meeting on the fifteenth and I thought at the time I could handle all of this. What made it worse was I had made my mind up to go and I resented the suggestion that I was pushed out. The key decision because of Luca's attitude was: do I reverse the decision and stand again? If I stood again, the teams would have announced their breakaway and that would have collapsed over the winter and things would have gone back to normal. I would have taken them on. But because of my son's death, I didn't want to go on. Had it not been for his death, I would have stood [for the FIA presidency] again and told them I would have looked forward to seeing how their breakaway got on. Looking back, you lose your resolve. You have to be tough and I wasn't then.'

Max Mosley could never be ordinary, nor could he be expected to escape the influence of parents who scandalised polite society. His mother Diana was one of the so-called Mitford girls, one of six daughters of the second Baron Redesdale and his wife, Sydney, who was a cousin of Clementine Churchill, Sir Winston's wife. Diana was a glacial beauty celebrated in elite London society, moving the novelist Evelyn Waugh to write that her beauty 'ran through the room like a peal of bells' – perhaps an overwrought description, but one that summed up her magnetism. She married Bryan Guinness, of the brewing dynasty, but was drawn to the charismatic Sir Oswald Mosley, the sixth Baron Ancoats. She left her husband abruptly, taking a few servants with her, to 'live in sin', as her family put it, with Mosley, who had been one of the nation's youngest MPs and whose speeches and rallies drew thousands.

Diana was already infatuated with Adolf Hitler and the Third Reich by the time she met the man who would become her husband, and father to her son, Max Rufus. Diana visited Germany with her sister Unity in the early 1930s (Unity was said at one time to have prayed to Hitler while giving the Nazi salute), but her relationship with Mosley deepened her belief in fascism. He was leader of the British Union of

Fascists, whose Blackshirt followers stoked riots and inflamed passions as Britain faced up to a war with Hitler that Oswald Mosley fiercely opposed. They audaciously married in Berlin at the home of Joseph Goebbels, the Nazis' propaganda minister, and the guest list included Adolf Hitler as a witness. When the war started, they were both incarcerated in Holloway Jail, the baby Max cared for by a nanny outside the prison walls.

Max has his mother's looks – described by one newspaper as being like 'a faded choirboy' – and a lot of her single-minded determination, and he has inherited the one quality from both parents: they were unafraid of public opinion and refused to be intimidated.

After attending boarding schools in Germany, and Millfield in Somerset, Mosley graduated from Oxford with a degree in physics, and then went on to study law. He became embroiled in the 'family firm', the British Union of Fascists, following his father around the country to rallies that sparked massive opposition from Jewish groups enraged by what they perceived as Sir Oswald's anti-Semitism. At one rally, Mosley was involved in violent exchanges, including one in which his father was knocked down by a mob. He was charged with threatening behaviour but cleared on the grounds that he was trying to protect his father. A photograph in *The Sunday Times* showed Mosley attempting to disrupt a rally in 1958 for the Conservative 'grandee' Lord Hailsham on behalf of his father's party, yet when Mosley went into the law, it was as a pupil in

Hailsham's chambers. In a picture from that rally, a young Mosley appears to be at the heart of a violent ruck. A profile in *The Sunday Times* described him as 'a thug'.

Almost sixty years on, Mosley looks much as he did then. The hair is still a slight sandy colour with flecks of grey, he stoops slightly but is still whippet thin and, like almost every other scion of motor racing, he is as deaf as a post, relying on high-tech hearing aids. His voice is soft, and as persuasive and convincing as ever, like a kindly uncle. The temper has subsided, but the rage is alive and well. His privacy battle with the *News of the World* coincided with the outbreak of revelations of phone hacking at the newspaper. Mosley had found a cause, and plenty of allies willing to help him pursue an end to the right of newspapers to publish stories like his.

Mosley handed Tom Watson, the Labour Party's deputy leader who was at the forefront of the privacy campaign, £500,000, while setting up a family trust fund in the name of his son Alexander to pour £3.8 million into a new press watchdog called Impress. At the same time, Mosley was guaranteeing the legal costs of some of the claimants in their court cases against the newspapers for phone hacking. Then Mosley went after Google, pursuing the search engine in Germany and France and winning the right to force them to remove photographs and videos from the *News of the World* article.

Inevitably, there was payback: Paul Dacre, the formidable editor of the *Daily Mail*, set himself up as Mosley's most dogged opponent. Mosley laughed off Dacre's accusation that what happened in the Chelsea apartment was 'unimaginable depravity', and Mosley regards the rush to condemn as somewhat hypocritical from an editor whose website had become a byword for salacious pictures and gossip. Mosley also remembered how quickly some of Formula One's biggest names rushed to disassociate themselves from the participant in the alleged 'sick Nazi orgy'. Mosley says in his autobiography that he was surprised when BMW and Mercedes both issued statements against him. 'The temptation to throw the stone back was irresistible. I put out a release reminding everyone of the involvement of both companies ... in the worst aspects of the Nazi regime while I was still in the nursery.'

Dacre unleashed his reporters to seek out anything in Mosley's past that could destroy his reputation. What Dacre's journalists found was unedifying, and pointed to Mosley being not just fascist, but racist. In 1961, Walter Hesketh – an eccentric who for some reason had run from Edinburgh to London in carpet slippers – had fought the Moss Side by-election in Manchester on behalf of Oswald Mosley's fascist Union Movement. The *Daily Mail* found an election leaflet that warned that coloured immigrants spread diseases such as 'tuberculosis, VD [venereal disease] ... and leprosy'. The publisher was Max Mosley.

In the turbulent battle for press freedom, which had Mosley on one side and Fleet Street on the other, this was devastating. Mosley's reputation was shredded within hours, compounded by a sweat-inducing television appearance on Channel 4 News, where the usually calm and forensic Mosley was reduced to bluster, squirming awkwardly in his chair under questioning. The irony is that the blow was wielded by a newspaper whose proprietor, Lord Rothermere, was an enthusiastic supporter in the 1930s of Hitler and his rule of Germany. More entertaining still, one new examination by Will Wainewright claims that Rothermere was so entranced by the British Union of Fascists that newsroom staff started to wear black shirts mimicking Mosley's troops.

Mosley doubted whether that inflammatory leaflet was endorsed by him and denies he is a racist and there seems little evidence in later life to signal that he was. When Lewis Hamilton was abused by spectators with blackened faces and wearing wigs during testing in 2008 at the Circuit de Catalunya in Barcelona, an angry Mosley immediately threatened to ban the Spanish Grand Prix.

Max Mosley's entire life has been overshadowed by his family, from the cradle to the grave of his son, but no one will force him to renounce them. John Hogan, who spent forty years in the top echelons of Formula One as the sponsorship fixer for the Philip Morris tobacco empire, remembers a lunch with Mosley. 'We were chatting about something when Max suddenly stopped and said: "I found some letters belonging to my mother the other day and, you know, she always referred to Hitler as Dear Führer. Isn't that funny?" I wasn't sure what to say, but it shows

Max has a totally different view of his family from the rest of the world.'

Mosley walked away from Formula One with barely a goodbye, except from Fleet Street, who threw a farewell dinner and presented him with a retirement gift – a whip. Mosley saw the joke and laughed uproariously.

Mosley has not been back to Formula One since. The separation is complete and irrevocable. One day I was with Ecclestone in his Princes Gate office, and he thought it might be fun to bring Mosley back to help dig Formula One out of the legislative mire it was sinking into. 'Brother Max,' Ecclestone said when Mosley picked up the phone at his mews house in London, 'I think you should make a comeback.' It was mischief, just like the mischief they had perpetrated in tandem on Formula One for years. Mosley saw the joke, but he was not for turning.

16

AGONY AND ECSTASY

YOU need only a few minutes in the company of Graeme Lowdon to understand the cruel ecstasy of Formula One. In the parlour of his cottage in Northumberland, there are piles of memorabilia, boxes of programmes and notes, race overalls and helmets, books and cards, picked up over a lifetime of overdosing on adrenalin at racetracks all over the world.

Then we move to the oak-beamed kitchen and Lowdon's voice softens as he takes me through every twist and turn of a young and ambitious racing team, from the wretched daily battle to find money to keep the show on the road, to the defining moment when a young man on the threshold of achieving his dream lost his life.

The Manor Formula One team – or Virgin, or Marussia, depending where in the story you start – was a host of epic narratives crammed into fewer than six seasons. The odds were stacked against them from the start and never seemed to offer a break. There was one lavish, hysterical moment of glory, on the grandest of all Formula One stages, before they fell back to sodden earth in pelting rain in Japan. Jules Bianchi, the burgeoning talent being groomed by Ferrari, had scored the only points in the team's short history in Monaco; barely four months later, he was on life support after suffering devastating head injuries in the final moments of the 2014 Japanese Grand Prix. Nine months later, he was dead at the age of just twenty-five.

Agony and ecstasy is a trite phrase, but one that is so apt to describe the slog, the torment and the trials of entrepreneurs who enter Formula One, full of courage and enthusiasm, only to end up clinging to existence on the most demanding and financially crippling of all sporting stages. The statistics tell a story: since the inception of the Formula One world championships in 1950, as many as 125 teams had gone to the wall up to 2016, when Marussia Manor Racing, as Lowdon's team was then called, folded. Admittedly, the early years were packed with fly-by-night operators and wealthy individuals who could put a car on the grid for a season or two of fun and frolics, but so many once-famous names have also gone – Lotus, Brabham, BRM, Arrows, Cooper, Maserati, March and Ligier, for example. Some were rescued and sold on, like Ken Tyrrell's team, which became British American Racing, then Honda, and eventually Brawn GP and Mercedes; Stewart Racing, founded by Sir Jackie, became Jaguar and then Red Bull, who also bought Minardi and turned it into Toro Rosso.

A financial playing field with a slope like the North Face of the Eiger has sent teams slithering to the bottom, unable to win or even get a sight of the podium because they are unable to keep up with the frantic spending among the handful of teams with massive manufacturer backing or a billionaire benefactor and the benefit of a bizarre and astonishingly unequal system of payments that was designed to keep the haves sweet and have-nots permanently in peril.

Bernie Ecclestone always rewarded success and scorned failure, and his prize payments system favoured the powerful over the weak. The crucial turn came when CVC Capital Partners bought Formula One with plans to float the business on the Singapore Exchange, where the big money would be. Estimates for the sale ranged anywhere between $6 billion and $10 billion, but first, Ecclestone had to guarantee potential investors that the marquee names would be on board – and that meant Ferrari, Mercedes, Red Bull and McLaren. They were the big attractions with the famous drivers, and they won all the races, and without them, there was no Formula One to sell. Ecclestone worked out a new payment schedule that would ensure they were in the fold. They would all get preferential payments based on a complex system that rewarded historical championship victories, a structure so complex and secret that few understood or knew about it. What it meant was the gap between the top and bottom of Formula One was a chasm – Ferrari picking up $180 million in prize money in 2017, while Haas were paid just $19 million. According to figures drawn up by the authoritative *Autosport* magazine, the Big Four teams – McLaren, Red Bull, Mercedes and Ferrari – were paid $609 million that year, with the other six teams sharing $330 million. It was a system almost designed to wipe out competition and force failure.

Lowdon thought that he could help break the system when Max Mosley decided he would impose a budget cap for the 2010 season that would rein in the free spending of the biggest teams and force a new era of more competitive sport.

The president of the FIA soon discovered fierce resistance to his proposals for a budget capped at just $40 million a year as established teams threatened a breakaway championship that would devastate Formula One. Mosley's answer was to find new teams and tempt them in with the budget proposals to ensure his racing series had a full grid, no matter what happened. When Lowdon heard, he saw an opportunity and rang his old pal and business partner John Booth, who had started Manor Racing in 1990 and become one of the most successful figures in the history of motor racing in junior series. Booth's teams had notched up 171 victories and nineteen titles in series like Formula Three and Formula Renault, blooding some of the best talent to reach Formula One, from Kimi Räikkönen to Lewis Hamilton. Lowdon reasoned that, with Formula One budgets restrained, how hard could it be to step up? Lowdon was already a millionaire as a result of his success as a tech entrepreneur helping start-up companies, he knew how business worked and knew that Booth understood racing.

'We weren't looking to be Ferrari. It didn't seem impossible, we just needed a plan. The problem was that the goal posts didn't change a bit, they changed a lot and often. Everything was tied up with what happened in Max's private life and when he had gone, things changed rapidly. The budget was going to be $20 million and then it went to $30 million and then dollars became pounds and so it went on, changing every day of the week and then there was no budget cap.'

Manor went ahead anyway, signing the Concorde Agreement, Formula One's commercial deal, in August 2009, but they had to be ready to race by March 2010 at the first grand prix in Australia. At the same time, a Spanish outfit called Hispania Racing Team – with an abbreviation of HRT, which caused much mirth among the English-speaking element in the paddock – and a revived Lotus founded by Tony Fernandes, the Malaysian airline entrepreneur, were joining.

The key for Manor was to find a sponsor. Sir Richard Branson had made an opportunistic entry into Formula One in 2009 with the new Brawn GP team, rescued by Ross Brawn after Honda Racing so abruptly pulled the plug on its Formula One operation. Brawn had cajoled enough money out of Honda to keep the team operating, but needed a title sponsor, while Branson wanted exposure for the Virgin brand and not the sort of eye-popping sponsor budgets that could reach £40 million a year and more for some teams. Branson got away with a one-off £6 million in cash and Virgin airline tickets to sponsor Brawn.

Lowdon had watched Branson's preening in the pit lane and his obvious enjoyment of life in the glamorous Formula One paddock, particularly during the 2009 Monaco Grand Prix where Button won and the championship beckoned. Lowdon wooed Virgin executives with his soft Geordie lilt, getting them to understand that if Mercedes became world champions, there would be no bargain basement deal for a second time in 2010. At the end of that championship-winning 2009 season, Brawn sold the team to Mercedes and Branson could see that sponsor prices would rocket. He walked away to put his name on Manor's car – but there was no money, just the chance to use Virgin as a brand leader, which Lowdon hoped would stimulate interest among other sponsors who would want to become associated with such an internationally famous name.

The maiden season of 2010 was a struggle against all the odds, and Branson soon lost interest in his new team. Life at the bottom of the grid lacked the cameras and the glamorous celebrities of the top. Lowdon found a new benefactor in Andrei Cheglakov, a Russian millionaire with ambitions to build a sports car range called Marussia. Virgin took second place in the team title in 2011. But there was little improvement for Marussia Virgin, except for the consolation that they weren't as bad as the Lotus and HRT teams that entered on the same wave of hope held out by Mosley's radical budget plan. At the inaugural Indian Grand Prix, Branson cut a lonely figure when I found him sitting alone in the team motorhome on a high stool, drinking coffee. There was no one else there, save for the motorhome staff and the odd mechanic passing through for supplies of food and drink. On the grid before the grand prix, he managed to infiltrate himself into the action, being pictured with Bollywood stars invited by Ecclestone to add some glitz to the occasion, but the association between Virgin and Formula One was over and Branson left at the end of the season.

In July of 2012, Marussia gave a test session to María de Villota, the daughter of Emilio, a one-time Formula One driver. The test was simple and should have been mundane, with De Villota required only to drive in a straight line at up to 150 mph on a runway at Duxford Aerodrome. She returned to the pits but somehow drove into the tailgate of one of the team's stationary trucks. An inquiry later found that the engine idle system was still on and, even though she hit the brakes, the revs were enough to push her into the truck. De Villota suffered horrible head injuries and lost an eye. The racers who spent their lives clinging on to beat their financial problems now found themselves dealing with the horror of a terrible accident. Marussia were at the Japanese Grand Prix in October the following year when they learned that De Villota had been found dead in her hotel bedroom in Seville. She had suffered a heart attack, aged just thirty-three.

The threadbare HRT team, underfunded and inexperienced and trying to operate out of a base in Madrid, staggered to the end of 2012 before they folded, while Tony Fernandes ran into legal trouble with the Lotus car company, Colin Chapman's legacy, over the use of the Lotus name. He had to change it to Caterham, the name of the sports car business he owned, but they, like Marussia Manor, had been ushered into a financial fairyland where normal rules didn't apply. At flyaway races, the teams were required to hire equipment from the circuit promoters – but that meant a single coat hanger could cost $50 because the promoters were trying to recoup some of their losses from staging the grand prix. At one race, John Booth told me with a wry smile that it cost so much to hire a forklift that it would be cheaper to buy one and drive it into the river on the Sunday night after the race.

Fernandes, who had appeared in Formula One bubbling with enthusiasm and predictions of huge success, was disenchanted with a sport that supported the biggest and most powerful. At the Monaco Grand Prix of 2014, his team established the record for the longest tenure in Formula One without scoring a point – eighty-three grands prix over almost five seasons – and his nose was rubbed in the mess of the sport's finances when Marussia finally rejoiced on the streets of the principality.

Jules Bianchi had shown promise ever since he had joined the fledgling team. Mechanics, engineers, motorhome staff and the management immediately took to this shy and self-effacing boy from Nice and relished his blossoming talent. He was being groomed in the Ferrari academy and had rare talent as well as being an engaging young man.

In Monaco, a few miles along the Côte d'Azur from his home, the Bianchi talent blazed. He dragged an uncompetitive Marussia around the twisting, narrow streets to finish eighth. A five-second penalty, caused by confusion at the start, relegated him to ninth, but it didn't matter – Marussia had finally achieved what had seemed impossible and scored two points. It justified the previous four years of struggle because the financial rewards would be huge in Marussia terms, worth about £30 million in prize money for the following season. Marussia had finally won in the Formula One casino in Monte Carlo.

Lowdon remembered fondly: 'There were so many false dawns over the years and there we were scoring championship points finally. Manor had raced all over the world in all sorts of formulas, so you never think you would cheer for an eighth-place finish, but we were all ecstatic.'

There were no celebrations, though, because the kit had to be freighted to the next race in Canada and the mechanics and motorhome staff worked into the darkness, not finishing until about 1 a.m. There was no relief from the quest for money, either. Lowdon was trying to snare new investors, and it seemed the timing of the Monaco result was perfect. He arranged for a group of potential sponsors to spend the Canadian Grand Prix weekend with the team. Lowdon got his numbers together and the team were primed to be on their best behaviour to create an impression, but the investors didn't turn up – their plane developed a fault and then air traffic problems meant they wouldn't arrive until minutes before the grand prix. 'We knew when they would land and had a car waiting at the square metre of runway they would stop at. We were so keyed up for the arrival of these money-men who could secure our futures to see this buoyant team. They finally got there, the Canadian Grand Prix started and the cars get to the first chicane where Max [Chilton, Marussia's second driver] and Jules crash into each other. That was both cars out on the spot at the exact moment the investors walked into the paddock. It's never straightforward, is it?'

Whatever trials there were at Marussia, Fernandes had made up his mind about Caterham's future. He stopped appearing at grands prix and instead installed himself in the executive box at Queens Park Rangers, the football club he had bought from Ecclestone and Flavio Briatore. Caterham was haemorrhaging money and he didn't want it to be his.

Four days before the 2014 British Grand Prix, the home race for the Caterham team based just thirty-five miles down the road from Silverstone at Leafield in Oxfordshire – once headquarters of the Arrows team – Fernandes announced he had sold the team to Engavest, a consortium of Swiss and Middle Eastern investors. Who they were and why they wanted Caterham was unclear, but in the background was Colin Kolles, the Romanian dentist turned motor-racing entrepreneur who was managing director of the Midland organisation that bought Jordan in 2005. Kolles had a dour, almost threatening look, and his only concession to high fashion was the occasional flourish of a scarf around his thick neck. In his time at Midland, his biggest achievement appears to have been performing dentistry on Tiago Monteiro before the Turkish Grand Prix of 2005 so that his driver could take part.

Engavest's investors were never seen nor identified and the paper trail led back to the offices of a Swiss lawyer called Stefan Gyseler, based in the tiny town of Baar near Zurich in Switzerland. Fernandes had washed his hands of the team leaving it to Engavest, and by October, the bailiffs had moved into the Leafield factory, taking a test car, wheels and tyres, steering wheels and equipment. Within days, it was over for Caterham, the workforce facing redundancy and only one man left behind, a confused, worried ex-footballer who was hired to clean the factory and somehow found himself in charge.

Constantin Cojucar was the most unlikely boss. The former Steaua Bucharest player had fallen on hard times after retirement and had moved to Britain, apparently with the approval of Kolles, to take a job as a cleaner at Leafield. Then, one day, he says he was packed off to London to sign documents and found himself the sole director in charge of a business he had bought for £1. From Domestos to high finance – or, perhaps, low finance at that price – in a day. When Smith & Williamson, the administrators, came in to clear up the financial mess, they found that a slightly dazed and confused Constantin had been sleeping on a camp bed in the managing director's office, worried that he had been left holding the financial baby, amounting to debts of about £16 million.

Finbarr O'Connell was in charge of the administration. His report to the High Court was damning, because there were implications of chicanery in the sale. Caterham's financial affairs were 'in total disarray', with records out of date and inaccurate. 'Assets had been appropriated by various parties,' the report added. 'We strongly suspect there had been improper activity.'

Constantin tracked me down, sending me a series of incomprehensible texts in broken English, wanting to sell his story to *The Times* because he was so hard up. Constantin fled the country when the storm broke but returned to London to meet me at a bar in Covent Garden. He brought a friend to interpret and was dishevelled and nervous, dressed in a windcheater on a sweltering day in London. His story was that he had no idea what was happening to Caterham or how he suddenly came to be the boss. It was a sad and odd tale, even though it seemed unbelievably naïve to get on a train to London and sign documents in a language you didn't understand for a purpose you didn't ask about. Four years on, O'Connell had sympathy with Constantin's predicament.

'I presume the plan was that he would be controlled by another party. Caterham was divided up into the team, car and intellectual property on the one hand and Constantin Cojucar ended up being responsible for the UK company that owed all the money and had no assets.'

O'Connell had been through the Leafield experience before – as an advisor when the Arrows team went under in 2002. Now he was back again and still mystified by a sport with so much money yet unable to sustain itself. 'As an outsider, I couldn't help feeling that if you wanted the spectacle, you needed a number of teams racing. With the amount of money available, it surely wasn't beyond the wit of man to make sure that teams could stay in the game and have enough to survive on.'

The usual – and easy – way out was to sell the assets and pay creditors, but O'Connell sensed an opportunity to keep Caterham alive if he could convince Formula One and the outside world that the team was still viable, for the bottom line was that forty people had been paid off in July and the jobs of another 230 were at stake. O'Connell wasn't to know, but he was launching his rescue attempt at the most critical and emotional time that the sport had seen in decades.

Both Marussia and Caterham were at the Japanese Grand Prix of 2014 for a race that was part lottery, part debacle after Typhoon Phanfone ripped through Mie Prefecture south of Nagoya. Suzuka's position on the coast facing out into the bay that leads to the Pacific Ocean is on the typhoon highway and October is typhoon season. Heavy rain drenched Suzuka on the Sunday of 5 October, and conditions were dreadful when the race started behind the safety car at 3 p.m. prompt for the benefit of the global television networks. Lewis Hamilton was on pole position, but even he could barely see where he was going in the spray from the safety car, and his pleas to halt the grand prix were heard by Charlie Whiting, the highly experienced race director, who called a halt after just two laps. After an interval of twenty minutes, the race restarted, although there were huge pools of standing water around the circuit. The late start, the delays and the slow speeds meant that the race was being dragged inexorably towards dusk. With seven laps to go, the skies were darkening when Adrian Sutil's Sauber veered off near the Dunlop Curve. Yellow warning flags were waved as a mobile crane came onto the circuit to lift his car clear. At that moment, Bianchi's Marussia arrived at the same corner and careered straight into the rear of the crane. His injuries were devastating. Lowdon and his Marussia team knew he was in trouble.

'I realised I couldn't see the car and if he had come off at the same place as Sutil it wasn't going to be good. There was no voice traffic of any sort, so we knew this was no straightforward crash where the driver hopped out and we recovered the car.'

The medical crew headed by Dr Ian Roberts, who took over from Professor Sid Watkins after his retirement, transferred Bianchi to the medical centre where Lowdon and the team waited, while the race was abandoned. Hamilton had displayed his extraordinary prowess in the rain with his victory, but that had become a side issue as the Formula One family held its collective breath to hear the fate of their young colleague. Because of the appalling conditions, Bianchi was taken by road to the nearest major trauma hospital twenty-five minutes away in Yokkaichi instead of by helicopter, with Lowdon and Booth following by car. 'We didn't know for a while that it was a head injury, but by the time we got to the hospital we started to understand what was happening. It was a horrible drive to the hospital. The weather was poor, we were extremely worried and I remember talking to Bernie, who was in London, on the way to the hospital.'

Formula One packed its bags and its vast freight trucks in gloomy silence, preparing to move on. The next grand prix, in Russia, was just a week away, and the sport had to pick itself up to be ready. It was also the inaugural Russian Grand Prix, a personal project of Vladimir Putin's, and the Marussia team was the nation's only representative. Now the Marussia squad of men and women would have to find the psychological resources to perform, while knowing their popular young driver was still in Japan in a coma.

Ecclestone remained in constant touch, offering advice and consolation, and his strength was invaluable to Lowdon and Booth as they waited at the bedside for Bianchi's parents, Philippe and Christine, to arrive from France. Ecclestone could relate to their anxieties, having suffered the loss of his close friends Jochen Rindt and Stuart Lewis-Evans, but did his best to buoy spirits as Formula One prayed that Bianchi would pull through.

'I was in constant contact with Bernie throughout, almost daily, keeping him informed and he was smoothing paths where he could,' Lowdon says. 'From what I have been told, Bernie had a very close relationship with Rindt and I have always wondered how much that affected him. There must be an indelible mark on him after that, but I guess he is the sort who would never talk about it. We had no idea of what the outcome was going to be with Jules. It must have been horrendous for his family to get on that plane and travel halfway around the world unsure what was happening to their son. I can't imagine what it would be like.'

Booth stayed in Japan, while Lowdon headed to Sochi to face the next huge hurdle. In all the pandemonium in Japan, it had been easy to forget that the Marussia team was close to extinction. After the trauma of Bianchi's accident and with his car company – trailed optimistically as a rival for Ferrari and Aston Martin – going nowhere, Andrei Cheglakov was closing his chequebook. Lowdon now had a driver in a coma in Japan, a shattered team, and his major shareholder preparing to quit at his home grand prix in Russia.

'We were very aware of how the team was feeling,' Lowdon says. 'Some of the people you think are hardest, who might step forward in a bar brawl, are the ones who need the most support. Sochi was hard – we have Jules to worry about, this is the first Russian Grand Prix and our owner is Russian and things were going badly financially. On top of all that, we still had to recognise that Formula One has to go on. We quickly made the decision that the right thing to do was to enter one car, yet prepare the second car properly, just as we would if Jules had been ready to jump into it. We wanted the mechanics to have something to focus on and something with meaning. We also wanted to send a clear message to Jules and his family that the team were behind him.'

Next door at Caterham, the new ownership had turned from dire to critical as the money ran out and the bailiffs moved in. Neither they nor Marussia would be at the next race in Austin for the US Grand Prix. All of Formula One's financial problems had been crystallised by the fortunes of the sport's two smallest teams, and emotions heightened by Bianchi's accident.

Bob Fernley, Mallya's deputy at Force India, had been warning for months that Formula One's smallest teams were on the brink, furious that CVC's investors were taking hundreds of millions of pounds out of the sport, while their plan for a flotation had led to a payments system that meant the sport was unsustainable for all but the quartet of leading teams taking 60 per cent of the prize pot. CVC were furious with Fernley's very public criticism, countering his accusation that they had 'raped' the sport by pointing out that the teams' prize money had grown hugely under their watch and were collectively better off than ever. But, for Fernley and the smallest teams, it was a vicious circle – no money meant no success meant fewer sponsors paying less.

Before the US Grand Prix, Ecclestone called me into his

private suite at the Circuit of the Americas. His smile was half-hearted, the customary left hand held out in greeting as though waiting for a kiss of the papal ring. He was pale, anxious and his honesty was searing. 'Frankly, I know what's wrong but don't know how to fix it,' he said. In a sentence, Ecclestone summed up a decade in which he had become an employee of CVC, turning from ringmaster and impresario of the Formula One show into the human cash machine, devoting himself to reaping millions for his shareholders. He had been remarkably successful for CVC, but at what cost to the sport? He knew the damage that the financial structure was doing to the small teams, and he was, like them, a racer at heart, used to overcoming the odds and challenging the system, but the old days when he could dispense the odd million here or there – his 'rain cheques' – to keep teams running were over and he was powerless to help. He was chief executive, but that was a job and not a reign, and CVC decided the priorities, not him. He was also trapped by the intransigence of the four big teams taking the lion's share of the pot because they sure as hell were not giving up their money. It was deadlock.

An angry Vijay Mallya demanded $20 million each for the four smallest teams – Lotus (which had been Renault), Sauber, Manor and Force India. 'Bernie wanted to take it out of the other teams because CVC wouldn't put their hands in their pockets. It was terribly unfair,' Mallya said.

Almost 5,000 miles from Austin, Finbarr O'Connell was launching his rescue mission for Caterham. His reasoning was sound: he was impressed by the dedication of the team and the power of Formula One to motivate. He believed that the 240 staff still there deserved a chance, and he planned to put the team back in the shop window at the final grand prix of the season at Abu Dhabi. There could be no more glittering showcase than the Yas Marina circuit, where the smell of money overpowered the ozone from the warm, blue waters of the Gulf. Just like Monaco, the powerbrokers met here, business people from Australia in the East to Los Angeles in the West. They would see a Caterham team and their cars in that familiar metallic green livery still in business.

Ecclestone was appalled when he discovered that O'Connell planned to ask fans to contribute by paying into a crowd-funding scheme. Holding out a begging bowl was definitely not Formula One, but it worked and the money rolled in. O'Connell rounded up the race team and paid them each £2,000 in expenses to get them there. The money was almost irrelevant as they were so excited to be back in the Formula One family. O'Connell also learned something about that family: although Ecclestone was dubious about the method, he pulled every string to help out. Caterham's kit was stranded in Austin, but Ecclestone had it all shipped to Abu Dhabi, and he arranged dispensations with the Total oil company for fuel, and free tyres from Pirelli. O'Connell was amazed when other teams – rivals – also rallied round and provided whatever kit and support was needed as the Caterham mechanics tried to sort themselves out into a race team once again.

O'Connell was swept away in the moment. An accountant used to poring over figures on paper, he was temporarily freed from the confines of the office and he could feel the thrill of the build-up to a grand prix and understand why entrepreneurs would gamble everything to be a part of this extraordinary show. By the time I met him in the Caterham motorhome, he was dressed to the nines in a team shirt, and he was, I suppose, for that weekend the team principal, just like Frank Williams or Toto Wolff.

O'Connell, who had never been to a race before, understood the financial inequity of Formula One easily enough, and how it translated to the track. When I asked if he would have any advice for his drivers, he said simply: 'Overtake and win.' I suspect his tongue was in his cheek and he was indulging in a little Irish irony, but the reality was simpler and more brutal. Caterham took part in their final grand prix, there was no buyer, the workforce was made redundant and the assets at Leafield sold off. The Caterham story was over.

'At the bottom end of the grid, everything is focused on cash flow. Where is the cash coming from because a team needs money just to get to the next race?' O'Connell says when we next meet up in the Smith & Williamson headquarters in the heart of the City. 'Mercedes spend a phenomenal amount, but you could spend a tenth of that and still do well and have a sport. The world just wants a spectacle. The sad thing is that unless there is a massive pile-up, a tenth or eleventh car is never going to be at the front because the whole sport is so orchestrated, controlled and engineered in every sense so that a minnow with lots of guts and spunk still can't have a chance of winning.'

Lowdon barely had time to worry about the demise of Caterham, although he desperately believed that Formula One needed entrepreneurs like Fernandes rather than be ruled by corporations with 'no skin in the game', as he put it. Although Marussia never made it to the US Grand Prix, Lowdon flew to Austin under his own steam, attempting to round up support to get Marussia, now Manor again, back into Formula One for 2015 and release the frustrating blockage to the £30 million owed for that points finish in Monaco – the points won by Jules Bianchi.

The trap is that word quickly gets around suppliers that a team is in trouble. Spooked that they will lose out, they demand their money, the banks squeeze the business and the structure collapses. In Manor's case, the best way forward, according to Lowdon, was to put the team into administration to restructure and cling on to the entry into Formula One for the 2015 season. Not that there would be support in the paddock – if Manor went down, so did the £30 million, which would then be split among the remaining teams, which is a crucial reason why so few rallied to their cause. 'The biggest threat was the team being wound up and we would have lost the prize money, our biggest asset. But here we were: a driver lying in hospital, a bunch of people who would like us to go under for the simple reason that they knew where the money would go and employees – brilliant people – who needed to know what was happening. Some teams had done budgets with and without us because it involved a few million quid either way.

'The frustration was overwhelming because I could see this opportunity wouldn't come around again. We made that business work on $10 million worth of prize money and now we have between $50 million and $60 million and not just for one year but two or three. With other guaranteed income like tax rebates and support from the creditors, then the team could go on and with a significantly better financial structure than ever.'

The FIA weren't giving any leeway, and they sent their invoice for $500,000 for the 2015 entry fee. The administrator didn't want to pay, so Lowdon paid half and the administrator paid the rest.

The White Knight on the horizon was an Irish entrepreneur, Stephen Fitzpatrick, who founded the Ovo energy business. From the start, he appeared to enjoy the energy in the paddock with its champagne lifestyle and revolving door of celebrities, but he was his own man and Lowdon and Booth, the founders who had lived and breathed their team through the toughest of times, both had to resign, while rumours flew that the now renamed Manor Racing was on the market for £85 million. Unfortunately, there were no takers and, at the end of 2016, the doors finally closed. The adventure that started as a dream in 2010 and soared on the Monte Carlo waterfront had come to a sad conclusion.

Virgin/Marussia/Manor punched briefly above their weight and the team of 220 people endeared themselves to the paddock for their struggle against the odds and the extraordinary climax – Bianchi's first points and then his sad death in hospital in his home city of Nice in July 2015, the first death of a driver in Formula One since Ayrton Senna a decade before.

'Key people in our team all went on to fantastic things at Mercedes and Ferrari and other teams, yet they still talk about those years with Manor,' Lowdon told me. 'Every year we would put everyone's name on the chassis and one year we were the most reliable team in the paddock. That was a period when several teams had problems with complicated hydraulics and the big teams would have an entire hydraulics department with half a dozen and more people, plus all the computer backup and everything that went with it. We had a department of one and he was the most reliable guy in F1. We didn't have anyone else, just him. It wasn't a fair fight, was it?'

17

LA BELLA FIGURA

LUCA Cordero di Montezemolo doesn't want to talk high-speed cars – he wants to talk high-speed trains. Ejected from Ferrari, to which he had devoted almost three decades of his life, Montezemolo concentrated on the train business. It was a risky venture, pitting his Italo trains against the state-controlled Trenitalia service, but a couple of days before I arrived in Rome for our meeting, he sold Italo for £2.2 billion.

Max Mosley, in one of his more colourful insults against the man who would eventually unseat him from power, once dismissed Montezemolo as a *bella figura*. It translates literally as 'beautiful figure', and Italians would take it as a compliment that the Ferrari boss made 'a good impression', as they would have it. But Mosley's sarcastic implication was that he was all style and no substance – or, as they might say in the north of England, fur coat and no knickers.

How wrong can a man be? Mosley underestimated Montezemolo, who used his charisma and powerful presence to round up warring Formula One team owners to unite against the FIA president, and he underestimated just how much Ferrari owes this extraordinary businessman. Not that you would know it today: Montezemolo's name has almost been expunged from Ferrari's history, and there is little sign of his once overwhelming presence in the Maranello factory. He was not even invited to the company's seventieth anniversary celebrations in 2017, despite his incredible role in Ferrari's survival and transformation.

I arrive at Montezemolo's three-storey palazzo in Rome on a freezing, wet day. The quiet street is in one of Rome's most exclusive quarters, a short walk from the Villa Borghese gardens, the 400-year-old park created by Cardinal Scipione Borghese, a nephew of Pope Paul V. There are expensive cars everywhere, but the homes are discreet and favoured by diplomats and businessmen. There are steps up to the double front door and I can see a dark-coloured Range Rover parked in the yard, Montezemolo's day-to-day transport. There is no family Ferrari these days, just the silver, custom-made Barchetta 360 given to him by Fiat's Gianni Agnelli, who was best man at his wedding. Montezemolo has barely driven it, and it stood for a long time in the factory, carefully tended by mechanics who watch over Ferrari's historic collection. He never seemed keen on open-top motoring anyway, moaning that 'it's got such a small windscreen, you need goggles and a helmet to drive it'.

The entrance hall is straight from the pages of *Vogue*, with white walls and tasteful art. From there I am ushered into the boardroom, where there is a long, polished wood table leading down to tall windows that look out onto the small garden. On the wall facing me is a huge mural of a desert road stretching to a distant horizon, while underneath the picture there is a line of perhaps two dozen miniature armchairs. I later learn that the chairs are tiny models from the high-end furniture manufacturer in which Montezemolo had an interest, which supplies the seats for his trains as well as the superb interior leather for Ferrari's road cars.

Montezemolo is never lost for words, and he has a lot to tell me about the sale of the train business he started with three of Italy's best-known businessmen in 2006. It was a long haul, bringing in the money, convincing the markets and then getting SNCF, the French railway operator, to take a stake and bring their know-how to the operation. He talks at machine-gun speed, his hand pointing east, west, north and south, to emphasise the destinations you can reach, from Rome to Milan or Pisa in these luxurious high-speed trains, with free Wi-Fi and all the trimmings of executive comfort – like those leather seats – even when you have not paid for the posh club class cabins. His take from the sale, according to friends, is somewhere around £215 million, so little wonder that on this day he is elated.

The Italo trains were his brainchild, but the photographs in his private office are of his passion, of historic Ferraris and memories of grands prix – as well as a picture of his 'dream team' that won six consecutive Formula One constructors' titles:

there they are at the 2000 Malaysian Grand Prix, celebrating the first of Michael Schumacher's run of five world championships in 2000, the first in twenty-one years for Ferrari – Montezemolo has his arms around Jean Todt, his sporting director, and the drivers Rubens Barrichello and Schumacher.

Being hounded out of Ferrari was like being evicted from his own home – and it still hurts badly, even though Montezemolo has a huge portfolio of business interests, including a private equity company. He has to keep busy because there are no calls from Ferrari these days, no invitations to a grand prix or a car launch. 'I have more contact with McLaren than Ferrari these days,' he says sadly. 'Everyone who was at the seventieth anniversary ceremonies was asking, "Where is Luca?" They didn't understand. I was six years as a team manager and twenty-three as president – almost thirty years, nearly half the life of the company.'

By the time Montezemolo left in 2014, production in the road car division had grown to more than 7,500 cars a year, and Ferrari drivers – Schumacher with five and Kimi Räikkönen in 2007 – had won six world championships in a decade, while Fernando Alonso had missed out on two more at the final race of the season. Maranello, once a motley collection of sheds, had become one of the most futuristic factories in the world, lauded from one side of the globe to the other. From a business on the brink of failure and with a Formula One team that had been humbled by the British *garagistes*, Ferrari was once again proud.

Montezemolo looked much younger than his seventy years, wearing a grey tweed jacket and dark grey trousers, woollen red tie and check shirt. There is the slightly foppish handkerchief tucked into the jacket pocket, and I forget to ask the brand of aftershave but I am betting on Acqua di Parma, his favourite fragrance; in fact, he liked it so much he bought the company – and sold it for a substantial profit. He still has the long, swept-back hair, only now starting to turn grey, which he flicks every now and again. His battle with Sergio Marchionne, the hard-nosed chief executive of the Fiat Chrysler group, Ferrari's owners, who took control of the Ferrari steering wheel for himself, seemed at one time to have wearied him, and he was obviously exasperated by a man who didn't share his vision for a brand that went to his core.

If there is an omission from his life, it is that he never entered politics, despite entreaties for him to run as president – yet you wonder how, given his extraordinary reach into Italian society. Montezemolo is almost a brand in himself and there is probably no businessman anywhere in the world who is so revered and loved across his nation, from housewives to an astronaut, as it happens. When Paolo Nespoli, the lone Italian astronaut on the International Space Station, was given one phone call, he called the president of Ferrari. As long as Nespoli wasn't paying the phone bill, it wouldn't be a problem, for Montezemolo is never short of conversation.

Montezemolo talks fluently with an easy charm that makes you feel you have been his best friend for years. He is not physically imposing, but rooms stop when he enters. He is conspiratorial and gossipy and smiles easily, even when we fell out during his years at the helm of Ferrari. He called me 'the polemical one', after I took him and his team to task for their habit of bending the rules and occasionally thumbing their noses at the spirit of the sport – like ordering Rubens Barrichello to move aside to allow Michael Schumacher to win the 2002 Austrian Grand Prix to howls of derision from spectators.

His ability to make his audience relax and become drawn in is one of his most potent weapons, which is why Gianni Agnelli, the godfather of Italian industry, and Enzo Ferrari found that confident young student so beguiling all those years ago. John Hogan, the man who took the Marlboro brand to Ferrari – still worth around $160 million a year to the Scuderia – discovered one of Montezemolo's tricks. 'We were discussing a deal and he was running out of time so we continued talking in his car. It turned out he was on his way to a big reception and he decided I was going with him. I really didn't want to go because I didn't know anyone and this was a high-powered event. Before we went in, I told Luca: "Look, I am really not comfortable with this." He just turned to me and said: "John. It will be fine. Just have a big smile. Smile."'

The smile masks the steel, though. One of Ferrari's senior Formula One engineers recalls a meeting when results were going badly. 'Luca was furious and banging the table so hard he drew blood. Believe me, we were straight to work after that,' he told me.

Montezemolo needed steel to carry Ferrari in the early days when he was only in his twenties and straight out of university, dealing with the irascible and unforgiving Enzo Ferrari and a bunch of disparate characters in Formula One, who were nobody's fools and always wary of intruders into their world.

After two world championships with Niki Lauda by 1977, Montezemolo was anxious to leave the claustrophobic world of Formula One, with its petty spats and internal wrangling. He moved to Switzerland to take over as managing director of Cinzano, the drinks business, and then launched Italy's first foray into the America's Cup. It was racing cars on water, effectively, and the landscape of organisation, discipline and getting the best people was familiar territory. The boat, named *Azzurra*, finished third and was celebrated in Italy – and, apparently, by hundreds of new parents, as Azzurra suddenly became one of the nation's favourite baby names.

His biggest challenge was ahead. In 1985, he was handed the task of running Italia '90, Italy's football World Cup. This was Italy's highest-profile encounter with the rest of the world since the Rome Olympics of 1960, and the nation was relying on Montezemolo to ease its long-term economic woes and lack of self-confidence with a spectacular tournament. It was about teamwork again, as Montezemolo set about pulling together warring politicians, divided cities and regions, and overcoming a national habit of leaving everything until the last minute. The stakes were high, for a disastrous World Cup would have embarrassed the nation, but a successful tournament would have all kinds of desirable effects on the psyche of the country and its economy. To put it into context, economists calculated that Italy's victory in the 2006 World Cup grew the gross domestic product of the country by 1 per cent – equivalent to more than £14 billion.

For Montezemolo, this was Ferrari writ large, a chaotic collection of personalities to be moulded, shaped, persuaded, cajoled and threatened. As at Ferrari, Montezemolo needed the best brains behind him, so he raided the corporate offices of some of Italy's biggest companies for talent, got eight major Italian businesses to come up with sponsorship, and mounted a huge campaign to license Italia '90 merchandise. Somehow, he also managed to sell tickets to games even before anyone knew who was playing and the tournament was a huge success.

Gianni Agnelli now wanted his protégé to wave his magic wand at the family football club, based in the city of Turin, where Fiat's headquarters were also located. This was not just any football club, but Juventus, the grand old lady of Italian soccer. The Agnellis had taken control of Juve, as it is popularly known, in 1923, and the club had won every honour there was to win, including the European Cup in the 1984–5 season. This was to be a rare failure for Montezemolo, who found the football world beyond his comprehension and, on his watch, there was no Juventus in European competitions for the first time in twenty-eight years. Asked by Italian interviewers if there was one year of his life he would erase, he replied immediately: 'It would be that year at Juve.'

Juventus's loss was Ferrari's gain. Three years after Enzo Ferrari's death in 1988, the Scuderia was drifting hopelessly, and it was time for the genius of Luca Cordero di Montezemolo.

I remind him that the first time we met was in 1993, more than a year after he had been brought back to Maranello at the request of Agnelli, the head of the Fiat family business, which had taken control after the death of Enzo. Ferrari was at rock bottom, still in mourning for the founder, and shrouded by an atmosphere of deepest gloom. The Maranello factory might have been legendary, but it was ramshackle and dowdy; work practices were hopelessly out of date, the Formula One team was rapidly becoming a laughing stock, and the road cars that had once been the most desirable in the world were rubbish – even Montezemolo thought so. Before he rejoined the company, he bought a Ferrari 348, and his verdict was short and to the point: 'It was not a Ferrari. The gearbox could have come from a truck. The road car business was being influenced by Fiat managers who wanted to put little components from Fiat cars into the Ferraris. Terrible. For the first time in history, we were forced to tell people to stay at home because we couldn't sell any cars. We sold only 2,000 cars in that first year. Our road cars were full of old technology – and then there was the factory. I was astonished when I came back to find it was 90 per cent the same as when I left it years before. Ralph Lauren [the American clothing designer] came to lunch at Maranello and I could tell he was disappointed. He told me that Ferrari was just an illusion and he expected more high-tech. That was the final straw.'

There was more: 'The Formula One team was a mess. We had not won a championship since Jody Scheckter in 1979. I arrived in December, and I asked who was designing the Formula One car and no one seemed to know. We had people coming from Fiat who knew zero about Formula One cars.'

Ferrari had come close to a world championship in 1990, after offering Alain Prost a way out of his internecine battle with Ayrton Senna at McLaren. The Frenchman pushed Senna hard and won five grands prix to finish second in the world championship, but it had been a turbulent year, typical of the internal warfare that plagued the Scuderia throughout its history. Prost had been hired as world champion to become number one alongside Nigel Mansell, but the Englishman took pride that he was the last driver to be personally selected by Enzo and had built up the idea that he was destined to lead the team back to glory. Prost had other ideas. The atmosphere turned ugly at the British Grand Prix: Mansell couldn't understand why his car was handling so differently from the way it had at the previous race in France, where he had taken pole position in the V12-powered Ferrari. In his autobiography, Mansell described how he discovered that Prost had decided that he wanted Mansell's car and the mechanics had swapped the chassis without telling him. Mansell was furious.

At the end of the season he moved to Williams Renault, where he would take his revenge and leave Prost to struggle.

Prost, then a three-times world champion, known as 'The Professor' for his calm, intelligent and smooth style of driving, did not hold back in his criticism of a team saddled with outdated V12 engines in 1991, when his main rivals were in cars powered by the lighter and more powerful V10s. After the Japanese Grand Prix, the penultimate race of the season, Prost chuntered: 'I've underlined the defects of the Ferrari throughout the season, but no one has listened to a word.'

Prost was sacked before the final race of the season and paid off so that he couldn't race for any other team. As the hapless Scuderia returned to Maranello, Montezemolo was walking into a team and a business at the lowest ebb.

That first full year back in charge was tough on the track. Williams dominated the 1992 season with Nigel Mansell, while Ferrari suffered twenty retirements with their two cars driven by Jean Alesi and Ivan Capelli, who was replaced for two races by Nicola Larini, not that it mattered. The only team that had been present in every season from 1950 could not buy a win after Prost's 1990 title challenge and there was almost no area in which Ferrari could claim to lead.

Traditionally strong on engines and mechanical components, Ferrari turned out to be largely clueless when it came to the advanced electronics and clever active suspension systems – a leap forward in ride and handling – that the

British teams were pioneering. 'We couldn't even complete a single lap with intelligent suspension,' Montezemolo says. 'When I was congratulated on opposing electronic driver aids, to be honest it was because Ferrari didn't have any.'

Ferrari was trapped in a time warp, in which a Formula One team and road car business looked back at the great days of Enzo and not forward to competing in the real world. Montezemolo knew he had to grab the business by the scruff of the neck and drag it into the future.

Montezemolo's first priority was to rebuild the ailing car business, and he started unconventionally, forcing his senior design team in the road car division to think beyond the confines of their dingy factory. He issued them all with subscriptions to glossy fashion magazines, like *Vogue* and *Vanity Fair*, so that they could absorb trends in materials and colours. It was a slow and time-consuming process, which meant he had little time for a Formula One team that was just as stagnant and lacking in imagination.

A major problem was Ferrari's location in Maranello, a small, unprepossessing town only notable for the symbol of the Prancing Horse that can be seen everywhere. Plonked in the Emilia-Romagna region, it sits squarely in the middle of northern Italy, just south of Modena, Enzo Ferrari's birthplace. But the Silicon Valley of motorsport was a thousand miles northeast in England, in the triangle bounded by McLaren in Woking, Surrey, Williams in Oxfordshire and what became Force India at Silverstone in Northamptonshire.

The most talented engineers lived and worked there and moved seamlessly between junior teams and Formula One.

'Even the big newspapers were saying it was impossible to do everything in Italy because there were not the people or the technical capabilities. I had to find a way and I needed someone who could help me to manage because I was busy trying to develop new road cars,' Montezemolo told me. 'I had to find a strategic injection of good people – aerodynamicists, engineers and suppliers.'

Formula One's ringmaster had an idea. Bernie Ecclestone had come across a Frenchman running the Peugeot World Rally and Le Mans teams with great success. Jean Todt was not much taller than Ecclestone, nowhere near as bustling and fun, but just as meticulous and wedded to detail.

'Bernie came to me and asked if he could find someone to help us,' Montezemolo remembers. 'And then he called me to tell me he had found this guy called Jean Todt. What I liked was that Todt was loyal for a long time to Peugeot. So, I gathered some information about him and talked it through with Bernie.'

Todt is about a year older than Montezemolo, born in 1946 in the small town of Pierrefort in the picturesque Auvergne region in the south of France, the son of a Jewish doctor, who fled Poland aged just seventeen at the start of the Second World War. Todt had a passion for cars and sometimes drove the family Mini in amateur rallies. His future, though, was as a co-driver, and between 1966 and 1981, he accompanied some of the world's finest rally champions, including Hannu Mikkola, Ove Andersson and Timo Mäkinen. Todt's reputation was burnished as a team manager when his Peugeot squads won four World Rally championships, four Paris-Dakar rallies and twice at the Le Mans 24 Hours Endurance Race. He might not have been involved in Formula One, but, like Montezemolo, he understood how to organise and inspire.

Their first meeting was inauspicious, thanks to one detail that the candidate for the job hadn't thought through. It was, if you like, an interview blunder, when he turned up at Montezemolo's home driving not a Ferrari, or even a Fiat, but a Mercedes. 'I invited Todt to my home outside Bologna and my son came running to me shouting, "Hey, Papa, this guy has come to see you driving a Mercedes." I grew up with Enzo Ferrari and had respect for the brand and my first impression of Todt was *that* Mercedes.'

It was a slow start after Todt joined Ferrari as general manager of the Racing Division in July 1993. Montezemolo found himself circling his curious new employee, who seemed hobbled by shyness, speaking with a slight lisp and rarely looking people in the eye, as well as gnawing at his fingernails until they were worn and bleeding. Todt likes mental arithmetic and puzzles, but admits to 'an anxious character'. But Montezemolo liked his meticulous approach. 'I delegated more and more to him month after month. He was a good organiser, a hard worker and, like me, had great attention to detail.'

But many people in Italy didn't like the idea of a Frenchman running the Scuderia, particularly when results were disappointing, with only a single victory in each of the 1994 and 1995 seasons. 'The press and the people were very against Todt because he was a foreigner as a Frenchman and he didn't come from a Formula One background,' Montezemolo says. 'We faced very difficult moments, from 1992 to 1997, when we had to explain to the Italian fans that they should be patient.'

There was still a missing link, the key to unlock whatever potential there was at Maranello. Meanwhile, Bernie Ecclestone needed box office again. He had lost his most precious star when Ayrton Senna was killed during the 1994 San Marino Grand Prix, but was surprised to discover the worldwide viewing figures had risen dramatically in the wake of the tragedy. His colourful and dangerous circus had suddenly become regulation Sunday afternoon viewing across the world again. Ecclestone engineered the brief return of Nigel Mansell to the Williams team alongside Damon Hill, but he needed Ferrari to break up the British domination of Formula One, and to revive the tarnished legend of the Prancing Horse. He had admired and respected Enzo Ferrari and had a soft spot for the new man trying desperately to turn around the Scuderia for a second time – and Ecclestone had an idea about how to achieve his objective.

Ecclestone had levered Michael Schumacher out of Jordan and into Benetton in 1991, when he recognised just how good the German was, and now he would give his blessing to Ferrari to snatch him away from Benetton. The German was on the radar at Maranello, and Montezemolo had decided he would break the bank if he had to. The result was a $60 million contract over two years, but Montezemolo wanted more – he wanted the whole shooting match from Schumacher's title-winning Benetton team: Rory Byrne, the chief designer who had left F1 to set up a scuba-diving school in Thailand, and Ross Brawn, who masterminded Benetton's leap from plucky also-rans, winning only seven grands prix in six seasons, to world champions. Within a year, Montezemolo had secured a clean sweep of a technical team that would become legendary in the history of Formula One, if depressing for the teams who had to watch the rise of Montezemolo's Ferrari. Montezemolo was betting the Maranello farm on this crew of men from France, England, South Africa and Germany. The salaries were high and so were the stakes – a total invest-ment of around $2 billion in people and facilities to win a world championship and bring Ferrari back to life.

Like Lauda during Montezemolo's first spell in charge at the Scuderia, Schumacher was the lynchpin. Montezemolo formed a close bond with his driver, a fearless and gifted character of extraordinary focus and discipline. Schumacher took fitness to new levels and, with Todt, developed a tightly knit community of engineers and mechanics. Each Christmas, the team members received a gift from their fabulously wealthy driver and he spent time with them, chatting and getting to know their families. The stiff-jawed German with his clipped English and apparent inability to see a joke was actually a reserved, intelligent and warm young man in private, and he was pioneering a new way of leading a Formula One team from the front. 'Michael was a team driver – when we won it was together, when we lost it was together,' Montezemolo says.

But Schumacher's determination could spill over into brutality, as the Ferrari president found out at the final grand prix of 1997. The championship went to the wire at Jerez, Spain, in the European Grand Prix, where Jacques Villeneuve and Schumacher battled for the victory. Schumacher led but his Ferrari developed a fault and, as Villeneuve attempted to pass, Schumacher turned his car into the Williams. It was scandalous and stupid – and Schumacher knew it. Villeneuve went on to win the world championship, but Schumacher was in despair, knowing he had ignited a furore that would end in ignominy and eventually his exclusion from the world championship.

Montezemolo had followed Enzo's lead by not attending races in person, fearing that the attendance of the president would be a distraction. His annual appearance on home turf at Monza for the Italian Grand Prix sparked a ruck of journalists, camera crews and autograph hunters crowding around the Ferrari motorhome. Montezemolo would move through the throng like a pope blessing his flock, but he would always be a distraction for a team trying to get on with the complex business of racing.

This time, he watched events in Jerez on television with mounting horror. He knew what Schumacher might be going through, and ordered his private plane to fly immediately from Bologna to Spain where a car was waiting to take him to the track. 'I used to go to races to protect the team when we weren't very good and I handed over power to Todt because I didn't want to get in the way. But I had to go to Michael. He was destroyed and I had to talk to him to tell him there would be other chances.'

There were, but 1997 was the first of that bizarre series of near misses that populated Montezemolo's reign. In 1998, Schumacher hounded McLaren's Mika Häkkinen to the final race in Japan, where a stall at the start and puncture finished his chances. In 1999, Eddie Irvine, signed as backup man for Schumacher, who had crashed and broken his leg at Silverstone, was on the brink of unlikely glory. Irvine went to the final grand prix in Japan relying on Schumacher to help him beat Häkkinen, perhaps incapable of forging his own destiny. 'Can you imagine Eddie, a mid-level driver, as a world champion?' Montezemolo mused. Clearly, no one else believed he was good enough, especially inside Ferrari. Irvine failed, but the silver lining was that Ferrari was the world championship constructor for the first time since 1983.

However, Montezemolo learned that Schumacher and Todt had grown close and viewed Ferrari as their team in an echo of the Old Man's suspicion and resentment of Montezemolo's first reign at the Scuderia. Almost three months after Schumacher broke his leg, Montezemolo wondered why his star driver hadn't returned to work. He rang Schumacher at his home in Switzerland to see how he was. Gina-Maria, Schumacher's daughter, answered the phone and said Daddy couldn't speak because he was outside playing football with her brother Mick. What followed was a blast from a hairdryer that would have made Sir Alex Ferguson proud: if Schumacher could play football, he could drive his Ferrari. Schumacher was back in the car for the Malaysian Grand Prix, where he set a qualifying time almost a second faster than Irvine, as if to underline the Ulsterman's inferiority. Irvine went to the final race of the season in Japan with the world championship within his grasp, four points ahead of Mika Häkkinen, but that wasn't in the script for Schumacher and Todt: Schumacher was supposed to be the first world champion in two decades, not the 'mid-level driver' signed as number two to the best of his generation. As it was, Häkkinen won the race and the title with Schumacher second – 90 seconds ahead of Irvine. It was the Irishman's final race for the Scuderia.

The following year was the moment of truth for Schumacher, Todt and Montezemolo, who had sunk everything into ending twenty-one years of hurt since Jody Scheckter had been crowned Ferrari's last world champion.

The 2000 Italian Grand Prix was a scene of celebration – and terrible tension; Monza was the first of a sequence of races that Schumacher had to win if there was to be any hope.

Under the trees in the royal park where the Monza track is situated, Ferrari erected a huge marquee for a dinner to celebrate the team's fifty-year participation in Formula One. It was a hollow anniversary given that the Scuderia had so little to celebrate – the team was a legend, it was beautiful, it was popular, but it had no champion. Montezemolo was desperate to win at last, desperate to justify his huge spending on Schumacher and his dream team and, more important, desperate to prove to the Italian nation that Ferrari was still their Scuderia.

Schumacher was a bundle of nerves, his thin face strained and pale. He found it impossible to smile, too difficult to laugh at the jokes. He sat quietly throughout the dinner, looking as though it was more wake than celebration. He left early and headed through the thousands of fans who had crowded around the marquee, waving their scarves and dressed in red, to contemplate what was ahead. On Saturday, he conquered his nerves to take pole position; on Sunday, he blasted away from the start and never relinquished his lead. It was his forty-first victory, equalling the record of Ayrton Senna, who had crashed in front of him six years earlier and died. When he was told he had equalled Senna's record, it suddenly became clear what a burden the weight of expectation had been since he'd joined Ferrari in 1996. At the official press conference, Schumacher – the hardest man in Formula One, the square-jawed German who seemed totally without sentiment – broke down in tears.

He left Monza two points behind Häkkinen, but focused as never before. He could feel the world championship within his grasp and smell the glory of becoming a champion in Ferrari red. Schumacher won the next three grands prix to be crowned world champion. It was just the start, for Montezemolo had once again taken Ferrari back to its place at the top of Formula One with Jean Todt as the architect. Schumacher won five titles on the run and, Felipe Massa would lose the title in the dying seconds of the final race in 2008, while Fernando Alonso was second in the 2010, 2012 and 2013 championships.

'From 1997, we won or lost the championship in the dying moments until 2012, and then Alonso is second again a year later. That was a fantastic performance,' Montezemolo says. 'To lose at the last race hurts but it was against different teams – McLaren, Williams, Red Bull and Renault. We have been in battle with all of the best for that long period. I am proud of that achievement. Todt proved them all wrong. Formula One is a long game that takes two or three or four seasons. Todt was with us for twelve years, Michael ten years. Teamwork and team spirit are in my blood and we had that.'

Schumacher was Ferrari's longest-serving and most successful driver, but it could not save him from being ruth-lessly culled when Montezemolo signalled the end of his era. Ferrari commanded the 2004 season, winning fifteen of the eighteen grands prix, with twelve victories for Schumacher. It was the most dominant performance anyone could remember since Jim Clark in his Lotus in 1963, but then came Fernando Alonso the following year, who won the championship with Renault from Kimi Räikkönen's McLaren; bizarrely, Schumacher won only a single grand prix just a year after having been so successful. Suddenly, there were questions about a thirty-six-year-old doing battle with these young guns, and the word 'retirement' leapt into the headlines.

Montezemolo – and Schumacher – had spotted his replacement years before at a private test at Mugello. Sauber, who used Ferrari engines, had a car there that was performing impressively. 'I remember Michael coming into the pits and asking who the driver was in the Sauber,' Montezemolo says. It was Kimi Räikkönen.

Before the start of the 2006 season, I took a call from Sabine Kehm, Michael Schumacher's public relations consultant, who asked if I wanted to talk to the most sought-after Formula One driver. Schumacher was at the first test of the new season, those days under cold skies when the drivers are rendered half-dizzy, driving around in endless circles so that engineers can hone their machines for the new season. Schumacher had become almost out of reach for any journalist, save for his scheduled official appearances, because the demands on him and his time were greater than on any driver in history.

When I arrived, Schumacher's car had broken down and he was killing time while he waited to go out again. Unlike most drivers (such as Lewis Hamilton, who thinks testing is 'boring'), Michael loved the hours he spent in the car and would take any chance to get onto the track, often pounding out mile after mile on Ferrari's own test track.

We were in Barcelona for this test and I found Schumacher dressed in a white T-shirt and jeans, his whippet-thin frame lounging on the sofa. Michael was the fittest driver of his generation, and it showed. He glowed with a skier's suntan and the muscles on his upper arms were lean and defined. The handshake was like a vice – only much tighter. Once the blood returned to my fingers, we exchanged pleasantries and then launched into a long chat about anything and everything, particularly his beloved football. He turned out regularly for a club near his estate in Switzerland, and we had played each other in a few knockabout matches before grands prix. We had arranged a match before a Belgian Grand Prix between the German and British media at the Royal Spa stadium, a down-at-heel lower-division ground with about 3,500 seats. The usual ragbag assortment of the good, the bad and the desperately unfit ran out onto the pitch in front of a few locals. We had played only about ten minutes when a ripple went through the ground and a substitute was called on – Michael Schumacher. He was the fastest man on the pitch by miles, and with a decent touch, yet the Germans could not break the invincible line of British defence led by Tony Jardine, ITV's Formula One pundit. Word reached the streets of Spa and the grandstands began to fill up with fans delighted to be within touching distance of the greatest driver of his Formula One era. With minutes to go, it was 1–1, and Michael had failed to score despite numerous efforts on goal. The minutes ticked by for an eternity as it became apparent that our referee, hired from a Belgian league, was willing Schumacher to score, presumably so that he could tell his grandchildren about the day he blew the whistle for Formula One's greatest champion. Eventually, after about ninety-eight minutes, Schumacher broke through an exhausted British defence and stuck the ball in the net. That was 2–1 to the Germans, with the congratulations to the winning scorer. You would think he would be used to acclaim, wouldn't you?

I reminded him of that game and he chuckled guiltily. You could tell how much he enjoyed that simple kickabout, ninety-eight minutes (eight too many from a British perspective) when there was media but no questions, no judgement and no cameras following his every move. Despite the bluster and the aggression on the track, I suspect he was shy. We talked about Corinna, his wife, and their then small children, Mick and Gina-Maria, and how they never went to grands prix, but watched on television. Michael revealed that Gina-Maria gave him good-luck charms, once a hairbrush, another time a locket that he kept in his overall pocket. At one race, Schumacher was distraught after he dropped the locket, but it was luckily returned by a laser-eyed photographer who had spotted it.

He assured me that his career was not over and he had no

intention of retiring, but Montezemolo was less sure. He felt his driver was prevaricating each time the issue was raised and decided he needed an insurance policy. He pounced on Räikkönen with the offer of a $45 million deal to leave McLaren. That was big money, and not even Montezemolo could afford two drivers on that sort of pay, which meant it would be Schumacher who had to leave. Todt didn't want to lose Schumacher, a driver who had become one of his closest allies and friends, and the rift between the president and his sporting director became a chasm.

Within minutes of victory at the 2006 Italian Grand Prix, Schumacher discovered that Ferrari had issued a press release announcing his retirement. He had won in front of the *tifosi* he had made proud again, but there was no way back for him now: Michael Schumacher, seven times world champion, was retiring. He won seven grands prix that season, but was second in the world championship to Alonso. His final race was in Brazil and his retirement gift was a lifetime achievement award from Formula One, presented by Pelé – one legend to another. In Kerpen, Michael's hometown not far from Cologne in Germany, they named a street after the local hero and held a Michael Schumacher Day in tribute to their most famous son.

That wasn't quite the end of Schumacher's Ferrari story, though. In 2009, Massa was hit on the head by a spring that bounced down the track during the Hungarian Grand Prix from the rear of Rubens Barrichello's Brawn GP car. He clung to life in a coma in a Budapest hospital while Montezemolo tried to work out where he could find a competitive driver for the next race in Valencia. He turned to his most successful driver.

'We were really nowhere after Felipe's crash. I called Michael and he came to Maranello, dressed all in white – shoes, shirt and trousers. I said, "Michael, we are in the shit. Please come back." After thirty minutes of talking, Michael looked like a child waiting for a present, his eyes lighting up with anticipation. He was silent for four or five seconds, then he suddenly said, "Yes, you are right. I have to give back to Ferrari for all that I have got today." At that moment, he was like a child, happy, and he went immediately to get a seat fitting and we organised a test for the day after in a two-year-old car at Mugello.'

Schumacher was quick but suffering neck pain as the result of a motorcycle accident. As soon as the test was over, he flew by private jet to see his doctor. Montezemolo says: 'At ten o'clock, he rang me in tears because his doctor told him that the injury was very dangerous and he could not drive for another two months. It is an irony that the two worst accidents that this wonderful driver should have would be on a motorcycle and skiing.'

Montezemolo had lost his man forever. By the end of the year, Schumacher had been wooed by Ross Brawn, his mentor at Benetton and Ferrari, and decided to join Mercedes, which had bought Brawn GP, while Massa recovered to drive again in 2010 alongside Fernando Alonso, who replaced Räikkönen. Montezemolo was upset by the launch of the Mercedes Formula One team in Stuttgart, for it featured Schumacher with a Mercedes sports car behind him – in Ferrari red. It felt as though the Germans were deliberately thumbing their noses at the Scuderia. Someone else was also learning to live with the Schumacher factor: Nico Rosberg was Schumacher's new teammate, but at the launch in the Mercedes-Benz museum in Stuttgart, no one wanted to speak to him. 'There were about 300 television crews but they all wanted Michael,' he said glumly.

The experiment to bring back a forty-year-old after a three-year absence was a failure. The car wasn't good enough and Schumacher's touch – and his drive – had gone. At an interview in Japan before he retired for a second time, Schumacher told me he was surprised it was so hard to come back, and you could tell from his demeanour that it was over. I had asked for an exclusive interview and got it immediately; no one else wanted to talk to the ex-champ, and there was no comet tail of followers through the paddock any longer.

Michael Schumacher's career ended for a second time in Brazil, but there was no lifetime award or garlands. He finished the race in seventh position. In December 2013, Schumacher fell while skiing during a family holiday in France and banged his head on a rock. He was airlifted to hospital in Grenoble and put into a medically induced coma for more than three months. He was returned to his home near Geneva the following September, but has not been seen since that day, when the life of one of the fittest men in the history of sport, who drove at speeds of 200 mph on tracks all over the world for more than twenty years, was changed forever. His family never speak of his condition, although it is known that he cannot walk or talk. He is seen by only the closest of his friends, like Todt and Montezemolo.

By then, Montezemolo had lost his 'dream team', and he remained in charge at Maranello only until Sergio Marchionne, the Canadian businessman of Italian extraction, eyed Ferrari's potential in the marketplace. He was on a collision course with Montezemolo, who held diametrically opposing views on Ferrari's place in the world: Marchionne wanted to build more and more Ferraris, but Montezemolo wanted to hang on to what he believed was the marque's biggest selling point, the same one that Enzo had taught him at the start of his career – exclusivity. Leave the buyers wanting something that they believe is difficult to buy.

Marchionne wasn't listening, and he went ahead with his plan to float part of Ferrari on the New York Stock Exchange. He raised $893 million with a share sale in 2015 that valued Ferrari at $10.4 billion – not bad for a business that was almost bust before Montezemolo moved in, and equally lucrative for Piero Lardi Ferrari, Enzo's illegitimate son, who held 10 per cent of the stock and became an overnight paper billionaire.

Montezemolo had resigned and hurriedly cleared his desk

a year before the float when he realised that Marchionne was intent on changing the nature of the business and switching attention away from the *bella figura*. Marchionne was prepared to pay £23 million in compensation to see the back of Montezemolo, who, like Enzo before him, had become a legend in his own lifetime in Italy. Ecclestone believes that Marchionne, who habitually wore crew-neck sweaters rather than Montezemolo's tailored jackets, was jealous of this dazzling icon of Italy and couldn't helping winding him up. 'He just wanted to be like Luca, the way Luca is popular with the people – but really he was a bully. When he came to his first team meeting – and only the team principals were allowed in – I asked him why he was there. There was him and Maurizio [Arrivabene, the team principal] together and I wanted to know what was going on because only one of them would be allowed to speak. When it came to the discussion, Arrivabene started to speak and Marchionne put his hand over his mouth to shut him up. Sergio always wore this blue sweater, so at the next meeting, I dressed up in a blue sweater just the same. He comes in and looks at me and I said, "Look at me, Sergio. I just wanted to dress like you to be a success."'

When Montezemolo left in September 2014, there were tears and a send-off from the entire workforce, who were gathered in a square outside what remains of the original factory built by Enzo. 'There were a lot of people crying; normally people can't wait to get rid of you,' Montezemolo remembered, his eyes misting at the memory. He was only half right, for while most of the workforce might have been sad, Marchionne was happy to see him go.

Marchionne's tenure at Ferrari was to be short: in July 2018 he died from complications after surgery at the age of sixty-six. Marchionne had been a tough negotiator and was hailed as a brilliant businessman who had turned around the Fiat-Chrysler conglomerate, reviving the associated Alfa Romeo and Maserati brands. And he was tough in Formula One, too, asserting Ferrari's place as the most important name in the sport, but the charisma of the Montezemolo years was gone. The team closed ranks, requests to go to Maranello were rejected and Ferrari, the team that added lustre to Formula One, simply got on with business.

I am about to leave Montezemolo when he becomes anxious that I have arranged a good dinner in Rome for the evening. I reassure him that I have spoken to his secretary, who reserved a table for me and my wife Jacqueline at some-where called Al Moro, around the corner from the Trevi Fountain. 'Ah, I will come too, with my wife,' he says enthusi-astically. Dinner is fixed. We are first to arrive at this very traditional Italian trattoria, all dark wood and white table-cloths with waiters in uniform and a wine list as thick as the *Encyclopaedia Britannica*. The staff are obviously primed to expect us and to perform. Unlike tourists, who are usually consigned to a back room, we are placed in the middle of the restaurant among the locals, our waiter speaks perfect English and is well informed about the menu. A few minutes later,

Montezemolo arrives with his wife and a friend who is over from America. There is lots of hugging and kissing and waving to diners around the restaurant. Everyone is seated but Montezemolo is still on the move, trawling the tables and making sure everyone has been spoken to. Ecclestone says Montezemolo is the world's best networker; I can believe it.

We feast on artichokes in olive oil and sensational pasta, but all the while Montezemolo keeps an eye on the door, checking as it opens to see who might be entering. If it is a friend or contact, he leaps to his feet for an embrace. It is bravura stuff – and that smile recommended to John Hogan is flashing like a beacon.

18

DECLINE AND FALL

L ISA Dennis was furious. She should have been relaxing in a lavish suite at one of the world's most luxurious hotels, sipping cocktails as she gazed out onto the still, blue waters of Lake Como. Instead, she was billeted on the industrial outskirts of Monza, stuck for four days in a hotel within sight of factory chimneys and a noisy six-lane highway. A statuesque blonde American, she had long ago learned to put up with the thin skin of Ron, her husband and the boss of McLaren, Britain's most successful Formula One team. But there were limits and this was it.

Anyone who was anyone in Formula One was staying at the famous Villa d'Este for the Italian Grand Prix weekend. The fabulous Renaissance building looked down on the shimmering lake, with its traffic of pleasure boats and ferries taking tourists on a journey that allowed them to gawp at the magnificent homes of the rich and famous, like that of George Clooney and his wife Amal, whose villa stood on a promontory, as if inviting stares.

This is where you went to see and be seen – but at a cost: a suite could be as much as £5,000 a night during the grand prix weekend. For Lisa Dennis, a gregarious party animal with a rich laugh and wide smile, this was where she had to be. Lisa and Ron had checked in to the Villa d'Este, but there were the logistics to take care of for the man in charge of a famous team bidding to win Italy's biggest motor race. The trip down to the circuit in Monza could take an hour by limousine, more if the traffic snarled as tens of thousands of *tifosi*, Italian fans, struggled to get through the narrow gates and into the royal park, which provides the setting for one of the fastest tracks in the world. Dennis was concerned he might be held up, and wanted to know if he could fly his helicopter into the hotel grounds to take him and his wife to Monza. The answer was a sympathetic no and a shrug of the shoulders from the elegant manager in his crisp white shirt and stylishly cut suit. He didn't want the whirl of helicopter blades to disturb the peace of his beautiful hotel and its gardens.

Ron was unhappy, but there was little he could do. The couple settled in, basking in the sumptuous surroundings of the villa. Until the sound of rotor blades could be heard coming closer and closer. A helicopter emerged from the treeline and set slowly down onto the lawn outside the hotel. Out stepped an unmistakable figure, his long hair disturbed by the rush of air as he scuttled towards the hotel entrance. It was Luca di Montezemolo, the president of Ferrari.

Ferrari was Dennis's nemesis in a rivalry that bordered on hatred. Dennis erupted and ordered his wife to pack. They were leaving immediately. This was nothing new: for Ron Dennis, taking umbrage was a way of life. The curled lip and the glowering eyes were the trademark of a man who could see insult at every turn or a plot to threaten him around every corner. For Ron Dennis, losing inflicts physical and mental pain – whether on the track or on the lawns of a plush hotel – and on that day, he had finished a poor second to his greatest foe.

History will judge Ron Dennis to be one of Britain's greatest entrepreneurs, a self-made man who rose from humble mechanic to creator and chief executive of one of the nation's most admired technology companies, as well as leader of Formula One's greatest team after Ferrari. He transformed a bunch of mechanics in a down-at-heel factory on an industrial estate on the outskirts of Woking into a shining example of British ingenuity. He was wooed by Prime Minister David Cameron and persuaded the Crown Prince of Bahrain to invest in his business. Dennis is worth more than £500 million, achieved by his own brilliance as a businessman and innovator. The empire he created now straddles some of the world's most exotic cars, and a company that generates technologies for everything from airports and hospitals to cycles for Britain's Olympic athletes. From 100 people in 1980, the McLaren Group employed 3,500 in a business with a turnover of £920 million by 2016, and with the road-car business close to hitting its production target of 5,500, almost as many as Ferrari makes in a year.

Yet Dennis is, to employ the words of Winston Churchill, a riddle wrapped in a mystery inside an enigma. He could be loyal yet ruthless; charming yet boorish; innovative yet trapped by old scores. As one rival team principal put it: 'Ron can be generous, funny, clever and he will always do what is right for Formula One, even if it is to the detriment of his own team. But he is still a c***.'

Christian Horner had direct experience of Dennis's mercurial moods when they were called to give evidence at an FIA inquiry together in Monaco. They travelled on Dennis's private plane and then he drove them from the airport, chatting so enthusiastically that they missed their junction for Monte Carlo. 'We really had an enjoyable day and had lunch in the Automobile Club of Monaco. The next time I saw Ron was at the French Grand Prix the following weekend and he was walking towards me in the paddock. I went to say, "Hi", and . . . nothing, not even a lift of the eye. It is Jekyll and Hyde. Here was this charming, interesting man, who was interested in what I had done and a chap I spent a day with. I see him three days later and he completely snubs me. I have a lot of respect for Ron and what he has built is unbelievable, but he is his own worst enemy sometimes.'

Dennis talks a lot about enemies and having a target on his back. His manner is occasionally brusque, possibly because he is constantly wary of being tripped up or embarrassed. Horner could see that Mosley had his measure and knew how to wind him up. 'Max had the ability to make Ron feel tiny,' he claims.

It is easy to suspect that Dennis harbours an inferiority complex as the former mechanic made good when seated across from men like Mosley and Montezemolo, with their high intellects and aristocratic backgrounds.

Stories of his temper are legion, like the outburst at a shooting party held by Jody Scheckter on his land in Hampshire. Dennis turned up in an immaculate new Mercedes 4x4 with a chauffeur and, when the rear of the custom-built vehicle was opened, it revealed special boxes for his guns and a cage for his Labrador. In between was a drinks compartment filled with champagne and six gold goblets engraved with 'Ron' and 'Lisa'. Once the bubbly was consumed, Dennis started to retrieve the goblets, only to find two missing and the rest of the party giggling because they had hidden them. He loaded his shotgun and pointed it at Scheckter's 4×4, threatening to shoot unless they were handed over. There was a sudden hush as the party wondered whether Dennis was serious. There is every chance he was and an equal chance that he knew how to get his revenge with a leg-pull of epic proportions, for Dennis is never far away from a joke or a prank.

The tale of how he had the gravel in his driveway removed to be washed and returned haunts every conversation about Ron Dennis, and how he once interviewed someone through his kitchen window because he didn't want the interviewee in his house wearing dirty shoes. Some are apocryphal; many are true.

On his desk in his office at the heart of the glittering McLaren Technology Centre in Woking, a £300 million monument to his achievement, his pens would be lined up neatly in order. The entire building is a blend of white, grey and black in steel and glass, almost as though colour might be an intrusion. Across the immaculate, curving entrance road, McLaren make some of the most beautiful and exciting cars on the road, fulfilling Dennis's lifelong dream of creating a British rival to Maranello. Enzo never chose any other colour than red, the colour of Italy, but papaya, a bright orange, was the traditional colour of Bruce McLaren, the founder in 1966 of the team Dennis took over – and Dennis hates orange. He likes grey.

Adrian Newey had a stormy relationship with Dennis, even though the pair won world championships together with Mika Häkkinen. He says that the ideal picture for Dennis is of a black, silver and grey McLaren F1 car in monochrome in a silver frame – and he should know because he gave his boss a seizure when he painted his own office blue.

The walls of the Williams headquarters are not monochrome, but they are corporate bland. It is a fifty-mile drive from Dennis's Bond-style headquarters in Woking, with its lake and futuristic gadgets, to Sir Frank's more humble factory in Grove in Oxfordshire. Next to the entrance to the main offices is a sign pointing to the museum, where some of the team's most famous cars are lined up, cared for by Jonathan Williams, one of Sir Frank's two sons.

On the second floor, Claire Williams is fretting. Although she is formally her father's deputy, his incapacity means she is effectively in charge, although unique among her peers as she is a mother. When we meet, she has a nanny crisis, and her time is limited because she needs to get home to her boy Nathaniel.

Claire Williams never expected to be in charge of her father's team as deputy principal, but, inevitably, it was Ecclestone's idea. 'Mum and Dad never wanted us to go into Williams ever. Dad was so opposed to nepotism and it was banged into us that there were no family rights in the team. As much as our whole world was Williams at home, it was never about a family dynasty.'

Ecclestone called Claire to his Princes Gate office in London where he posed the simple question: 'How do you feel about taking over the team?' She was taken aback. 'I was flattered, but no way was I ready and I didn't feel capable, I would let everyone down, I was too young and a girl. He reassured me, but I still refused.' Ecclestone was persuasive and cunning and dragged Claire to a birthday lunch for his daughter Tamara. 'Bernie spent the whole lunch telling me it would be fine and he would support me if I did the job – and all the while I was getting daggers from Tamara because we had intruded on her birthday lunch. I felt so sorry for her.'

Sir Frank knew nothing of the machinations, but Claire consulted her mother Virginia. The only worry was her brother Jonathan, who had worked his way through the team, starting as a van driver, and might have expected to be first in line for succession. 'Jonathan is the eldest son and primogeniture would dictate that he would take over, but it didn't happen. It was other people's choice, it was the board's choice and I was deeper into the heart of the organisation. It isn't nice. That's a problem with a family business.'

Dennis was a regular visitor to the Williams home, sometimes chasing the children wearing a Tommy Cooper-style arrow-through-the-head illusion, or tossing the remains of a lobster shell into their beds. It was the side of Formula One life hidden from public view.

'There's something about Ron that I love,' Claire says. 'We had amazing Christmas parties and lots of Formula One people would come. Ron would always come upstairs to see us and have some bag of tricks with him. Dad didn't have a world outside of Formula One. He has no mates. He isn't interested in anything else. If people want to talk to him about Formula One, or if it is his side interests of planes or Hitler, he is fine with that. After that, he is glazed because his first passion is Formula One, his second is his family. We don't mind that because we understand it.'

This single-mindedness peppers any discussion about Britain's foremost team owners in Formula One. Frank Williams and Ron Dennis came through Formula One together, rising to dominate their sport in tandem, snatching victories from each other, nicking each other's staff and drivers and luring away sponsors. Between 1984 and 1999, the only name to come between McLaren and Williams as world champion constructor was Benetton, in 1995; otherwise it was their show. Bernie Ecclestone could never understand why they were so friendly when they were at each other's throats on the track, but their relationship was different and their similarities were forged by their desire to race – and win.

Dennis forged a hugely successful partnership with Mercedes-Benz when the German carmaker returned to Formula One as an engine supplier in 1994 after an absence from the sport of almost four decades. There were world championships for Mika Häkkinen and Lewis Hamilton, and McLaren Mercedes were in the front rank, until Dennis decided he must realise his ambition to build his own road cars. That would inevitably bring him into conflict with Mercedes, whose business is on the road. Spygate, quickly followed by Liegate, was too much for the corporately correct Germans and they struck out on their own to buy Ross Brawn's team to race alone from 2010. For the first time in fifteen years, McLaren were a customer for engines and not the team who got first call on the best power in Formula One.

Williams had a similarly tense relationship with BMW when they came in as the team's engine supplier in 2000. He and Patrick Head had no truck with the efforts of BMW, led by Mario Theissen, a precise and prim head of motor racing for the company, to run the show, and Williams was happy to wind up the German executives at every opportunity. A keen student of the Second World War, Williams is also a plane enthusiast and on good terms with the powers-that-be at Royal Air Force Brize Norton, near his Oxfordshire factory – and he loved a flypast. Claire Williams remembers: 'Dad had Mario and a contingent from BMW arriving. So, Dad got on the phone to the RAF and told them he had a party of Germans coming in and requested a flypast. He sent the co-ordinates and they did. Dad thought it was hilarious, Mario not so much.'

After six seasons without a championship, relationships deteriorated as BMW blamed Williams for not producing cars worthy of their engines – and their vast investment. The Germans took their millions and bought Sauber to start their own team, where they were not much more successful, managing only a single victory. At the end of 2009, BMW gave up and attempted to sell the team to a mysterious consortium called Qadbak Investments. BMW wouldn't have needed the prowess of a private investigator to discover that Qadbak was a shell company set up by a convicted fraudster who was behind a dubious plot to buy Notts County Football Club, installing former England coach Sven-Göran Eriksson as manager. It took BMW a while to cotton on, until they realised there was no money or investors and sold the team back to Peter Sauber.

If BMW were embarrassed, Williams were being humbled. The days of multiple world championships and heroic drivers like Nigel Mansell were over. There was only a single victory since 2004, although it was both remarkable and memorable, for it coincided with Sir Frank's seventieth birthday, something the family feared they would never see, and it was also the final time Virginia Williams would attend a grand prix.

Pastor Maldonado was an unpredictable driver, and in the Williams team thanks to £29 millions' worth of sponsorship from the state-owned PDVSA oil company from his homeland of Venezuela. But something strange happened at the 2012 Spanish Grand Prix, where he started from pole position, and led to the chequered flag, for the most unlikely victory anyone could remember. The Williams team were ecstatic and the champagne flowed, while rivals lined up to congratulate a popular team that had fallen on hard times. And then, as mechanics and staff lined up to listen to a thank-you speech from Sir Frank, the garage exploded in flames.

I was on the balcony of the media centre at the Circuit de Catalunya when I noticed smoke billowing from the pit lane. Jake Humphrey, the BBC anchor, started leading his pundits to the safety of the paddock exit, while Ted Kravitz, the Sky Sports pit-lane reporter, began running in the opposite direction, towards the flames. His cameraman helped pull mechanic Martin 'Barney' Betts from the blaze, and Force India crew in the garage next door dashed to wheel Sir Frank clear. It was an extraordinary end to an extraordinary day.

'I always think that there was some mystical power at play,' says Claire Williams, who was standing by her father when the explosion happened. 'Blowing the garage up was so

Williams. How none of us had a heart attack in that garage, I don't know.'

Equipment and laptops were destroyed, with the Monaco Grand Prix just two weeks away. Formula One rallied round and teams donated computers and tools to ensure Williams were on the grid for the biggest grand prix of the year, and able to celebrate that lone victory.

Ten months later, Claire Williams was in charge. The announcement was delayed until after the funeral of her mum, Virginia, the rock who had supported her husband through some of the worst times as he struggled to establish himself and then recover from the horrific accident that had robbed an active man of his ability to move. Ginny Williams had always been unable to fathom his insatiable need to go to the edge, sometimes driving along country lanes around their home with his headlights switched off for the thrill of it. Their home was transformed after his accident by the arrival of nurses needed for his round-the-clock care and, in her autobiography, she complained that her husband changed. She tells the story of the day Iain Cunningham, Williams's nurse, wheeled her husband out of the family home after they had decided to split up. She opened the car door for him, puzzled that he was showing no feelings. She asked if he cared. Williams replied: 'Emotion is weak, Ginny.' The split turned out to be temporary, and the psychological wounds healed, but Williams's response to his wife was telling: like Ecclestone, Dennis and the rest, there was no place for emotion in Formula One.

Claire Williams had time after her mother's death to digest the enormity of what was to come, not just as the only woman around the Formula One table (after Monisha Kaltenborn quit in June 2017 after a brief tenure at Sauber), but also as the custodian of the Williams brand and its reputation. So much has changed since her father launched himself with an overdraft into the realm of entrepreneurs racing for the love of it and then notched an astonishing nine constructors' world championships and seven more world titles for drivers like Keke Rosberg, Damon Hill, Alain Prost and Nigel Mansell. Williams were once the biggest players, but the competition now comes from the big battalions of multinational companies – Mercedes, Honda, Ferrari, Red Bull, Renault – who have the financial firepower to spend whatever they need to win. It is a depressing scenario for a team that has remained independent. In an interview for *The Sunday Times*, she told me: 'I have come to terms with the fact that no one outside the Big Three of Ferrari, Mercedes and Red Bull can win. The financial gap is now so insurmountable that it is not now possible. I think that is so sad. That is the difference between an independent team like Williams where we are in this sport, have always been in it and will always be in it unless outside circumstances dictate otherwise.

'These bigger teams can leave when they feel like it, so we need to protect the teams for whom Formula One is a livelihood. When I took on this role, I genuinely believed we could win, but now I don't know how we could do it. You always have to have hope and I always had that naïve spirit and that if you work hard you get your just rewards, but how do you do it? I just don't know.'

Success ran dry at McLaren, too. Ron Dennis could measure his life in Formula One by statistics – McLaren's 182 grand-prix victories and twenty world championships, almost entirely during his reign. He could measure success by the status of his champions, like Alain Prost, Lewis Hamilton and Ayrton Senna, as drivers rated among the greatest, but his team was in decline as Dennis was shoved towards the exit of the company he created.

Once Mercedes had gone, they convinced Hamilton, the jewel in McLaren's crown, to follow and cash in on their huge investment. Hamilton was released from the straitjacket of a McLaren environment that had constrained his desire to be his own man. His final grand prix with McLaren symbolised the end of a relationship that had soared and fallen back to earth with a bump. Hamilton led the 2012 Brazilian Grand Prix, but was punted off the track by Nico Hülkenberg's Force India car. Jenson Button went on to win, the last victory for a McLaren car before the team fell into the middle of the pack as an also-ran instead of standing as a beacon of innovation and strength.

The car that won in Brazil was the fastest on the track, and Martin Whitmarsh, Dennis's successor as team principal, had a choice for 2013: stick with the MP4/27 – which won seven races – or go radical and design an entirely new car. He chose the wrong option and the newly designed car was no winner.

This was to be McLaren's critical year. Vodafone, the title sponsor paying as much as $75 million annually, decided to end their sponsorship, and then it emerged that Mansour Ojjeh, Dennis's long-time partner, was seriously ill and needed a double lung transplant. There were back-room suggestions from Ojjeh's advisers that Dennis should buy his 25 per cent shareholding, which would cost about £250 million and make Dennis an equal partner with Mumtalakat, the Bahrain sovereign wealth fund that owned half the shares in McLaren. Dennis had been busy attempting to raise finance for McLaren's road car business, eventually persuading Peter Lim, the Hong Kong billionaire, to invest an initial $50 million. There was a catch, though: Dennis had decided to retire on his seventieth birthday in June 2017 and Lim warned that no Dennis meant no investment. Talks started to extend Dennis's contract, but when Ojjeh returned to work after a lung transplant, Dennis felt that his one-time partner appeared to resent the idea of his once friend and partner trawling the Far East for money to buy him out.

In the meantime, Whitmarsh was sacrificed for his errors in allowing Hamilton to slip through his fingers and then ditching the successful 2012 car. Dennis had treated Whitmarsh as a protégé, but Whitmarsh lacked the fire that had made Dennis so successful – he was too nice, too reasonable. Whitmarsh left at the end of a dire 2013 season with a severance payment substantially north of £6 million.

By then, Whitmarsh had already persuaded Honda to

return to Formula One to supply engines, triggering jubilation among fans at the resurrection of a partnership that had been one of the most glorious in the history of motor racing, when Ayrton Senna and Alain Prost had swept all before them and McLaren had been the most powerful name in the sport. Remarkably, Fernando Alonso was also persuaded to put his tortured year of 2007 behind him when he had caused so much grief for Dennis and his team during Spygate to rejoin the team. It was another 'dream team' as he was partnered with Jenson Button, which meant two world champions alongside each other and Honda for the 2015 season – what could go wrong? Everything.

Alonso was ruled out of the Australian Grand Prix, supposed to be his first race back with McLaren, after knocking himself unconscious during testing. He didn't miss much: his replacement Kevin Magnussen didn't make it to the starting grid because his car developed a fault.

The first season for the new partnership was a disaster: Honda simply could not fathom the complex hybrid engines and McLaren were paying Alonso, a two-times world champion, £20 million a season to drag around at the back of the field, if he finished at all. He suffered seven retirements in eighteen grands prix, and ended the season seventeenth of the twenty drivers, a testament to a Honda-powered car that was not just under-powered but horribly unreliable.

The McLaren Technology Centre, the vast, shiny temple to

excellence, was under siege. By September 2016, all trust between the main players had broken down and the relationship with Honda was at rock bottom. Dennis had presented his vision for the future of McLaren – but there was no future for him in the business he had created. He was asked to resign from the company he had built from a racing team in junior series to a powerful, global business with one of the biggest trophy cabinets in the world of sport. Dennis was humiliated and angry and determined not to go without a fight. He went to the High Court for an injunction to prevent Ojjeh and Mumtalakat placing him on gardening leave while they thrashed out the future for McLaren. The injunction was refused, partly because Sir Geoffrey Vos, Chancellor of the High Court, said in his judgement that he believed both sides could resolve their differences, but the board meeting that followed showed that they couldn't. Mumtalakat appointed three new directors before the vote, perhaps as insurance to make sure they got their way, although, in the event, Dennis had no option but to go. He sold his shares worth an estimated £275 million and walked out. That was in November 2016 – and he has not been back.

The farewell was typically Ron Dennis – only the best would do. He hired the Royal Albert Hall and Cirque du Soleil in January 2018 at a cost of £450,000 and bussed in 3,500 of his former employees, sponsors, friends, drivers and the former colleagues he had left behind more than a year earlier for a night of free entertainment. Bernie Ecclestone and Dennis had locked horns over Formula One's finances for decades, yet he was there with his wife Fabiana and there was a mutual admiration and respect.

'I am probably Ron's biggest supporter,' Bernie said. 'If I had a team, I would want Ron to run it. He was the best at his job in the sport. The only thing that upset me with Ron was the trouble with Mansour and how it all went wrong.'

The warmth that emanated from the crowd in that vast arena was genuine, and they stood to applaud his valedictory speech, which was a moving account of his life in Formula One. Many had worked at McLaren for decades, their families had become part of the McLaren fabric, while sponsors and associates had become friends as Dennis built his empire, culminating in the huge Norman Foster-designed headquarters that looms over a roundabout on the way into Woking. These people were testament to his career as much as the statistics. I asked Dennis why so many turned up.

'The key is respect. If you live up to your standards, you achieve a lot more because everyone is pointing in the same direction. I have always had phenomenal loyalty. You can't know everyone's names, but you build a DNA, which is in the company. I wanted to find a way to say thank you to those people who had believed in my values and the principles by which I had built the company. It had to be a way which gives them something more than an object, it had to be a memory because I am a great believer in memories. I hope they all stood and applauded because I was open and honest about my own fragility and emotion.'

I sat in a box with Anthony Hamilton, who had seen his son transformed from aspiring karter to world champion, thanks to Ron Dennis's patronage. We agreed that neither of us could figure out this extraordinary, complex man. I remembered that when Ray Matts, my *Daily Mail* colleague, had a heart attack before an Australian Grand Prix, Dennis immediately offered to fly his wife Valerie out to Melbourne and put her into a hotel, all expenses paid. When Tony Jardine's wife Jeanette was involved in a horrific accident, losing her arm, Dennis rang the former ITV pundit almost daily, offering to fly in top surgeons. The stories of his kindnesses are many, but not broadcast.

Dinner with Ron is a laugh-a-minute extravaganza, with terrible jokes, lots of gossip and fun. With Lisa, he entertained the British media one Friday night at Imola before the San Marino Grand Prix. It was raucous, so much so that one leading broadcaster was unfit for work the next day and a journalist from the *Daily Mail* was not seen until thirty minutes before the race on Sunday because his hangover was so huge.

Dennis's work with the charity Tommy's, which funds research into premature birth, miscarriages and stillbirths, is tireless, and has raised tens of millions of pounds, and he is also a passionate promoter of Britain as a business ambassador for the government.

He is immensely loyal to those who are loyal to him, but

ruthless with those who break ranks. Adrian Newey was told to clear his desk within minutes of telling Dennis he was leaving for Red Bull, their friendship and time together no barrier to an abrupt dismissal. Trust is fundamental to his relationships, as I found out covering his team year after year and then dining with him and sharing conversations that were to remain private. Of all the team owners, I found Dennis the most fascinating for his kindness, generosity and humour yet laced with occasional anger, coldness and an obsession with correctness that come straight from the pages of a Dickens novel: this is a man who refused to allow his staff to have coffee cups on their desks because they would spoil the vista of his space-age headquarters, for heaven's sake. But he can't help himself: at his farewell, he related the story of how he was late to a meeting to address his staff. On his way out of his office, he spotted a stray piece of paper on the floor and walked past it – but he couldn't leave it behind even though it would delay him, so he returned to put it in the shredder. As he leaned forward, the shredder took the paper and his tie and chomped it in half. He paid the price for his obsession and had to address the staff with the half-eaten tie tucked into his jacket.

He hates social media and cut off two friends because they posted pictures of a party he threw. 'Be there for the experience and enjoy the moment but don't expect to make me happy if you start putting things on social media. Two friends have fallen out with me for that and are not my friends any more. It is not the way life is. It's not me,' he said in his interview for the American Academy of Achievement.

David Coulthard was Dennis's longest-serving driver, spending nine seasons as a fixture in the team, yet he never felt as though he was given the same treatment as his team-mate Mika Häkkinen, who won two world championships in their time together. 'The first grand prix I drove for Ron in Melbourne in 1996, we went into the debrief. I was on one side of the table with my engineers and Mika was on the other side. Ron walked in and I stood up to shake his hand, but he ignored me and sat on Mika's side and asked, "So, what are we doing?" I listened to what Mika's engineer said about Mika's car, and then Ron pointed at me and said, "And what are they doing?"'

At the final grand prix of the 1995 season in Adelaide, a tyre burst on Häkkinen's McLaren and he flew into the barriers, suffering a fractured skull. His life was in peril and he was in hospital for two months, with Dennis fretting over the health of his young driver, who was only twenty-six and had his life ahead of him. 'Ron finally admitted that Mika had almost died in one of his cars and he had gone through the experience of watching his driver in hospital in Adelaide, lying there on a ventilator and clinging on to life,' Coulthard says. 'As soon as he told me that, the conversation was over because I realised why he favoured Mika.'

But Dennis was loyal to Coulthard because his driver committed himself to the McLaren cause. 'I made a commitment and it warranted commitment in return in Ron's eyes.'

By the end of 2017, the relationship with Honda was over and McLaren were forced to pay £60 million to get out of their contract with the Japanese manufacturer, who moved to Red Bull. A sixth season of trawling around at the back of the field, this time with Renault customer engines, was in prospect, and Zak Brown, a marketeer hired by Dennis and now running the team, was forced to admit that it could be years before a McLaren mounted the winner's rostrum again. Next door at Williams, there was only despair for 2018: Martini, the team's title sponsor, were walking away and so was Lawrence Stroll, the Canadian entrepreneur bankrolling the career of his son Lance by pouring as much as £20 million a season of his own money into the team.

McLaren and Williams. They were Britain's motor-racing royalty, the best of the best built by the proudest of men. Sir Frank, sidelined by age and disability, was powerless to steer his team back to greatness, and Dennis, perhaps the biggest figure in Formula One after Ecclestone, had left behind the team he created for good.

19

THE RINGMASTER

15 SEPTEMBER 2016: it felt like a metaphor for what was to come. Bernie Ecclestone was guiding his party of VIPs into the brilliantly lit paddock, as teams prepared for the Singapore Grand Prix. Ecclestone always attracted a crowd at a race, with camera crews hounding him and journalists seeking one of his ready quips.

But tonight, no one was looking at the man who made all of this happen, for the cameras were all pointed at a short, stocky American with neat grey hair and a moustache that would not have looked out of place on a Victorian mill-owner. Chase Carey was now the big man in town and, as he walked, cameramen backtracked trying to get him in focus. Carey, chairman of Liberty Media, Formula One's new owners, was being introduced to Formula One – and it couldn't have been at a more startling venue. The Marina Bay circuit sparkled under the banks of floodlights that illuminate a racetrack around the streets of the richest city-state in the world. It felt unreal, a fantasy scene that could have come from a science-fiction movie. But it was real, and it was worth eight billion of

Liberty's dollars to own the sport that would fill Singapore's gilded streets.

Ecclestone was walking further and further from the main group, being pushed aside by the crowd, until he was knocked by a photographer and stumbled. Bewildered, he staggered to his feet and everyone stopped for a moment before the train of VIPs moved on, leaving the eighty-six-year-old Formula One chief executive behind to dust himself down. Ecclestone was yesterday's man, aware that Formula One, his sport, was finally slipping into the possession of the corporate suits from America.

No one knows more about Formula One than Bernie Ecclestone: he was a trusted friend of Enzo Ferrari, had seen Juan Manuel Fangio race and shaken hands with Jim Clark. He had been to more grands-prix venues than anyone could count, and he had milked billions from the sport, but he made sure that plenty of others profited, too.

He sold the rights to the sport when he believed he might not survive his heart operation and regretted it ever since, because the day Formula One was bought by CVC Capital Partners in 2006 he became an employee, ceding ultimate control to City bankers whose mission was to extract as much money from the sport as they could in the shortest time. For all of Ecclestone's faults and the accusations of avarice that ran through his long career, he was a racer who dedicated his life to Formula One. CVC tried to ease him out, an old man still obsessed with secrecy and prone to extraordinary gaffes, like praising Adolf Hitler as a man 'who got things done'. They approached Sir Stuart Rose, the former chairman of Marks & Spencer, and tried to lever Paul Walsh, the ex-Diageo chief executive, into place, but Ecclestone saw them off his premises. He wasn't for moving. In fact, CVC should have been grateful, even if he had dragged them through some of the most turbulent times their business would ever see. From their initial $2 billion investment, the City money-men had reaped an estimated $5 billion by letting Ecclestone bring in the money. And then they sold Formula One to Liberty Media, an American media company, for $8 billion in 2016, an extraordinary sum for a sport that forty years before had been little more than a bunch of enthusiasts racing on a shoe-string for the love of it.

Everyone was happy – except Bernie Ecclestone. He had made a fortune from Formula One, but lost the thing he loved above all else. He claimed to know little of the sale when the news burst into the public domain at the Italian Grand Prix, eleven days before that 2016 Singapore Grand Prix. I called his mobile after the race at Monza and he was on a private plane home with Donald Mackenzie, the lugubrious CVC chairman. 'I don't know what's happening. You had better ask Donald.' Donald didn't do talking to the media. The following January, Carey made the phone call to tell Ecclestone he was no longer chief executive and running the show, but he could be something called chairman emeritus, an advisor. Ecclestone had no idea what that meant and he has not been asked to advise since.

There will never be another Bernie Ecclestone. They called him the ringmaster because he was the man leading his extraordinary flying circus, putting on a show from one corner of the globe to the other.

He has been unconventional in every way, and the only thing you could expect from him was the unexpected, and his tactic was to keep everyone off balance. The first time we met, I held out my hand in greeting only to be met with, 'Oh, so you're the guy writing all this shit about Formula One.' I was unnerved, but discovered this was a favourite ploy and the test was whether you bounced back. Just calling him was a cloak-and-dagger affair, though, with the office telephonist answering simply, 'Treble-six-eight.' There were no niceties, no proud response of 'Formula One Ltd', just the anonymous, ex-directory phone number and you either had it, or you didn't. But he always called back. Always, even answering calls from obscure websites and magazines all over the world who managed to secure the number. Whether any of them understood him is another matter, for interviews could sometimes require the code-breaking skills of Alan Turing. On occasions, he was doing the fishing for opinions, on others he had a message to plant and wanted it to be read by his co-conspirators or rivals in the teams. Either way, it could be a minefield.

His contacts book ranged through royalty, pop stars, movie actors, the world's top chief executives and, of course, a president – Vladimir Putin – and he would catch you off-guard: when I told him I had just interviewed Sepp Blatter and couldn't understand why the FIFA president was resisting the introduction of goal line technology, Ecclestone said: 'Quite right. The technology would mean no controversy and you have to have controversy. I told Sepp last week over lunch.'

He knew everyone – at least everyone worth knowing. All this was some achievement for a man from a tiny village in rural Suffolk, who insists he is 'only a second-hand car dealer'.

But he is much more than that. Small in stature, he is big in personality, and his method of winning is to play the best hand in any deal. The handshake remained his currency, whether it was with a dealer for a Ford Escort or with a king for a grand prix. 'One of the race promoters called me the other day,' he told me months after he was out of Formula One. 'He asked if I realised that we had worked together for thirty-four years and never had a contract. That could never happen now.'

His way of conducting business belonged to the past, and the modern world caught up with him when a deal with a handshake came back to haunt him. Gerhard Gribkowsky, chief risk officer at BayernLB, was the bank's man overseeing Formula One after EM.TV and then Kirch's business collapsed and CVC stepped in to buy. German prosecutors discovered that Ecclestone and the Bambino family trust had paid the banker $44 million, while Ecclestone had taken a $41 million 'finder's fee' in commission, which he didn't declare to CVC. Ecclestone denied any wrongdoing and his evidence was that Gribkowsky was trying to 'shake him down' by reporting him to the British tax authorities, which would have tangled him in years of paperwork. Gribkowsky was sentenced to eight and a half years in jail and prosecutors in Munich put Ecclestone in the dock in 2014 for what was the most high-profile bribery trial in German history. This was serious for the 'Teflon Man', who usually seemed able to get out of any mess. As Max Mosley once said: 'Bernie is very good at getting out of scrapes he got into in the first place.'

He used the tried-and-tested technique of diversion when it came to his evidence. Bemused prosecutors heard how he dodged the V-1 flying bombs that pounded London during the Blitz before he moved on to a description of his daughter Petra's wedding to James Stunt, and how appalled he was at the £12 million cost of the extravaganza in an Italian castle to entertain more than 250 guests drinking Château Pétrus, said to cost £250 a bottle. Ecclestone didn't touch a drop, sticking to his customary half of beer, of course. The trial went nowhere and Ecclestone used German law to settle the case, paying $100 million to walk free without any admission of guilt. He left the court telling reporters: 'I'll be back at work tomorrow.' And he was.

It had been bruising, though. In the run-up to Munich, Ecclestone looked ragged. The impish humour had dried up as he seemed to be fighting fires – perhaps ones he started – on all fronts against restless teams, corporate giants and now lawyers.

Before Munich, Ecclestone had been in the High Court in London where Mr Justice Newey was less entertained by

Ecclestone's apparent loss of memory and diversions. Ecclestone had started in style, amusing photographers by entering a revolving door and emerging back into the street immediately, as though coming through the curtains of the London Palladium like Bruce Forsyth. The court, though, was business-like as it trawled through reams of evidence from Constantin Medien, another German media company, which was suing Ecclestone, Bambino, Gribkowsky and Stephen Mullens, the former family lawyer, for $144 million it claimed it lost through the sale of Formula One to CVC.

I sat behind Fabiana Ecclestone throughout her husband's evidence and she never took her eyes off him as the lawyers talked through hours of complex financial deals. At the end, Mr Justice Newey had no doubt that Ecclestone entered a 'corrupt agreement' with Gribkowsky and the $44 million handed to the German banker was a bribe, describing Ecclestone as 'neither a truthful or reliable witness'. It could have been crushing for Ecclestone, and the string of legal actions shook CVC, whose plans to float Formula One on the Singapore Stock Exchange were shelved.

The judge dismissed Constantin's claim, though, and Ecclestone lived to fight yet another day, his humour briefly revived. He spotted me with Jonathan McEvoy of the *Daily Mail* and Tom Cary of *The Daily Telegraph*, who had sat with me during long hours of boredom and bafflement as the High Court evidence disappeared into a maze of complicated details of shares and loans.

'I looked at you three down there and could see you didn't have a clue what was going on,' he said. I admitted we didn't understand a word. 'Neither did I, as it happens,' he chuckled.

The case did throw up one fascinating twist: Mullens, who rented an office in Ecclestone's Princes Gate headquarters, had represented his wife Slavica when she divorced Ecclestone. The High Court heard that Mullens and his family were victims of an 'horrific robbery' in April 2009. Mr Justice Newey said that 'it went through [Mullens'] mind for one second' that Ecclestone might have been responsible for sending in a gang to rough up his former lawyer. The robbery was so frightening that Mullens was on the point of giving up his law practice and fleeing the country. Mullens changed his story and decided that 'a very large number of other people with whom [he had] dealings, professionally and personally, may have been involved'. Ecclestone simply dismissed the idea that it was anything to do with him but, by 2010, the relationship with the man who had set up the huge Bambino family trust was broken and Mullens was removed from Ecclestone's life in Formula One.

Had Ecclestone's reputation followed him? He may have had plenty of dealings with the High Court, and in early 2018 he was interviewed under caution about a possible £1 billion owed to Britain's tax authorities, part of a long-running dispute with Her Majesty's Revenue & Customs over the Bambino family trust, but there is no suggestion of wrongdoing and he has never been convicted of a criminal offence.

But that constant flow of controversy has marked his life – the sale of F1, women as white goods, Hitler, Putin. He says what he thinks because he believes it, but each blunder stains a career that bears examination for its achievements. When Susie Wolff wanted to launch her campaign to encourage girls into motor racing, and not as white goods, Ecclestone was the first to donate to the cause. Sacha Woodward-Hill was his closest confidante and legal advisor for years. He doesn't do sexism, only for mischief.

He has lived his life in Britain, shunning the idea of fleeing to a sunny tax haven, like Monaco, where his friend Prince Albert would welcome him and he would have a home among Formula One characters, such as David Coulthard, Alex Wurz, Lewis Hamilton and Eddie Jordan.

Tom Bower, a hard-nosed investigator who wrote an acclaimed biography of Ecclestone in 2011, believes he should be regarded as one of Britain's great entrepreneurs, and the case for acknowledging Ecclestone's part in transforming Formula One into the driver of Britain's thriving motor-racing industry is a strong one. Max Mosley nominated his friend for a knighthood in 1995, pointing out that Ecclestone could lay claim to having created and maintained 50,000 jobs in the British motor-racing industry. Support came from Silvio Berlusconi, the former Italian prime minister, but other letters were from more surprising sources: Edson Arantes do Nascimento, the Brazilian Minister for Sport, wrote of Ecclestone helping Britain achieve 'pre-eminence in motor racing and its highly-competitive technology upon which much of the progress in the development of modern road vehicles is based'. We know that former sports minister simply as Pelé. If that letter wasn't persuasive enough, here is a paradox for Ecclestone's critics: Prime Minister John Major also received a letter supporting Ecclestone's nomination from Nelson Mandela. The pair had met when Ecclestone was attempting to get motor racing back into South Africa after apartheid, and this unlikely couple – the south London car dealer and the president elevated to near-sainthood – became friends.

Ecclestone's refusal to bow to the establishment and the persistent rumours that he might be involved in some sort of corruption no doubt haunted ministers who worried that handing a gong to such a controversial figure might backfire spectacularly. I asked Ecclestone if he was insulted and he smiled. Ecclestone sees life simply: you don't get something for nothing, and a politician who offers something with one hand will want something in return with the other. He was bruised by Blair over the 'cash-for-ash' affair and will never forget nor forgive. Mosley reckons he wouldn't have accepted a title anyway, because 'Bernie wouldn't want to be part of their club'. But he adds: 'What he did for the reputation of the country is huge. Compare that to some other people who get awards of one kind or another, and for what?'

Ecclestone refuses point-blank to answer questions about his charitable giving. However, friends reckon he has handed out more than £100 million, with favourites, like the Great Ormond Street Hospital for Children in London, benefiting hugely from his generosity, buying expensive equipment, organising auctions, or just handing over a cheque. At the other end of the scale was the local church in the village of St Peter, where he'd been christened before his family moved from Suffolk to Dartford. When they needed money to repair the roof, Ecclestone didn't bother with a donation: he just sent them a cheque for the full £20,000 cost.

There is one anecdote I put to him involving a young woman who worked for the FIA in Paris. She needed expensive cancer treatment, and the workers in her office had a whip-round. Ecclestone heard about it and a banker's draft arrived the next day for €100,000. 'It is an aspect of you that people don't know about,' I told him, hoping he might shed some light on how much of his fortune has gone to good causes. 'It's better they don't know,' he said quietly, looking down at his handmade leather shoes.

Christian Horner became a close friend, despite a forty-three-year age gap. The Red Bull team principal has seen both sides of Ecclestone, from tough negotiator to big softie, but he also recognises that Ecclestone doesn't like to be seen as an easy touch and has no time for hangers-on or people who expect something for nothing. 'Bernie has a big heart. He has given millions and millions. What he has done for Great Ormond Street, or for the tsunami victims in Japan has been incredible. He will never talk about it, but he must be one of the biggest donors in the UK. For him, it is all about kids and animals because he feels that they don't want something, they're innocent. He can't help himself. He came to visit us when the farm next door had been lambing. There were about 200 new lambs and he asked me what would happen to them. I guessed they would end up in Waitrose. He was horrified. "They can't do that," he said. "Tell you what, I'll buy them and you look after them. They can't go to Waitrose, they need a chance to live."'

Bernie wouldn't like the fuss of a gong anyway. For all the worldwide publicity he has garnered, Ecclestone is essentially private, and a contradiction: he has private jets, a priceless car collection and a yacht, and he owns swathes of property across London and Europe – yet at heart he is a beer and chips man. He drinks very little, perhaps sipping at half a pint of lager at lunch or dinner, and his champagne glass is never emptied. He lives quietly without any trappings of wealth, save for an art collection that is a hobby.

The choice of daily transport is significant, the type of Range Rover that thousands of middle-class housewives choose for the school run. There is no fleet of Rolls-Royces and security men that have become a feature of the lives of his daughters. Despite his obvious affection for his two girls, the fact they live their lives in the spotlight clearly pains him. When Ecclestone and I meet one day, Tamara, the elder, has just appeared the night before in her own reality series on Channel 5 called *Billion $$ Girl*. The clue to the content is in the title, and Ecclestone seemed mystified as to why she needs to chase publicity and turn herself into a target for critics and online trolls. 'I think she has a fashion business she is trying to promote. I really don't know,' he said with a sigh. One person who didn't appear in the series, which took viewers inside Tamara's £70 million home in Chelsea and let them see the hugely expensive gifts lavished on her daughter Fifi, was Ecclestone. He refused to watch the shows and is clearly wondering why his ability to spot a trap has not been inherited by his elder daughter, particularly when she was filmed pondering the meaning of toast.

Ecclestone's anxiety over his daughters' high profile is understandable. He has been the victim of two vicious muggings and, in 2016, Fabiana's mother, Aparecida Schunk, was kidnapped from her home near São Paulo with a ransom demand for £28 million. Ecclestone was typically belligerent: the São Paulo police wanted him and Fabiana to stay away, but he wanted to meet the kidnappers face to face to negotiate. Some might think this was bravado after the event, but I believe he meant it; Ecclestone really doesn't fear anyone and he understands the percentages. 'Why would they kill me?' he said. 'If I have the money, they need me alive, don't they?' Fortunately, police found her captors and she was released after ten days, but it was demonstration enough to Ecclestone that the safety of his family was becoming paramount, despite his own disregard for personal safety around London. His haunts are well known to the paparazzi and he and his new wife Fabiana are regularly pictured leaving restaurants and hotels.

Their wedding reception was at least hidden from prying camera lenses. Then again, Fabiana got a wedding reception, unlike his first two wives who soon discovered his intense devotion to work. Ecclestone was still running his motorcycle showroom in 1952 when he took half an hour off to marry Ivy Bamford, a telephone operator, at Dartford Register Office. According to the account by Susan Watkins, as soon as Ivy and Bernie were declared man and wife, Ecclestone turned and marched off. 'Haven't you forgotten something, Mr Ecclestone,' said the registrar. 'What?' Ecclestone asked. 'Your bride,' came the puzzled reply.

Thirty years later, Ecclestone encountered a six-foot-tall Croatian model called Slavica Malic loitering in the pit lane at Monza before the Italian Grand Prix. Even glamorous models weren't allowed to litter his immaculate pit lane, and Ecclestone ordered her out. Her response was feisty, a precursor of what was to come in their relationship. 'If you come any nearer, I'll kick you,' she is reported to have threatened. The relationship was fiery, to say the least. Slavica had a temper and an attitude, but Ecclestone was fascinated enough to end a half-hearted seventeen-year relationship with his lover Tuana Tan for this Amazonian, dark-haired creature. The deal was sealed when Slavica revealed she was pregnant. In June 1984 she gave birth to Tamara, and Slavica warned the father that she would be going back to Croatia unless they married and set up home in London. Thirteen months later, Bernie Ecclestone and Slavica attended the Kensington and Chelsea register office on the Kings Road, ready to be wed. They were ready, but the registrar wasn't when he discovered that the bride-to-be couldn't understand enough English to repeat the vows. Max Mosley was called to be a witness and he brought along his Colombian housekeeper. A hurried call was made to his secretary to translate so the service could go ahead. There was no photographer to record the occasion and no guests. 'It was all so hurried,' Mosley says. 'Quite strange because it seemed to be over in minutes once we got under way and we were out on the street again.'

The bride wanted a reception, but the groom was restless. He made a desultory attempt to get a table at the popular Langan's Brasserie, just off Piccadilly, but there was no room, so Ecclestone went back to work, telling his new wife that she should catch a taxi home. In the years that followed, Ecclestone was devoted to his wife, despite her volatile nature and regular tantrums that once resulted in him allegedly ending up with a black eye. They were an odd couple, she tall and willowy and towering over her diminutive, and much older, husband.

Eventually Slavica tired of Ecclestone's obsession with Formula One, his constant travelling to grands prix and new locations to assess their suitability for races. He was constantly on the move, or at Princes Gate, poring over contracts. When he was at home, he ate in the kitchen, sometimes alone, demanding nothing more exotic than egg on toast. This was not the high-life that Slavica thought she had signed up for, with only the occasional meal in Ecclestone's favourite West End haunts or a trip to Waitrose for the weekly shop. In 2009, Slavica was granted a divorce after twenty-three years of marriage, taking a £740 million cash settlement. It was not all it seemed, though, for it emerged that a twist in their arrangements meant that the family trust had to pay him $100 million annually. In Bernie's world, finances are always complex.

Fabiana Flosi was vice president in charge of marketing at the Interlagos circuit in São Paulo when she first met Ecclestone. Their relationship was kept under wraps until their engagement was announced, in April 2012, with the appearance of a diamond ring estimated to be worth £100,000. It was the talk of the Formula One paddock as Fabiana – forty-seven years his junior – appeared at Ecclestone's side at grands prix, but she rapidly established herself as a favourite with everyone in the paddock. By August, the couple were married, and this time there was at least something of a celebration, despite the intervention of the groom at the wedding ceremony. Inevitably, there was mischief.

Christian Horner was Ecclestone's best man, accompanied by Beverley, his then partner, while Fabiana's mother was also there to witness the ceremony. The service was conducted in the register office in Gstaad, close to Ecclestone's £23 million chalet, Le Lion. As the female registrar went through the vows, Ecclestone suddenly stopped her with a raised hand. 'Our jaws dropped and we wondered what the hell he was going to say,' Horner told me. Ecclestone asked quietly, 'Excuse me, but do you do the divorces in the same building?' The registrar replied, somewhat baffled, that divorces were indeed carried out next door. 'That's okay then. Just checking,' Ecclestone said. 'Carry on.' A champagne dinner smoothed over the event and Ecclestone chuckled at the memory. 'Fabiana was okay with it – she knows what I'm like,' he said.

Fabiana has to know what her husband is like because the wind-ups come thick and fast in Ecclestone's world and no one is spared.

Ecclestone has always loved and admired the drivers, forming close bonds with Stuart Lewis-Evans and Jochen Rindt as contemporaries, but later he was fond of Niki Lauda and Ayrton Senna, who was like an uncle to his girls. He is still close to Lauda today, and the pair are wonderfully conspiratorial and politically incorrect. Sebastian Vettel, too, became a favourite as he swept up four world championships. They would play backgammon together in Ecclestone's motorhome after the Formula One day was finished and, one year, the young driver was invited with Christian Horner and an old pal of Ecclestone's called John onto his yacht during the summer break.

Vettel was still in training, so every day would don his Speedos and swim furiously around the bay where the yacht was docked. Ecclestone waited as Vettel emerged dripping wet and said he was impressed, but he bet that the world champion couldn't beat his mate John. Vettel looked at John, lying on a sunbed with his red face and generous belly, cocktail in hand, reading the paper. 'You must be joking,' said Vettel. 'I am twenty-five and he must be about seventy-five.' Ecclestone persisted, insisting that John had been an international swimmer in his day. The bet took off and was in the thousands of dollars by the time a race was set up for 9 a.m. the next day.

Ecclestone lined up the contestants: Vettel, his body lithe from training, wearing his tight Speedos and hopping from foot to foot, ready to launch himself into the blue waters, and John, grey and balding in his baggy shorts, yawning and wanting his fry-up for breakfast. Ecclestone takes up the story: 'The deal is that we play to John's rules and they have to swim from the yacht to a buoy about fifty metres away. John then decides he wants his breakfast, so Sebastian has to have breakfast to John's rules. So, ten o'clock arrives and finally they are ready to go. And then I tell Sebastian that John can't swim without a pint of water. Sebastian is fine with that rule, too, and a crew member brings two glass cups in stainless-steel holders on a tray. John takes his and downs it. Sebastian picks his up and realises it is boiling water. While he is blowing on it and waving his hands to cool it down, John is in the water and swimming. By the time, Sebastian hits the water, John is on his way back and wins easily.'

The stitch-up. An essential part of Formula One life, when humour could be quick and cruel. And, in Vettel's case, expensive. Ecclestone's payoff was a life lesson: 'You just learned that if it looks that easy, son, it probably isn't.'

It was never made easy by Ecclestone, the perfectionist. The tics and manias range from the absurd to the amusing. Ecclestone was neurotic-in-chief, and his Formula One paddock was spotless. Anyone caught throwing litter would have followed the offending paper or plastic to the dump. His fastidiousness even applied to the gleaming fleet of silver Formula One trucks that travel to each European grand prix; when they arrived at the circuit, they were lined up in number plate order, each one measured and spaced perfectly and parallel all down the line.

There is another anecdote that dates back a few years to an Australian Grand Prix. The Albert Park circuit is less than a mile inland from the Melbourne shore and prone to inclement weather. Ecclestone was guiding VIPs around the garages when he was told that the pit aprons – the box into which the cars drive for a change of tyres – were damp. The slippery conditions were hazardous, and fears were growing that a driver would miscalculate and slither into his pit crew. Ecclestone ordered one of his team to buy rolls of substantial tape to add grip to the surface, but to make sure he came back with enough in team colours in line with the colour-coded appearance of his pits. Next thing, he was on his hands and knees with a pair of large scissors, cutting and positioning tape to demonstrate exactly how and where it should be. It not only had to be safe, it had to be perfect.

For all the money, Ecclestone was a racer, and cared passionately for his sport and its participants. He lived and breathed Formula One, at the track or at his lair in Princes Gate, perfectly positioned a couple of blocks from the Royal Albert Hall and on the threshold of London's museums district. He bought the building in 1985 from Adnan Khashoggi, a Saudi arms dealer apparently famous for sex orgies, and then spent £2 million – cash, of course – fitting it out.

After his divorce from Slavica, Ecclestone lived 'over the shop' in a penthouse at the top of the building, coming down in the lift each day to work. He had tried fancy addresses, such as in 2001 when he bought the grandest house in Kensington Palace Gardens, the most expensive street in London. The house was said to be the most expensively refurbished property in Britain after Windsor Castle, and featured a Turkish bath and marble from the same quarry in Agra that supplied the Taj Mahal, as well as an underground car park for twenty cars. Slavica hated it and Ecclestone said he only went there three times. He bought it for £50 million and sold it to Lakshmi Mittal, the Indian steel magnate, for a £7 million profit.

He has thought of selling Princes Gate now it has been cleared of its small coterie of staff, who have moved to Liberty's grand new offices in Piccadilly, but will probably stay on, fearful of missing the rabbit warren of small rooms.

You have to press a button to be admitted to a narrow

hallway, where you are still greeted by a single receptionist at a small, plain desk. Visitors shown to the waiting room are drawn to the model of $100 bills, stacked up into a $1 million mini-mountain – a suitable in-joke for a man who counts his cash in billions. Walls were covered in artwork about Formula One, with more piled up waiting for a space – race posters, a huge canvas depicting Ayrton Senna and Ecclestone together; another of Ecclestone with Niki Lauda, who drove for him at Brabham and became a three-times world champion as well as a lifetime friend; then a large painting of Mike Hawthorn, the first British world champion, and many more reminders that Formula One was more than a passion, it was his life. In between the motor-racing memorabilia was a poster for *The Thomas Crown Affair*, the 1968 Hollywood movie starring Faye Dunaway and Steve McQueen. It is one of his favourite movies. Oh, and he knew McQueen, a motor-racing obsessive like him. Inside his office, the first sight to catch the eye is a helmet, complete with spike, perched on the end of the vast glass desk; it is his fireman's helmet, he says, for putting out those fires of his.

About a year on from his 'sacking' by Liberty, as he likes to call it, Ecclestone called a small press conference. He had missed the banter and mischief and asked the assembled hacks: 'Well, what do you want to know?' The only break in the conversation came as tea and coffee was served by one of his secretaries. As she passed on her way out of the room,

Ecclestone looked up and said with a mischievous grin, 'Why haven't you got a mini-skirt on?' The eyebrows of the man from the *Guardian* shot up into his hairline, but it was objective achieved for Ecclestone, a minor shockwave to liven up the discussion.

Then to lunch, it was decided. I knew where: Bar Boulud, the Michelin-starred bistro underneath the Mandarin Oriental Hotel, about half a mile down the road from Princes Gate. The bistro is a favourite haunt and his chosen spot for entertaining journalists. A *Financial Times* hack treated to lunch asked Ecclestone if he was a regular, only to be told, 'No. Not really', as the waiter handed over menus and inquired, 'Your usual, Mr Ecclestone?' Ecclestone's usual was a burger without the top bun and fries. Bar Boulud it was, then.

It was freezing but Ecclestone decided he was going to walk, sending his wife Fabiana ahead in the couple's chauffeur-driven Range Rover. He wore a light, zip-up jacket and must have been perished, but Ecclestone was relishing the attention and the conversation, and so were we until we reached the traffic lights in Knightsbridge outside the Harvey Nichols department store. Clearly unused to being a pedestrian, Ecclestone stepped out onto the busy road without looking, forcing a London bus to pull up. Unfazed, Ecclestone walked around the front of the bus, reached through the side window and shook the driver's hand. 'Thanks, sport,' he offered cheerily before marching on across the road.

There was a surprise at lunch – no burger, but prawns and a

small glass of lager. Then, he talked Formula One, and she talked the future. Fabiana is an attractive, dark-haired former lawyer, who became one of Ecclestone's greatest assets in her short time in the paddock, making sure guests were at ease and her man was properly looked after. Cynics will leap to the conclusion that she is a gold-digger, but they haven't seen how attentive she is with him and how she watches him: she adores Bernie and he adores her.

She sat to her husband's left, close enough to ensure that his mobile phone – the technological bane of Ecclestone's life – was properly tuned to his hearing aids. For a man who presided for so long over a sport so steeped in technology, he never quite got a grip of how it all worked. Not long after he launched his pioneering high-definition television channel, he caught me in the paddock at Monaco. 'Have you seen it?' he asked excitedly. 'It's fantastic.' Unfortunately, I hadn't, because I was always at grands prix, so he collared me and the *Daily Express*'s Bob McKenzie and dragged us into 'the Kremlin', his motorhome, to show off his new toy. You took your shoes off at the door of the Kremlin, by the way, just to make sure the pale grey carpet wasn't marked. He switched on his flat-screen television and started flicking through channels. 'That's MTV, Bernie,' I said, as we watched Take That or some boy band. 'No, that's Channel Four. Now you are on Eurosport.' This went on for some minutes until, frustrated, Ecclestone threw the remote control across the motorhome onto the sofa, having failed to locate his channel. 'Well, I'm telling you, it is brilliant,' he said, and we left. It probably was, but his timing was, for once, wrong, and the channel crashed costing him £50 million.

Technology of even the simplest kind defeated him in his days at Brabham, according to Charlie Whiting, Ecclestone's then chief mechanic, who became the FIA's race director. Whiting says that Ecclestone would jump up to the pit wall clutching a pair of stopwatches, spend ages pressing buttons without having a clue and then throw them aside, cursing them.

The mobile phone was a constant source of frustration. Although he had his most important numbers on speed-dial, others were carefully printed out and taped to the back of a fairly basic Nokia-style phone. One day he wanted to show me a joke that had been sent as a text; that was on Thursday evening in the paddock in Shanghai and he finally found it on Saturday morning. Imagine how baffled I was at lunch one day when Ecclestone suddenly started a new conversation looking down at a shiny new smartphone; it turned out Fabiana had found a device that linked by Bluetooth from the phone to the hearing aids he has in both ears. There was no taped list of numbers on the back either. It was a startling moment.

After making sure her husband was connected, Fabiana told of her plans for her new coffee business, based on production from the ranch Ecclestone has bought outside São Paulo. Called Celebrity Coffee, she is striving to get the brand into roasteries and top-of-the-line coffee bars, and her husband seemed enthused by this new venture, a long way from the roar of the racetrack. She told how when Ecclestone bought the plantation, the couple toured their land to meet the thirty or so workers they had inherited. 'There was one woman who never looked at us or smiled. Then we realised she had no teeth,' Fabiana said. 'Bernie looked around the houses on the estate and decided he had to do something, so he demolished the lot and built new homes, as well as a medical centre and a dental surgery. Sometime later, we came back from London and there was this woman – and she had the biggest smile for us with lots of shiny, white new teeth. It was fantastic.'

It was a simple act of kindness, but one that changed a life, and one that – again – Ecclestone wasn't so keen to talk about, pushing his prawns around his plate. Dessert was his treat and he ordered for everyone at the table his favourite chocolate soufflé. When the bill came, Ecclestone reached into his pocket for his traditional roll of 'readies', but there weren't enough £50 notes to cover it, so out came an American Express card – a black one, the highest value card you can get. On the way out, a young man leapt from his table and asked for a selfie and Ecclestone, slightly uncomfortable, obliged, and then he was off in the Range Rover back to Princes Gate.

There was one last memorable moment for me in Princes Gate. Ecclestone was just coming down from the penthouse when I arrived and he was already grinning. He was dressed in his customary crisp white, button-down shirt, but with tight grey jeans that drew the eye to his spindly legs. He is not as sprightly as he was, and the expanding waistline tells the tale of a satisfying private life, but, at eighty-seven, an age when most pensioners are contemplating the care home and remaining years of daytime television, Ecclestone was bouncing with energy – and mischief.

Ecclestone waved me forward and then took me by the arm into his office where he wanted to show me what had been the hub of Formula One for more than thirty years. The last files were bundled up and the big glass desk was clear of Formula One business for the first time in years. 'All ready to go,' he said, with not a hint of sadness. He was up to something, though. Ecclestone took my arm again and steered me through a side door into an anteroom. 'Look at this. What do you think?' he asked, pointing at a stainless-steel box on the wall with a circular glass door and a large red button on one side and a green button on the other. 'Erm, are you going into the laundrette business now you are done with F1?' I said, wondering what was going on. 'That's it,' Ecclestone chuckled. 'It's for money-laundering. You pop the money in here like a washing machine and press the green button.'

The irony of the joke was inescapable, a laundering machine for the man with more money than he could ever have dreamed of growing up in Suffolk and southeast London and who had laughed off suggestions he was behind the Great Train Robbery. Even now, I am not sure whether I was the victim of another monumental Ecclestone wind-up.

20

THE END OF
THE ERA

L EWIS Hamilton folds his arms across his chest and sits
motionless in the claustrophobic cockpit as six white-
shirted mechanics pull his long, sleek Mercedes back into the
garage. They wipe and shine and stroke and prod the car, as
though it was an opera diva being preened ready to walk out
on stage. For a moment, there is quiet amid the din of practice
for the ultimate motor race, the one everyone wants to go to,
the one that has taken its place in sporting history and evokes
all the enduring images of Formula One.

Hamilton has won the Monaco Grand Prix twice and
knows all about what it means for his place in the pantheon
of Formula One. I watch him practising for the 2018 grand
prix around the narrow, winding streets in an almost impossible combination of physical endurance and mental agility.

I am wired in to Hamilton's communications system with
Pete Bonnington, his race engineer, and Ricky Musconi, his
performance engineer, for the practice session, positioned over
the garage entrance alongside Geoff Willis, one of Formula
One's most experienced executives, who has been given one of

those titles that needs two doors – director of digital engineering transformation technology. He has a laptop, at least, and, like me, a set of headphones to monitor the car-to-pit conversations. Practice is a constant stream of information: while Hamilton negotiates the tightest turns and then accelerates to 180 mph with steel barriers either side of him and then ahead as he hits the brakes, Bonnington is talking him through the corners where he is losing the most time, and it might only be fractions of a second. Bonnington has the reassuring calmness of a British Airways pilot; he could almost be talking Hamilton through the journey to his next holiday, when the meals will be served and his arrival time at the chequered flag. In the car, Hamilton is occasionally breathless, clearly fighting the strain of being buffeted by the G-forces.

His steering wheel could come from a fighter jet, with its buttons offering dozens of combinations of settings for brakes, fuel, tyres – almost anything but the Drivetime show on Radio Two. It seems like the racing equivalent of patting your head and rubbing your stomach at the same time as doing *The Times* crossword.

This is how he described it to me after we emerged from his garage overlooking the harbour front at Monaco: 'Things are coming at you at ridiculous speeds and your body is contorting the whole time, your body is constantly tense and every muscle is firing. Sometimes there is a build-up of things after I have been at a grand prix and I hit the wall and don't leave the apartment for days and don't get out of bed, but people will be watching on their sofa having a cup of tea and thinking, "Oh, it looks easy".'

Perhaps they thought it was easy when his hero Ayrton Senna performed his most celebrated lap of Monaco – some say the greatest lap of any racetrack anywhere by any driver. It lasted 1 minute 23.998 seconds, an exhibition of bravery and brute force as he wrestled with the wheel of his red-and-white McLaren MP4/4 in qualifying for the 1988 Monaco Grand Prix. It is an iconic image of a man who says he zoned out during the lap, almost taking leave of his body. Thirty years on, in 2018, Hamilton set a time of 1 minute 11.232 seconds in qualifying for the Monaco Grand Prix.

Technology, safety, speed and money have been transformed in Formula One. The days when Bernie Ecclestone's Brabham team would load two cars into trucks and trundle across Europe with a handful of mechanics, never knowing whether they would have a spare seat on the return journey after the death of a driver, have disappeared into the mists of time. It took 1,500 people to produce the machine that carried Lewis Hamilton in Monaco and a budget nearing £300 million. Ecclestone's budget would have done well to reach seven figures. Ayrton Senna argued with Ron Dennis over $1 million but, in Monaco, Hamilton was about to sign a deal worth $40 million a year. In reality, both drivers would have taken to the track for free, though, because the need for speed is insatiable.

The men who run the sport have changed, too. As I leave the garage and the army of technicians hunched over their computers, I bump into Toto Wolff, the head of Mercedes Motorsport and the leader of the new breed of team principal. He was wealthy before he entered Formula One, but now has a stake in the Mercedes team worth more than £140 million, after winning four consecutive world championships with Hamilton and Nico Rosberg. Wolff runs the team, but is answerable to the boardroom in Stuttgart where the long-term future of Mercedes in Formula One will be decided. When the corporates have had their return, they will pull the plug on the sport because they are not like the *garagistes* with their obsession with racing and their history of struggle and success.

Wolff was with a small boy, who was barely waist-high to the tall Austrian. His name was Andrea Kimi Antonelli and he was twelve years old. The name 'Kimi' is no accident, for his father is a Formula One fan and his little boy is now the hottest ticket in junior karting – so hot that he has already been signed by Mercedes.

'If you want to find the next Lewis, you need to look that early because all of the great champions were impressive at that very early age,' Wolff says. Graham Hill didn't pass his driving test until he was twenty-four before winning the world championship twice, and Nigel Mansell had to wait until he was thirty-nine to become world champion.

How far the world of Formula One has come since Bernie Ecclestone and his gang wheeled and dealed their way around the world. The sport is now the property of an American media company, whose first act was to put out more messages on social media – something that baffled Ecclestone – while the fans raged about the dullness of the sport and the domination of Wolff's Mercedes.

The question might be asked what legacy those extraordinary entrepreneurs have left after their decades of creating Formula One in their own image. In their heyday, it was easy: build a car, put petrol in it and then drive like hell. The only threat to their way of life was that the cash would run out.

Now the threats are existential as life evolves away from the thunder of petrol power and car companies start to invest their billions in battery power. Formula One once claimed the high ground, as a technological leader, often developing systems and components that would trickle into the conventional motor industry and cars on the roads. Yet today, teams spend millions on pointless aerodynamic tricks devised by hundreds of highly qualified scientists and indulge in a hybrid engine system that is not only complex and hugely costly but has turned off millions of fans with the puny noise emitted from the exhaust. Meanwhile, Formula E – an all-electric series – has stolen the technological thunder by going straight to the battery science that most carmakers believe is the future. While Formula One has been unable to attract carmakers back to its fold, Formula E has recruited Jaguar, Audi, Mercedes and others to its ranks who race in choice locations, such as the centre of Berlin, Paris, Hong Kong and New York – venues that Formula One would dearly love to lure.

The days of switching on the BBC to listen to Murray Walker guide you through a race in some exotic, far-off land which was an essential part of the Sunday ritual are over. Pay television companies, like Sky Sports, have swept up the broadcasting rights around the world as sport swaps eyeballs for hard cash. The English Premier League led the charge onto satellite stations, but Formula One has been quick to follow and Sky Sports in Britain is the sole broadcaster of the sport from 2019. When Jenson Button won the 2011 Canadian Grand Prix – one of the most dramatic of all-time with a two-hour rain delay before he came from last to victory – it was watched by 8.5 million on the BBC; in 2017, Sky's average audience was 652,000 but Sky's deal is said to be worth more than £1 billion.

At the same time, the conventional model of getting bums on sofas to watch television is over. Youngsters watch phones and iPads and, as other sports are finding, getting them to sit down to watch a 90-minute event unfold is almost impossible. Instead, money is drifting into something called eSports, essentially motor racing without the sweat, the danger or even having to step outside. Mercedes recruited their first eSports champion, a former kitchen porter called Brendon Leigh, in the summer of 2018 to lead their eSports team. With the best will in the world, Leigh was hardly Lewis Hamilton. He won the first Formula One eSports championship in Abu Dhabi before the 2017 grand prix – he had never been out of Britain before or even on a plane.

Technology has sucked the life out of Formula One, too. Now a computer transmits data to an engineer who tells his driver what the weather is like, what his car is doing and even how to drive. At the 1999 French Grand Prix, Eddie Jordan sent a mechanic on a scooter to some outlying fields to watch the rain clouds. The mechanic telephoned in to say he could see rain was on its way to Magny-Cours, so Jordan altered Heinz-Harald's strategy and he won the race. Now every team has satellite traces and a cohort of boffins back at their headquarters predicting every outcome of every possibility using supercomputers.

The visceral appeal of Senna at Monaco – raw power, strength, danger and speed – has been neutralised by laptops and algorithms.

Formula One enjoyed a thrilling and lucrative past, but what is the future? Mark Gallagher, Eddie Jordan's commercial director and now a leading pundit, writer and consultant in motor racing, has an interesting take.

'The future may well lie in the past,' he says. 'There are profound decisions to be made, but perhaps it is the horse racing solution: we stopped using horses as a mode of transport more than 100 years ago, but people still watch the Grand National and the Derby and they generate hundreds of millions of pounds with jockeys and horses that become legends. When cars are driving themselves, I will tell my grandchildren to watch real people driving real machines with real danger.

When the dust had settled after the Liberty takeover and Ecclestone was officially out of work for the first time in his life at the age of eighty-seven, we met up at Princes Gate. The sun streamed through the windows of his office, which looked out over a small, neat garden. Our conversations in the past would have ranged from which driver was going where to which team was demanding more money, but now we wondered where the series that had been his life for more than fifty years and that he nurtured and loved would end up.

Ecclestone had only memories, for he is no wiser than the rest what will happen when he is long gone. 'I told Fabiana to put me in a box and put me out with the rubbish when I go,' he smiles.

I told him his departure from Formula One was the last of the gang who created the sport, the end of the era of Enzo, Ron, Luca, Max and all the rest. Ken Tyrrell had been dead since 2001, Tom Walkinshaw since 2010, while Sir Frank's health wanes. All the rest had been swept aside by events as the world moved on and their era was declared over.

Ecclestone looked out of the window for a moment, as if absorbing the meaning of the statement, casting his mind over the years of struggle, the growth of the sport, the loss of friends and the eventual ending.

'End of an era?' he said. 'Maybe it's right that the old-timers move out and let someone else have a go. We had our time and it was a good time. We would never regret any of it.'

And not regret the money they all made? Ecclestone leaned forward and cupped his chin in his hands. 'The thing is that all the people you have just mentioned, including me, all of us, didn't do it for the money. Ron, Frank, all of us were racers. We made money because of Formula One. We didn't go into the business to make money. We went into it to race and, if we made some money, then good. But we were racers.'

POSTSCRIPT

A T my farewell from Bernie's flying circus, the tributes kindly described me as the doyen of Formula One journalism, mainly thanks to age rather than talent, and happily also came in my favourite liquid form – gin. Daffy's, sponsor of Manor Racing, came up with this recipe for the Doyen cocktail. Mix and raise a toast to the men who made Formula One: 50 ml Daffy's Gin, 100 ml cranberry juice, half-teaspoon of Duerr's 1881 Golden Orange Conserve, top with champagne, garnish with hibiscus flowers & fresh lime wedges, shake and strain the gin, cranberry juice and marmalade – then top up with fizz. Good health.

ACKNOWLEDGEMENTS

It happened at every dinner party and during any casual chat in a pub. As soon as people discovered I was journalist in Formula One, the questions would come: 'What's Bernie Ecclestone really like?' Or, 'I can't stand that Lewis Hamilton. Is he really that arrogant?' This book is, I hope, the answer to some of those dinner party questions. I was always amazed that people could only see the worst in Formula One, despite its incredible success and my reassurances that the characters in it could be just like them: they had families and worries, tempers and tantrums, highlights and lowlights, for Formula One is the ultimate soap opera, and set a template for so many other sports with its glitz and glamour.

I have not attempted to tackle the complexities of the sport in detail, but tried to paint portraits of people I dealt with over 20 years of reporting from tracks all over the world. To delve into the history that helped create these characters, I relied on the excellent biographies of Bernie Ecclestone by Tom Bower and Susan Watkins, and the detailed account of

ACKNOWLEDGEMENTS

The Piranha Club, by my old colleague Timothy Collings, as well as Christopher Hilton's wonderfully thorough *Grand Prix Century*, plus the biography of Enzo Ferrari by Richard Williams. I was too late to know the great Enzo and I have to thank Brenda Vernor, his former secretary, for her accounts of life at Maranello. We spent an enjoyable day together close to the Ferrari factory.

I also have to thank the main players for giving up their time to speak to me to go over memories, some flattering, some not so. Thanks to Eddie Jordan, Christian Horner, Flavio Briatore, Graeme Lowdon, David Coulthard, David Richards, Mark Gallagher, Sir Jackie Stewart, Vijay Mallya, Claire Williams, Anthony Hamilton, Toto Wolff, Paul Stoddart, John Hogan, Finbarr O'Connell and Oliver Weingarten for their time, company and honesty in helping me order my thoughts. I have also drawn on interviews from past years, particularly Niki Lauda, Sir Frank Williams, Sir Stirling Moss and Michael 'Herbie' Blash, one of the longest-serving – and nicest – men in formula one. And I would like to pay tribute to Charlie Whiting, who so sadly passed away after the writing of this book. He was always kind and helpful. He will be much missed. Thanks, too, to my old mates in Fleet Street – Jonathan McEvoy of the *Daily Mail* and Bob McKenzie, late of the *Daily Express* – for jogging my ageing memory. And to Bradley Lord, communications director at Mercedes, for ensuring I had time with Lewis Hamilton, a young man I first met when he was only 15 years old.

Last but definitely not least, huge thanks to the 'Big Beasts' of Formula One, who probably did most to shape the sport over decades – Bernie Ecclestone, Ron Dennis, Max Mosley and Luca di Montezemolo. They didn't have to bother, but their kindness and generosity helped me to some sort of vague understanding of Formula One – and kept me in a job.

PHOTO ACKNOWLEDGEMENTS

The author and publisher would like to thank the following for permission to reproduce photographs:

Bernard Cahier/Getty Images, Fox Photos/Getty Images, Victor Blackman/Express/Hulton Archive/Getty Images, Daily Express/Hulton Archive/Getty Images, Joe Bangay/ Daily Express/Hulton Archive/Getty Images, Grand Prix Photo/Getty Images, Sergio del Grande\Mondadori Portfolio via Getty Images, Ercole Colombo Motorsport, Brenda Vernor, Paul-Henri Cahier/Getty Images, Dave Benett/ Getty Images, REUTERS/Matt Dunham, Fairfax Media via Getty Images, Mark Thompson/Getty Images, Clive Mason/Getty Images, ANTONIO SCORZA/AFP/Getty Images, Francois Durand/Getty Images, The Times, Peter J Fox/Getty Images, XPB Images, Clive Mason/Getty Images, Action Images, Mark Thompson, Mark Sutton Motorsport, ANDREJ ISAKOVIC/AFP/Getty Images

Other photographs from private collections.

Every reasonable effort has been made to trace the copyright holders, but if there are any errors or omissions, Hodder & Stoughton will be pleased to insert the appropriate acknowledgement in any subsequent printings or editions.

GLOSSARY

A

Giovanni 'Gianni' Agnelli (born 1921, Turin, Italy. Died 2003) – head of the Fiat family car firm and the richest man in Italy, who took control of Ferrari after Enzo's death.

Mario Andretti (born 1940, Motovun, Croatia) – American with twelve career grands-prix victories and the world championship in 1978 for Lotus.

Fernando Alonso (born 1981, Oviedo, Spain) – two-times world champion with Renault. Started his career with Minardi and finished it in 2018 with McLaren after 32 victories.

Alberto Ascari (born 1918, Milan, Italy. Died 1955) – Ferrari's first world champion in 1952 and 1953, but killed testing at Monza. His father Antonio died at the 1925 French Grand Prix.

B

Rubens Barrichello (born 1972, São Paulo, Brazil) – started more than 300 times in Formula One with Jordan, Stewart, Ferrari, Honda, Brawn and Williams. Eleven victories.

Gerhard Berger (born 1959, Wörgl, Austria) – drove for Arrows, Benetton, Ferrari and McLaren and took ten victories. Great friend of Ayrton Senna.

Lorenzo Bandini (born 1935, Marj, Libya) – drove for Ferrari, but killed at the 1967 Monaco Grand Prix after a single career victory.

Tony Brooks (born 1932, Dukinfield, England) – dentist turned racer who recorded the first grand-prix win for a British constructor in a Vanwall shared with Stirling Moss at the 1957 British Grand Prix.

Jenson Button (born 1980, Frome, England) – joined Formula One as a twenty-year-old and recorded 306 starts and 15 victories, as well as the 2009 world championship.

Jean-Marie Balestre (born1921, Saint-Rémy-de-Provence, France. Died 2008) – autocratic president of the Federation Internationale de l'Automobile overthrown by Max Mosley and Bernie Ecclestone.

C

David Coulthard (born 1971, Twynholm, Scotland) – joined F1 in 1994 with Williams, longest-serving McLaren driver until joining Red Bull in 2005. Thirteen career wins in 246 starts. Television producer and, until the end of 2018, a Channel 4 F1 pundit.

John Cooper (born 1923, Surbiton, England. Died 2000) – with father Charles inspired the rise of the British constructor. Apart from sixteen F1 victories and two constructors' world championships, Cooper was also responsible for the successful Mini Cooper road car.

Peter Collins (born 1931, Kidderminster, England. Died 1958) – charismatic Ferrari teammate to Mike Hawthorn, killed at the 1958 German Grand Prix.

D

Ron Dennis (born 1947, Woking, England) – former mechanic, who took control in 1981 of McLaren, a team which has notched twelve drivers' championships and eight as a constructor. Left after a boardroom row in 2016.

E

Bernie Ecclestone (born 1930, St Peter, Suffolk, England) – amateur racer, second-hand car dealer turned billionaire leader of F1 for almost forty years. Controversial and outspoken, deposed as F1 chief executive in January 2017.

F

Enzo Ferrari (born 1898, Modena, Italy. Died 1988) – founder of F1's most famous and successful team, the only one to have competed in every year of the modern world championship since 1950.

Giuseppe Farina (born 1906, Turin, Italy) – winner of the first Formula One world championship grand prix at Silverstone on 13 May 1950, and the first world champion.

Juan Manuel Fangio (born 1911, Balcarce, Argentina. Died 1995) – Argentinian thought by many to be the greatest driver of all time, with five world championships.

G

Grimaldi – the ruling family of Monaco, who started the world's most famous grand prix, in 1929. Now ruled by Prince Albert II (born 1958), who succeeded his father Prince Rainier, the husband of Hollywood star Grace Kelly.

H

Mike Hawthorn (born 1929, Mexborough, Yorkshire, England. Died 1959) – Britain's first F1 world champion, driving a Ferrari, in 1958. Killed in a road accident just six months after retiring.

Mika Häkkinen (born 1968, Vantaa, Finland) – twice a world champion with McLaren, including twenty victories under Ron Dennis.

James Hunt (born 1947, Belmont, Surrey, England. Died 1993) – playboy F1 favourite, who won a famous 1976 world championship for McLaren. BBC television pundit, died of a heart attack aged just forty-five.

Christian Horner (born 1973, Leamington Spa, England) – team principal of Red Bull, which won four constructors' world championships and four drivers' titles for Sebastian Vettel (2010–2013).

Patrick Head (born 1946, Farnborough, England) – co-founder of Williams Grand Prix and technical director, guiding the team to nine constructors' world championships. Retired in 2004.

Lewis Hamilton (born 1985, Stevenage, England) – Britain's most successful driver. Has more wins than any driver except Michael Schumacher and record number of pole positions and by 2018 held four world championships.

I

Eddie Irvine (born 1965, Newtownards, Northern Ireland) – Ulsterman who was beaten to the world championship in 1999 by two points with Ferrari before moving to Jaguar. Four career victories.

J

Eddie Jordan (born 1948, Dublin, Ireland) – former owner of Jordan Grand Prix turned television pundit with Channel 4. Started in F1 in 1991 and sold his team to Midland F1 in 2005.

K

Korean Grand Prix – held between 2010 and 2013.

L

Niki Lauda (born 1949, Vienna, Austria) – three-times world champion, who drove for March, BRM, Ferrari, Brabham and McLaren. Airline magnate and chairman of the Mercedes F1 team. Underwent lung transplant in July 2018.

M

Vijay Mallya (born 1955, Kolkata, India) – owner of the only India-backed team in F1 history. Bought Spyker in 2007 in £80 million deal, but team taken over by a consortium headed by Canadian businessman Lawrence Stroll after falling into administration in 2018.

Dietrich Mateschitz (born 1944, Sankt Marein, Austria) – co-owner of Red Bull drinks brand and among the top 50 richest people in the world with a $21 billion fortune. Owns Red Bull and Toro Rosso teams in F1.

Giancarlo Minardi (born 1947, Faenza, Italy) – founder of Minardi F1 team, sold to Paul Stoddart in 2001.

Stirling Moss (born 1929, London, England) – considered the best driver never to win the world championship, Moss was the first British F1 winner, in 1955 at the British Grand Prix in a Mercedes. Knighted in 2000.

Max Mosley (born 1940, London, England) – lawyer turned driver, co-founder of the March team before becoming president of the Fédération Internationale de l'Automobile (1993–2009) to govern F1 for almost two decades.

Luca Cordero di Montezemolo (born 1947, Bologna, Italy) – turned Ferrari into the most successful team in F1. A protégé of Enzo Ferrari and Gianni Agnelli, he left Ferrari in 2014 after almost 30 years running the company.

N

Adrian Newey (born 1958, Stratford-upon-Avon, England) – F1's most successful designer, winning world championships at Williams, McLaren and Red Bull. His cars have won ten constructors' championships and F1 world titles for six drivers.

O

Mansour Ojjeh (born 1952, Saudi Arabia) – former partner of Ron Dennis and still a major shareholder in McLaren.

P

Alain Prost (born 1955, Lorette, France) – four-times world champion, who drove for Ferrari, McLaren and Williams before retiring at the end of 1993 with 51 victories. In 1997, bought the French Ligier team, but the team crashed in 2002 with $30 million worth of debt.

R

Jochen Rindt (born 1942, Mainz, Germany. Died 1970) – F1's only posthumous world champion after being killed in a Lotus car at the Italian Grand Prix at Monza. Close friend of Bernie Ecclestone.

S

Ayrton Senna (born 1960, São Paulo, Brazil. Died 1994) – three-times world champion with McLaren. Moved to Williams in 1994, but was killed in a crash at Imola during the San Marino Grand Prix. Forty-one career wins and 65 pole positions.

Jody Scheckter (born 1950, East London, South Africa) – drove for McLaren, Tyrrell and Wolf and won the 1979 world championship with Ferrari.

Michael Schumacher (born 1969, Hürth, Germany) – most successful and richest driver in history with 91 victories, seven world championships and a fortune estimated at more than £600 million. Completed 307 F1 starts with Jordan, Benetton, Ferrari and Mercedes.

Jackie Stewart (born 1939, Milton, Scotland) – three-times world champion and former owner of Stewart Grand Prix. Formidable safety campaigner and winner of 27 grands prix from 99 starts. Knighted in 2001.

Paul Stoddart (born 1955, Melbourne) – Australian airline magnate who bought Minardi in 2001 and sold to Red Bull in 2005.

Silverstone – Britain's most historic racetrack, in Northamptonshire, England, and the site of the first grand prix of the modern world championship on 13 May 1950.

T

Ken Tyrrell (born 1924, East Horsley, England. Died 2001) – pioneer of the British F1 scene, winning three world championships as a constructor with Jackie Stewart in 1969, 1971 and 1973. Sold the team to British American Racing in 1999.

Jean Todt (born 1946, Pierrefort, France) – world championship-winning rally co-driver and successful team manager with Peugeot, winning Le Mans. Sporting director of Ferrari in 1993 where he won six consecutive constructors' championships. Succeeded Max Mosley as FIA president in 2009.

V

Gilles Villeneuve (born 1950, Saint-Jean-sur-Richelieu, Canada. Died 1982) – Ferrari favourite who won six grands prix, but died at the 1982 Belgian Grand Prix. Father of Jacques, the 1997 world champion with Williams.

Wolfgang von Trips (born 1928, Cologne, Germany. Died 1961) – German nobleman on course for the 1961 world championship when he crashed during the Italian Grand Prix at Monza and was killed along with 15 spectators.

Sebastian Vettel (born 1987, Heppenheim, Germany) – one of the most successful drivers of all-time with four world championships with Red Bull before moving to Ferrari.

W

Sid Watkins (born 1928, Liverpool, England. Died 2012) – acclaimed neurosurgeon who became F1's first full-time medical officer, from 1978 until retirement in 2005.

Tom Walkinshaw (born 1946, Mauldslie, Scotland. Died 2010) – European Touring Car champion turned engineering director at Benetton where he orchestrated two world championships for Michael Schumacher. Bought the Arrows team in 1996 but it folded in 2002.

Frank Williams – (born 1942, South Shields, England) – Britain's most successful constructor with nine world championships. Knighted in 1999. Started his first team in 1966. Confined to a wheelchair after breaking his neck in a car accident in 1986.

Claire Williams (born 1976, Windsor, England) – daughter of Sir Frank and deputy team principal of the Williams Formula One team.

Toto Wolff (born 1972, Vienna, Austria) – former Williams shareholder, who joined Mercedes in 2013 and became head of Mercedes Motorsport.

INDEX

INDEX

INDEX

INDEX

INDEX

INDEX